The Duel

The Duel

Pakistan on the Flight Path of American Power

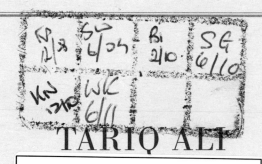

TARIQ ALI

SCHUSTER

London · New York · Sydney · Toronto

First published in Great Britain in 2008 by Simon & Schuster UK Ltd
A CBS COMPANY

1 3 5 7 9 10 8 6 4 2

Simon & Schuster UK Ltd
1st Floor
222 Gray's Inn Road
London
WC1X 8HB

www.simonsays.co.uk

A CIP catalogue for this book is available
from the British Library

ISBN: 978-1-84737-355-7 (Hardback)
ISBN: 978-1-84737-363-2 (Trade paperback)

Printed in the UK by CPI Mackays, Chatham ME5 8TD

for
Tahira, Tauseef, Kamila, and Mishael,
four generations of Lahoris

CONTENTS

BOOKS HAVE A DESTINY. THIS
The first, *Pakistan: Military Rule o* ...)69
and predicted the breakup of the sta... ... ... ran. Critics of every persuasion, even those wh... ..., thought it was
going too far in suggesting that the stat... ... disintegrate, but a few
years later that is exactly what happened. Just over a decade later I wrote
Can Pakistan Survive? The question mark was not unimportant but
nonetheless struck a raw nerve in General Zia's Pakistan, where to even
pose the question was unacceptable. The general himself was extremely
angry about its publication, as were sections of the bureaucracy, willing instruments of every despotism. Zia attacked both me and the book
at a press conference in India, which was helpful and much appreciated
by the publisher's sales department. That book too was banned, but to
my delight was shamelessly pirated in many editions in Pakistan. They
don't ban books anymore, or at least not recently, which is a relief and
a small step forward.

When I left in 1963, the country consisted of West and East Pakistan. Eight years later the East defected and became Bangladesh. The
population of the Western wing was then 40–45 million. It has grown
phenomenally ever since and is now approaching the 200 million
mark. The under-thirties constitute a majority.

This book centers on the long duel between a U.S.-backed politico-
military elite and the citizens of the country. In earlier years the State
Department would provide the seconds for the duel, but with U.S.

troops now in neighboring Afghanistan and U.S. bombs falling on homes inside Pakistan, the conflict is assuming a more direct form. Were it to proceed further, as some have been arguing in Washington, there is a distinct possibility that serious cracks would threaten the much-vaunted unity of the Pakistan military high command. The relationship with Washington, always controversial in the country, now threatens the Pakistan army. Political commentators in the United States together with a cabal of mimics in Pakistan regularly suggest that an Islamist revolution is incubating in a country that is seriously threatened by "jihadi terrorists." The only function of such a wild assertion is to invite a partial U.S. occupation and make the jihadi takeover a self-fulfilling prophecy.

The most important aspect of the duel is not the highly publicized conflict in Waziristan, but the divide between the majority of the people and their corrupt, uncaring rulers. This duel is often fought without weapons, sometimes in the mind, but it never goes away. An important reason for the deep hostility to the United States has little to do with religion, but is based on the knowledge that Washington has backed every military dictator who has squatted on top of the country. With Pakistan once again a strategic asset, the fear is that Washington will do so again, since it regards the military as the only functioning institution in the country, without showing any signs of comprehension as to why this is the case. This book might help in this regard.

What explains my continuing interest in Pakistan? I was born and educated there. Most of my family still lives there, and in periods when I haven't been banned from entering the country, I visit regularly. I enjoy running into old friends and acquaintances, especially now that most of them have retired from important positions and can speak openly and laugh again. I never feel alone in Pakistan. Something of me stayed behind in the soil and the trees and the people so even in bad times I am welcome.

I love the mountains. At least they can't be skyscrapered and forced to look like Dubai. Palm trees, Gulf kitsch, and the Himalayas don't mix, not that it prevents some from trying. The cityscapes are something else. They have greatly changed over the years; new unplanned and poorly designed buildings have wrecked most of the larger towns.

In Islamabad, the capital, one of the U.S. architects who built the city in the late sixties, Edward Stone, was unhappy with the site because it sat on a geological fault line and had weak soil. He advised that no building higher than three stories should ever be built there. He was ignored by the military dictator of the day. When a massive earthquake hit the country in 2005, buildings trembled all over Islamabad. I was there during the aftershocks, which were bad enough.

It was not only the earthquake that hurt Pakistan. This latest tragedy brought other wounds to the surface. A deeper and darker malaise, barely noticed by the elite and taken for granted by most citizens, had infected the country and was now publicly visible. The earthquake that killed tens of thousands of people shone a light on a country tainted by corrupted bureaucrats, army officers, and politicians, by governments rotten to the core, by protected mafias, and by the bloated profits of the heroin industry and the arms trade. Add to this the brutal hypocrisy of the Islamist parties, which exploit the state religion, and the picture is complete. Many ordinary people on the street, unsurprised by tales of privilege and graft, viewed the disaster in this context. At a state school in Lahore, students collecting toys for the children who'd survived the tragedy were asked whom they would like to address them. They voted unanimously against any politician, army officer, or civilian bureaucrat. They wanted a doctor.

None of this, of course, explains the urge to keep writing about a country. The reason is simple. However much I despise the callousness, corruption, and narcissism of a degenerate ruling elite, I have never allowed that to define my attitude toward the country. I have always harbored a deep respect and affection for the common people, whose instincts and intelligence, despite high levels of illiteracy, consistently display a much sounder appreciation of what the country requires than those who have lorded it over them since 1947. Any independent-minded Pakistani journalist or writer will confirm this view.

The people cannot be blamed for the tragedies that have afflicted their country. They are not to blame for the spirit of hopelessness and inescapable bondage that sometimes overcomes them. The surprise is that more of them don't turn to extremist religious groups, but they have generally remained stubbornly aloof from all that, which is highlighted in every election, including the latest, held in February 2008. Given the chance, they vote in large majorities for those who promise social change and reforms and against those in power. They are always disappointed.

COLIN ROBINSON, my long-standing editor, first at Verso, later at the New Press, and now at Scribner, was strongly convinced that I should write this book long before I was. His persistence paid off. His instincts were better than mine. As I was working on the book, Mary-Kay Wilmers, stern janitor of the *London Review of Books,* plucked a lengthy extract from the work-in-progress on Benazir Bhutto's return home. It was, as readers will discover, sharply critical. Two weeks after I delivered it, as I was working on this manuscript, Bhutto was assassinated. Sentiment dictated I soften the prose, but despite my sadness and anger at her death, I resisted. As the German writer Lessing once remarked, "The man who presents truth in all sorts of masks and disguises may be her pander, but never her lover." And truth usually visits Pakistan in whispers. We owe it to the people to speak our minds. The death of Benazir, whom I knew well over many years, was undoubtedly tragic. But not sufficient reason to change my assessment. That she handed over her party to her husband till her son came of age was a sad reflection on the state of democratic politics in Pakistan and confirmed my judgment. The country needs a break from uniforms and dynasties.

My thanks are due to numerous people in Pakistan from all walks of life, from peasants and trade unionists to generals, civil servants, and old friends, who spoke without inhibition during my trips over the last few years. Naming them would not necessarily be construed as friendly. Thanks also, as always, to Susan Watkins, my companion for almost three decades, a friendly but firm editor of the *New Left Review,* as many contributors (myself included) have discovered.

When I began to write this book a London friend asked, "Isn't it reckless to start a book while the dice is still in the air?" If I waited for the dice to fall, I would never have written anything on Pakistan.

TARIQ ALI
APRIL 5, 2008

The Duel

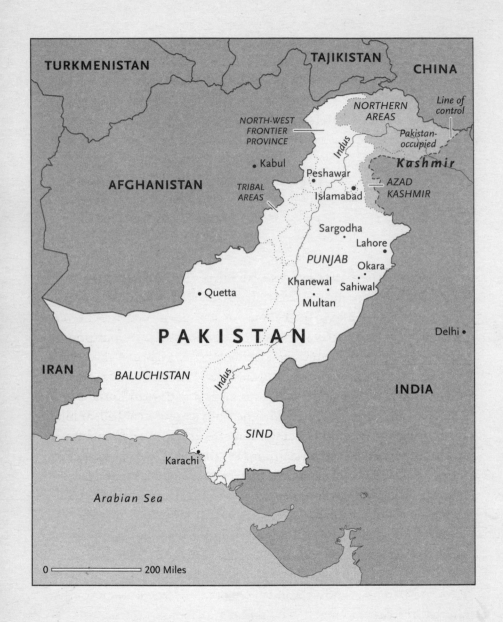

1

PAKISTAN AT SIXTY

A Conflagration of Despair

THE TWENTIETH CENTURY WAS NOT KIND TO PAKISTAN. THE LAST three decades, in particular, had witnessed a shallow and fading state gradually being reduced to the level of a stagnant and treacherous swamp. Business, official and unofficial, flourished at various points, but without the aid of education, technology, or science. A tiny number of people acquired gigantic fortunes, and the opening of a Porsche showroom in Islamabad in 2005 was greeted with loud hurrahs and celebrated as one indicator among others of a country that had, at long last, achieved modernity. What was forgotten were the latest malnutrition statistics that revealed a startling fact: the height of the average citizen was on the decline. According to the latest United Nations Population Fund figures, 60 percent of children under five were moderately or severely stunted.

Few among the rich cared about the underprivileged. The needs of ordinary people, their tattered lives, the retreat to religion, a thriving black market, armed clashes between different Muslim factions, war on the western frontier, and assassination of political leaders—none of this affected the rich too much. The thunder of money drowned out all other noises. Most of the mainstream political parties, like their Western cousins, no longer subscribed to programs rooted in ideology, but instead became dependent on cronyism, clientilism, and soulless followers. The organizational goal has become strictly personal: sinecures, money, power, and unquestioning obedience to the leader or, in some cases, to the army as collective leader. Notables in each party are hostile to every genuine talent. Political positions as well as parliamentary seats are rarely determined on merit. A pure character or a sharp intellect is virtually a disqualification.

When an individual turns sixty s/he gazes in the mirror and is either pleased or filled with discomfort. It's a great pity that a country cannot view itself in similar fashion. It becomes necessary for someone else— artist, poet, filmmaker, or writer—to become the mirror.

The sixtieth anniversary year of Pakistan, 2007, when power appeared to be draining away from the dictator, seemed a good moment to observe the country firsthand. The cities of the plain are best avoided in August, when the rains come and transform them into a huge steam bath. When I lived there, we usually fled to the mountains, where the Himalayan breezes keep the atmosphere permanently refreshed. In 2007 I stayed put. The monsoon season can be hazardous but needs to be experienced once in a while, simply to access the old memory bank. The real killer is a debilitating humidity. Relief arrives in short bursts: a sudden stillness followed by the darkening of the sky, thunderclaps sounding like distant bombs, then the hard rain. Rivers and tributaries quickly overflow. Flash floods make cities impassable. Sewage runs through slums and wealthier neighborhoods alike. Stench transcends class barriers, and even those accustomed to leaping from air-conditioned rooms to air-conditioned cars can't completely escape the smell.

The contrast between climate and the hopeless world of official politics could not be more striking. The latter is a desert. The reliction is complete. Not even an imaginary oasis in sight. Popular disillusionment and resentment is widespread. The large hoardings promoting the cult of the Big Leader (General Musharraf)/Small Leader (provincial shadows with no personality of their own) have assumed a nauseating and nightmarish quality. One of the older sources of official legitimacy—the cultivation of anti-Indian/anti-Hindu fervor—has also run dry. August 14, the country's red-letter day marking its independence, is even more artificial and irritating than before. A cacophony of meaningless slogans impress nobody, as countless clichés of chauvinistic self-adulation in newspaper supplements compete for space with stale photographs of the country's founder, Mohammed Ali Jinnah, and the eternal poet laureate, Allama Iqbal, that have been seen on hundreds of previous occasions. Add to this banal panel discussions in the videosphere, all reminding us of what Jinnah had said or not said. As ever, this is accompanied by a great deal of whinging about how the perfidious Lord Mountbatten and his "promiscuous" wife, Edwina (her love affair with Indian leader Jawaharlal Nehru is treated as a political event by Pakistani blowhards), had favored India when it came to a division of the spoils. It's true, but who cares now? The odd couple can't be blamed for the wreck that the country has become. In private, of course, there is much more soul-searching, and one often hears a surprising collection of people who now feel the state should never have been founded.

Several years after the breakup of the country in 1971, I wrote a book called *Can Pakistan Survive?* It was publicly denounced and banned by the dictator of the day, General Zia-ul-Haq, the worst ever in the country's history. Under his watch the country was heavily "Islamized," its political culture brutalized with dissidents flogged in public. His ghastly legacy appears to have left a permanent mark. My book was pirated in many editions and, as I was later told, read carefully by a number of generals. In it I argued that if the state carried on in the same old way, some of the minority provinces left behind might also defect, leaving the Punjab alone, strutting like a cock on a dunghill. Many who bitterly denounced me as a traitor and renegade are now asking the same question. It's too late for regrets, I tell them. The country is here to stay. It's not the mystical "ideology of Pakistan" or even religion that guarantees its survival, but two other factors: its nuclear capacity and the support it receives from Washington. Were the latter to decide that Pakistan needed a soft balkanization—for instance, the detachment of the North-West Frontier Province and its merger with a NATO-occupied Afghanistan—then China might feel obliged to step in to preserve the existing state. One of the basic contradictions confronting the country has become even more pronounced: thousands of villages and slums remain without electricity or running water. The wooden plow coexists with the atomic pile. This is the real scandal.

On the country's sixtieth birthday (as on its twentieth and fortieth anniversaries) an embattled military regime was fighting for its survival: an external war was being waged on its western frontier, while at home it was being tormented by jihadis, lawyers, and judges. None of this seemed to make much impact on the young daredevils in Lahore, who were determined to commemorate the day in their own fashion. Early in the morning, young males on motorbikes, bull and bullfighter in one, took over the streets to embark on what has become an annual suicide race. As if the only thing worth celebrating is their right to die. Only five managed it in 2007, a much lower figure than in previous years. Maybe this is a rational way to mark a conflict in which more than a million people hacked each other to death as the decaying British Empire prepared to scuttle off home.

Meanwhile another uniformed despot was taking the salute at a military parade in Islamabad to mark Independence Day, mouthing a bad speech written by a bored bureaucrat that failed to stifle the yawns of the surrounding sycophants. Even the F-16s in proud formation failed to excite the audience. Flags were waved by schoolchildren, a band played the national anthem, the whole show was broadcast live, then it was over.

The West prefers to view Pakistan through a single optic. European and North American papers give the impression that the main, if not the only, problem confronting Pakistan is the power of the bearded fanatics skulking in the Hindu Kush, who, as the papers see it, are on the verge of taking over the country. In this account, all that has stopped a jihadi finger from finding its way to the nuclear trigger has been General Musharraf. It was already clear in 2007 that he might drown in a sea of troubles, and so the helpful U.S. State Department pushed out an overinflated life raft in the shape of Benazir Bhutto. But what, some of us were asking months before the tragedy of her assassination in December 2007, if they were to sink together?

In fact, the threat of a jihadi takeover of Pakistan is remote. There is no possibility of a coup by religious extremists unless the army wants one, as in the 1980s, when General Zia-ul-Haq handed over the Ministries of Education and Information to the Jamaat-e-Islami, with dire results: Islamist gangs extinguished all democratic opposition on the campuses, and Jamaati propagandists became embedded in the media. Serious problems confront Pakistan, but these are usually ignored in Washington, by both the administration and the financial institutions. The lack of a basic social infrastructure encourages hopelessness and despair, but only a tiny minority turns to armed jihad.

During periods of military rule in Pakistan three groups get together: military leaders, a corrupt claque of fixer-politicians, and businessmen eyeing juicy contracts or state-owned land. Each is by now sufficiently versed in deception and well trained in concealing petty rivalries and jealousies for the sake of the greater bad. The bond that unites them is money and the primitive accumulation of property in town and country. Politicians ill-favored by the military wonder what they've done wrong and queue up to correct misunderstandings and win acceptance. The country's ruling elite has spent the last sixty years defending its ill-gotten wealth and privilege, and the Supreme Leader (uniformed or not) is invariably intoxicated by their flattery.

What of the official opposition? Alas, the system specializes in producing MNAs (Members of the National Assembly) who, in the main, are always on the lookout for ready cash. Brutal and coarse with raucous voices and a sly cunning, they're experts in cultivating paymasters who become dependent on them. They would be intensely comic figures were they not so dangerous: silkily affectionate when their needs are met, merciless when frustrated. What have the people done to deserve this?

Corruption envelops Pakistan like a sheet of water. The late Benazir Bhutto and her widower, Asif Ali Zardari, had, after two terms in office, accumulated assets of $1.5 billion. The twice prime minister Nawaz Sharif and his brother, with their intimate knowledge of the business cycle, probably netted double that amount. Given the inspiration from above, lesser politicians, bureaucrats on every level, and their counterparts in the armed services have had little trouble in building their own piles. The poor bear the burden, but the middle classes are also affected. Lawyers, doctors, teachers, small businessmen, and traders are crippled by a system in which patronage and bribery are trump cards. Some escape—twenty thousand Pakistani doctors are working in the United States alone—but others come to terms with the system and accept compromises that make them deeply cynical about themselves and everyone else.

MEANWHILE THE ISLAMISTS, while far removed from state power, are busy picking up supporters. The persistent and ruthless missionaries of Tablighi Jamaat (TJ) are especially effective. The name *Tabligh* means the "propagation of true Islam," and the sect has many similarities with born-again Christian fundamentalists in the United States. Sinners from every social group, desperate for purification, queue to join. TJ headquarters in Pakistan are situated in a large mission in Raiwind. Once a tiny village surrounded by fields of wheat, corn, and mustard seed, it is now a fashionable suburb of Lahore, where the Sharif brothers built a Gulf-style palace when they were in power in the 1990s. The TJ was founded in the 1920s by Maulana Ilyas, a cleric who trained at the orthodox Sunni seminary in Deoband, in Uttar Pradesh. At first, its missionaries were concentrated in northern India, but today large groups are in North America and Western Europe. The TJ hopes to get planning permission to build a mosque in East London next to the site of the 2012 Olympic Games. It would be the largest mosque in Europe. In Pakistan, TJ influence is widespread. Penetrating the national cricket team and recruiting stars has been its most conspicuous success: Inzamam-ul-Haq and Mohammad Yousuf are activists for the cause at home, while Mushtaq Ahmed works hard in their interest in Britain. Another triumph was the post-9/11 recruitment of Junaid Jamshed, the charismatic lead singer of Pakistan's first successful pop group, Vital Signs. He renounced his past and now sings only devotional songs—*naats*.

The Tablighis stress their nonviolence and insist they are merely broadcasting the true faith to help people find the correct path in life. This may be so, but it is clear that some younger male recruits, bored with all the dogma, ceremonies, and ritual, are more interested in getting their hands on a Kalashnikov. Many commentators believe that the Tablighi missionary camps are fertile recruiting grounds for armed groups active on the western frontier and in Kashmir.

The establishment has been slow to challenge the interpretation of Islam put forward by groups such as Tablighi. It is not groups of this sort that threaten Musharraf's rule. It is the legal profession that has fought the regime to a virtual standstill. On March 9, 2007, Musharraf suspended Iftikhar Muhammad Chaudhry, the chief justice of the Supreme Court, pending an investigation. The accusations against Chaudhry were contained in a letter from Naeem Bokhari, a pro-government lawyer. Curiously, the letter was widely circulated—I received a copy via e-mail. I wondered whether something was afoot, but decided the letter was just sour grapes. Not so: it soon became clear that it was part of a plan. The letter began with a few personal complaints before extravagant rhetoric took over:

> My Lord, the dignity of lawyers is consistently being violated by you. We are treated harshly, rudely, brusquely and nastily. We are not heard. We are not allowed to present our case. There is little scope for advocacy. The words used in the Bar Room for Court No. 1 are "the slaughter house." We are cowed down by aggression from the Bench, led by you. All we receive from you is arrogance, aggression and belligerence.

The following passage should have alerted me to what was really going on:

> I am pained at the wide publicity to cases taken up by My Lord in the Supreme Court under the banner of Fundamental Rights. The proceedings before the Supreme Court can conveniently and easily be referred to the District and Sessions Judges. I am further pained by the media coverage of the Supreme Court on the recovery of an [abducted] female. In the Bar Room, this is referred to as a "media circus."

Chief Justice Chaudhry was beginning to embarrass the regime. He had found against the government on a number of key issues, including the rushed privatization of the Pakistan Steel Mills in Karachi, a pet project of the then prime minister, Shaukat "Shortcut" Aziz. The case was reminiscent of Yeltsin's Russia. Economists had estimated that the industry was worth $5 billion. Seventy-five percent of the shares were sold for $362 million in a thirty-minute auction to a friendly consortium consisting of Arif Habib Securities (Pakistan), al-Tuwairqi (Saudi Arabia), and the Magnitogorsk Iron & Steel Works Open JSC (Russia). The privatization wasn't popular with the military, and the retiring chairman, Haq Nawaz Akhtar, complained that "the plant could have fetched more money if it were sold as scrap." The general perception was that the president and the prime minister had helped out their friends. A frequenter of the stock exchange told me in Karachi that Arif Habib Securities, which now owns 20 percent of Pakistan Steel Mills, was set up as a front company for Shaukat Aziz. Tuwairqi, the Saudi steel giant, acquired 40 percent. Musharraf is reportedly on close terms with this company and had previously turned up to open a steel plant set up by the group on 220 acres of land rented from the adjoining Pakistan Steel Mills. Now they have a stake in the whole thing.

After the Supreme Court insisted that "disappeared" political activists be produced in court and refused to dismiss rape cases, some in Islamabad worried that the chief justice might even declare the military presidency unconstitutional. Paranoia set in. Measures had to be taken. The general and his cabinet decided to frighten Chaudhry by suspending him. On March 9, 2007, the chief justice was arrested and kept in solitary confinement for several hours, manhandled by intelligence operatives, and traduced on state television. But instead of caving in and accepting a generous resignation settlement, the judge insisted on defending himself, triggering a remarkable movement in defense of an independent judiciary. This was surprising. Pakistani judges are notoriously conservative and have legitimized every coup with a bogus "doctrine of necessity" ruling. When Musharraf took over, a handful of judges refused to swear an oath of loyalty and resigned, but not Chaudhry, who was elevated to the Supreme Court a year later, in January 2000, and became chief justice in 2005. Prior to this appointment, little or nothing indicated that he was a judicial activist.

When I visited Pakistan in April 2007, the protests were getting bigger every day. Initially confined to the country's eighty thousand lawyers and several dozen judges, unrest soon spread beyond them, which was again unusual in a country whose people have become increasingly alienated from elite rule. But the lawyers were marching in defense of the constitutional separation of powers. Street demonstrations occurred in virtually every city, and the sight of men in black being confronted by cordons of armed policemen became commonplace. The independent TV stations—Geo, Indus, Aaj, and others—provided daily coverage of events. Musharraf and his ministers were subjected to sharp and critical interviews that must have made the president yearn for the comparative safety of CNN and BBC World. The general would regularly upbraid journalists for not treating him with the same deference shown to Bush and European leaders by Western networks.

This delightfully old-fashioned struggle involved neither money nor religion, but principle. Careerists from the opposition (some of whom had organized thuggish assaults on the Supreme Court when in power) tried to make the cause their own. "Don't imagine they've all suddenly changed," Abid Hasan Manto, one of the country's most respected lawyers, told me. "They're cut from the same cloth as the rest of the elite. On the other hand, when the time comes, almost anything can act as a spark."

Most people in the Islamabad bureaucracy soon recognized that they had made a gigantic blunder in arresting Chaudhry. But as often happens in a crisis, instead of acknowledging this and moving to correct it, the perpetrators decided on a show of strength. The first targets were independent TV channels. In Karachi and other cities in the south, three channels suddenly went dark as they were screening reports on the demonstrations. There was popular outrage. On May 5 Chaudhry drove from Islamabad to give a speech in Lahore, stopping at every town en route to meet supporters; it took twenty-six hours to complete a journey that normally takes three or four. In Islamabad, Musharraf plotted a counterstrike.

The judge was due to visit Karachi, the country's largest city, a sprawling, anarchic mass of 15 million people, on May 12. Political power in Karachi rests in the hands of the MQM (Muttahida Qaumi Movement/United National Movement), an unsavory outfit created in 1984 during Zia's dictatorship. It began life in 1978 as a student group set up by Altaf Hussain with a membership restricted to Urdu-speaking students in the Sind. These were the children of Muslim refugees who had fled India in 1947 and sought a new home in Pakistan. Many remained poor and suffered from job discrimination. The new organization played on these resentments and gave them voice, but soon acquired notoriety for its involvement in protection rackets and other kinds of violence. It has supported Musharraf loyally through every crisis.

Its leader, Altaf Hussain, fled the country in the 1990s to avoid prosecution. He was given asylum in Britain and now guides the movement from a safe perch in London, fearful of retribution from his many opponents were he to return. In a video address to his followers in Karachi just prior to Chaudhry's arrival, he said, "If conspiracies are hatched to end the present democratically elected government, then each and every worker of MQM . . . will stand firm and defend the democratic government." On Islamabad's instructions, the MQM leaders decided to prevent the judge from leaving the airport and addressing his supporters, who were assaulted in different parts of the city. Almost fifty people were killed. After footage of the violence was screened on Aaj TV, the station was attacked by armed MQM volunteers, who shot at the building for six whole hours and set cars in the parking lot on fire.

Senior police officers, the chief minister, and the governor all failed to intervene, and a successful general strike followed, which further isolated the regime. A devastating report, *Carnage in Karachi*, published in August 2007 by the Human Rights Commission of Pakistan, confirmed in great detail what everyone already knew: the police and army had been ordered to stand by while armed MQM members went on the rampage:

> . . . a matter of grave concern from the perspective of the institutional integrity of the state is the virtual withdrawal of the state's security apparatus for almost 20 hours and the actual takeover of the city by armed cadres of more than one political party. The spectacle of a *disarmed* police force operating on the direction of *armed* cadres was highly disturbing, especially since key officers of the state were reduced to expressing their helplessness.

Musharraf, trying desperately to keep a grip on the country, was now confronted with the possibility that a popular movement in defense of the chief justice might become uncontrollable, especially if the events in Karachi were repeated elsewhere. Fearful of the consequences of further repression, he had little alternative but to sound a retreat. The chief justice's appeal against his suspension was finally admitted and heard by the Supreme Court. On July 20 a unanimous decision reinstated him, and shamefaced government lawyers were seen leaving the precincts in a hurry. A reinvigorated court got down to business. Hafiz Abdul Basit was a "disappeared" prisoner arrested for "terrorism" without any specific charge. The chief justice summoned Tariq Pervez, the director general of Pakistan's Federal Investigation Agency, and asked him politely where the prisoner was being kept. Pervez replied that he had no idea and had never even heard of Basit. The chief justice instructed the police chief to produce Basit in court within forty-eight hours: "Either produce the detainee or get ready to go to jail." Two days later Basit was produced and then released, after the police failed to present any substantial evidence against him. Washington and London were not happy. They were convinced that Basit was a terrorist who should have been kept in prison indefinitely, as he certainly would have been in Britain or the United States.

The Supreme Court then decided to consider six petitions challenging Musharraf's decision to contest the presidency without relinquishing his command of the army. Even though parliament had passed the President to Hold Another Office Act in 2004 to circumvent a challenge to Musharraf's decision to stay on as army chief while president, the Supreme Court had accepted an appeal against this decision, saying that the language of the amended law was not in conformity with the constitution. There was also the question of term limits: Pakistan's constitution permits the president only two terms in office. Musharraf had assumed the presidency in June 2001. This was followed by a referendum in 2002 that he claimed was a "democratic mandate" and therefore, his opponents argued, constituted a second term. An added problem was that he was over sixty and, according to government rules, should therefore have retired as chief of army staff. Having done so, he would then have faced a two-year bar on any government employee seeking elected office. Unsurprisingly, there was much nervousness in Islamabad. The president's supporters threatened dire consequences if the Court ruled against him. But to declare a state of emergency would have required the support of the army, and at that stage, soon after the Karachi killings, informal soundings had revealed a reluctance to intervene on the part of the generals. Their polite excuse at the time was that they were too heavily committed to the "war on terror" to be able to devote resources to preserve law and order in the cities. They would later, with a bit of encouragement from the U.S. embassy, change their minds.

As THE JUDICIAL crisis temporarily ended, a more somber one loomed. Most of today's jihadi groups are the mongrel offspring of Pakistani and Western intelligence outfits, born in the 1980s when General Zia was in power and waging the West's war against the godless Russians, who were then occupying Afghanistan. It was then that state patronage of Islamist groups began. One beneficiary was the cleric Maulana Abdullah, who was allotted land to build a madrassa in the heart of Islamabad, not far from the government buildings. Soon the area was increased so that two separate facilities (for male and female students) could be constructed, together with an enlarged Lal Masjid, or Red Mosque. State money was provided for all this, and the government was the technical owner of the property.

During the 1980s and 1990s this complex became a transit camp for young jihadis on their way to fight in Afghanistan and, later, Kashmir. Abdullah made no secret of his beliefs. He was sympathetic to the Saudi Wahhabi interpretation of Islam and during the Iraq-Iran war was only too happy to encourage the killing of Shia "heretics" in Pakistan. Shia constitute 20 percent of the Muslim population in Pakistan, and prior to Zia's dictatorship there was little hostility between them and the majority of the Sunnis. Abdullah's patronage of ultrasectarian, anti-Shia terror groups led to his own assassination in October 1998. Members of a rival Muslim faction killed him soon after he had finished praying in his own mosque.

His sons, Abdul Rashid Ghazi and Abdul Aziz, then took control of the mosque and religious schools. The government agreed that Aziz would lead the Friday congregation. His sermons were often supportive of Al Qaeda, though he was more careful about his language after 9/11. Senior civil servants and military officers often attended Friday prayers. The better-educated and soft-spoken Rashid, with his lean, haggard face and ragged beard, was left to act as spin doctor and was effective in charming visiting foreign and local journalists.

But after November 2004, when the army, under heavy U.S. pressure, launched an offensive in the tribal areas bordering Afghanistan, relations between the brothers and the government became tense. Aziz in particular was livid. When, according to Rashid, "a retired colonel of the Pakistan army approached us with a written request for a fatwa clarifying the Sharia perspective on the army waging a war on the tribal people," Aziz did not waste any time. He issued a fatwa declaring that the killing of its own people by a Muslim army is *haram* (forbidden), "that any army official killed during the operation should not be given a Muslim burial," and that "the militants who die while fighting the Pakistan army are martyrs." Within days of its publication the fatwa had been publicly endorsed by almost five hundred "religious scholars." Despite heavy pressure from the mosque's patrons in the ISI (Inter-Services Intelligence), Pakistan's military intelligence, the brothers refused to withdraw it. The government response was surprisingly muted. Aziz's official status as the mosque's imam was ended and an arrest warrant issued against him, but it was never served, and the brothers were allowed to carry on as usual. Perhaps the ISI thought they might still prove useful.

Set up in 1948 with officers of the three services of the Pakistan military, the ISI was originally a routine intelligence directorate specializing in the gathering and analysis of information and focused largely on India and local "Communist subversion." Its size and budget grew at a phenomenal rate during the first Afghan war against the Soviet Union. It worked closely with U.S., French, and British intelligence services during that period and, as described later in this book, played a central role in arming and training the mujahideen and, later, infiltrating the Taliban into Afghanistan. With a level of autonomy no greater than that allowed the CIA or the DIA in the United States, the ISI operated throughout with the official approval of the military high command.

Earlier in 2004 the government had claimed to have uncovered a terrorist plot to bomb military installations, including the GHQ (general headquarters) in Rawalpindi and state buildings in Islamabad, on August 14. Machine guns and explosives were found in Abdul Rashid Ghazi's car. New warrants were issued against the brothers and they were arrested. At this point the religious affairs minister, Ijaz-ul-Haq, General Zia's son, persuaded his colleagues to pardon the clerics in return for a written apology pledging that they wouldn't become involved in the armed struggle. Rashid claimed the whole plot had been scripted to please the West and in a newspaper article asked the religious affairs minister to provide proof that the minister had supposedly asked for the undertaking. There was no response.

In January 2007, the brothers decided to shift their focus from foreign to domestic policy and demanded an immediate implementation of Sharia law. Until then they had been content to denounce U.S. policies in the Muslim world and America's local point man, Musharraf, for helping dismantle the Taliban government in Afghanistan. They did not publicly support the three attempts that had recently been made on Musharraf's life, but it was hardly a secret that they regretted his survival. The statement they issued in January was intended as an open provocation to the regime. Aziz spelled out his program: "We will never permit dance and music in Pakistan. All those interested in such activities should shift to India. We are tired of waiting. It is Sharia or martyrdom." They felt threatened by the government's demolition of two mosques that had been built illegally on public land. When they received notices announcing the demolition of parts of the Red Mosque and the women's seminary, the brothers dispatched dozens of women students in black burkas to occupy a children's library next to their seminary. The intelligence agencies appeared to be taken aback, but quickly negotiated an end to the occupation.

The brothers continued to test the authorities. Sharia was implemented in the gender-segregated madrassas (religious schools) housed in the mosque complex, and there was a public bonfire of books, CDs, and DVDs. Then the women from the madrassa directed their fire against Islamabad's upmarket brothels, targeting Aunty Shamim, a well-known procuress who provided "decent" girls for indecent purposes, and whose clients included the local great and good, a number of them moderate religious leaders. Aunty ran the brothel like an office: she kept office hours and shut up shop at midday on Friday so that clients could go to the nearest mosque, which was the Lal Masjid. The morality brigades raided the brothel and "freed" the women. Most of the girls were educated, some were single parents, others were widows, all were desperately short of funds. The office hours suited them. Aunty Shamim fled town, and her workers sought similar employment elsewhere, while the madrassa girls celebrated an easy victory.

Emboldened by their triumph, the brothers next decided to take on Islamabad's upmarket massage parlors, not all of which were sex joints, and some of which were staffed by Chinese citizens. Six Chinese women were abducted in late June and taken to the mosque. The Chinese ambassador was not pleased. He informed President Hu Jintao, who was even less pleased, and Beijing made it clear that it wanted its citizens freed without delay. Government fixers arrived at the mosque to plead the strategic importance of Sino-Pakistan relations, and the women were released. The massage industry promised that henceforth only men would massage other men. Honor was satisfied, even though the deal directly contradicted the Sharia, which usually decrees the death penalty for homosexuality. The liberal press depicted the antivice campaign as the Talibanization of Pakistan, which annoyed the Lal Masjid clerics. "Rudy Giuliani, when he became mayor of New York, closed the brothels," Rashid said. "Was that also Talibanization?" Rashid, were he alive, would have strongly supported the "resignation" of Governor Spitzer.

Angered and embarrassed by the kidnapping of the Chinese women, Musharraf demanded a resolution to the crisis. The Saudi ambassador to Pakistan, Ali Saeed Awadh Asseri, arrived at the mosque and spent ninety minutes with the brothers. They were welcoming but told him that all they wanted was the implementation of Saudi laws in Pakistan. Surely he agreed? The ambassador declined to meet the press after the visit, so his response remains unrecorded. His mediation a failure, Plan B was set in motion.

On July 3, the paramilitary Rangers began to lay barbed wire at the end of the street in front of the mosque. Some madrassa students opened fire, shot a Ranger dead, and for good measure torched the neighboring Environment Ministry. Security forces responded the same night with tear gas and machine guns. The next morning the government declared a curfew in the area, and a weeklong siege of the mosque began, with television networks beaming images across the world. Rashid, infatuated with publicity, must have been pleased. The brothers thought that keeping women and children hostage inside the compound might save them. But some were released and Aziz was arrested as he tried to escape in a burka, only to be released quietly a week later and allowed to return to his village.

On July 10, paratroopers finally stormed the complex. Rashid and at least a hundred others died in the ensuing clashes. Eleven soldiers were also killed and more than forty wounded. Several police stations were attacked, and ominous complaints came from the tribal areas. Maulana Faqir Mohammed, a leading Taliban supporter, told thousands of armed tribesmen, "We beg Allah to destroy Musharraf, and we will seek revenge for the Lal Masjid atrocities." This view was reiterated by Osama bin Laden, who declared Musharraf an "infidel" and said that "removing him is now obligatory for Muslims."

I was in Pakistan in September 2007 when suicide bombers hit military targets, among them a bus carrying ISI employees, to avenge Rashid's death. But in the country as a whole the reaction was muted. The leaders of the MMA (Muttahida Majlis-e-Amal), a coalition of religious parties that governed the Frontier Province and shares power in Baluchistan, made ugly public statements, but took no action. Only a thousand people marched in the demonstration called in the provincial capital, Peshawar, the day after the deaths. This was the largest protest march, and even here the mood was subdued. There was no shrill glorification of the martyrs. The contrast with the campaign to reinstate the chief justice could not have been more pronounced. Three weeks later, more than one hundred thousand people gathered in the Punjabi city of Kasur to observe the 250th anniversary of the death of the great seventeenth-century poet Bulleh Shah, one in a distinguished line of Sufi poets who promoted skepticism, denounced organized religion, and avoided all forms of orthodoxy. For Bulleh Shah a mullah should be compared to a barking dog or a crowing cock. In response to a question from a believer as to his own religious identity, the poet replied:

Who knows what I am,
Neither a believer in the mosque,
Nor an unbeliever worshipping clay,
Neither Moses nor Pharaoh,
Neither sinner nor saint;
Who knows what I am . . .

That this and similar poems are regularly performed throughout Pakistan is one indication that jihadis are not popular in most of the country. Nor is the government. The mosque episode raised several important questions that remain unanswered. Why did the government not act in January when the vigilantes first poured out? How did the clerics accumulate such a large store of weapons without the knowledge of the government? Was the ISI aware that the mosque concealed an arsenal? If so, why did they keep it quiet? What were the relations between the clerics and government agencies? Why was Aziz released and allowed to return to his village without being charged?

I wondered if I might find answers to these questions in Peshawar, the capital of the North-West Frontier Province, a few miles from the Khyber Pass and Afghanistan. I had not visited the city for over a quarter of a century, not since it had become the headquarters of the anti-Soviet jihad in the 1980s and its governor, a close colleague of General Zia's, had defended the heroin trade. On that occasion in 1973 I had crossed the Afghan border and returned without a passport, just to see if it could still be done. Pleased with my success I then took a bus to Rawalpindi. I still remember the thrill of catching sight of a bloodred sunset filling the sky as we crossed the river Indus on the bridge at Attock.

The old bridge always brings back memories of childhood and youth. The sight of the turbulent waters below helps recall the history that had, in the shape of successive conquerors from Europe and Central Asia, marched through here on its way south and long before Alexander. How many soldiers had died making the crossing on makeshift rafts? The Mogul emperor Akbar had built a giant fort just upstream from where the Kabul River merged noisily with its more famous cousin. Its strategic aim was to house a garrison that could ward off invaders and crush local rebellions and, no doubt, tax merchants.

Thirty-four years later, on my way by car from Islamabad, I could not suppress my excitement. I stopped the car to take a look at the river and the fort above. The fort is now a notorious political prison, a torture center used by successive Pakistan governments and not just the military kind. I tried but could not see the two black rocks that, as I remembered, jutted from the river just below the fort. Where were they? Perhaps they could only be seen from the old nineteenth-century bridge, a masterpiece of Victorian engineering, surrounded by Mogul ruins, including an old gravestone labeled "prostitute's tomb" (a punishment inflicted by a queen on her husband's favorite mistress) that used to make us giggle as children.

The two rocks had been named after two brothers, Kamal-ud-Din and Jamal-ud-Din, who were flung down from their peak into the river below on the orders of the great Mogul emperor. Akbar's toleration of dissent has been greatly exaggerated. Its true that while the Catholic Inquisition was sowing terror in Europe, Akbar, himself a Muslim, ruled that "anyone is to be allowed to go over to a religion that pleases him." The interreligious debates he organized in Agra included Hindus, Muslims, Christians, Parsis, Jains, Jews, and the atheists of the Carvaka school, who argued that Brahmans had established ceremonies for the dead only "as a means of livelihood" for themselves.

But Akbar sometimes flouted his own injunctions when his power was challenged. Hence his deep anger with the rebellious Pashtuns from Waziristan and their challenging philosophy. The brothers were members of a sixteenth-century Muslim sect, the Roshnais, "Enlightened Ones," founded by their father, Pir Roshan. They rejected all revealed religions and hence the Koran. They argued against the mediation of prophets or kings. The Creator was alone and each person should relate to Him as an individual.* Religion was a personal matter between Allah and a believer.

Akbar was busy trying to create his own synthetic religion as a way of bridging various confessional and class divides and uniting India. The persecution of this sect, however, was not the outcome of ideological

---

*Similar ideas were floating around Christian Europe at the time and were subsequently deployed by Oliver Cromwell to topple Charles I and execute him.

rivalry. The Enlightened Ones were popular among the peasantry in the region, and their approach to life was often used to justify rebellions against the central authority. The Mogul king, who founded the city of Peshawar as a military and trading base, regarded this as intolerable.

Peshawar, now a city of over 3 million, has trebled in size over the last thirty years. Most of its new inhabitants consist of three genera-tions of refugees, a result of the interconnected Afghan wars unleashed by the big powers (the Soviet Union and the United States respectively) in the twentieth and twenty-first centuries. The colonial city built by the British was designed as a cantonment town, to house a garrison that protected the northwestern frontier of British India against czarist and Bolshevik intrigues. This function has been preserved and expanded.

Peshawar remains a border city, but it is not the case, as the *New York Times* reported on January 18, 2008, that "for centuries, fighting and lawlessness have been part of the fabric of this frontier town." This view is derived from the minstrel of the British Empire, Rudyard Kipling, whose descriptions were mistakenly read as history. In a dis-patch from Peshawar, a location he characterized as "the city of evil countenances," to the *Civil and Military Gazette* in Lahore on March 28, 1885, hostility to the British presence was described as follows:

Under the shop lights in front of the sweet-meat and *ghee* seller's booths, the press and dins of words is thickest. Faces of dogs, swine, weasels and goats, all the more hideous for being set on human bodies, and lighted with human intelligence, gather in front of the ring of lamp-light, where they may be studied for half-an-hour at a stretch. Pathans, Afridis, Logas, Kohistanis, Turcomans, and a hundred other varieties of the turbulent Afghan race, are gathered in the vast human menagerie between the Gate and the Ghor Kutri. As an Englishman passes, they will turn to scowl upon him, and in many cases to spit fluently to the ground after he has passed. One burly big-paunched ruffian, with shaven head and a neck creased and dimpled with rolls of fat, is specially zealous in this religious rite—contenting himself with no perfunctory performance, but with a wholesouled expectoration, that must be as refreshing to his comrades, as it is disgusting to the European, sir. . . . But he is only one of twenty thousand. The main road teems with magnificent scoundrels and handsome ruffians; all giving the on-looker the impression of wild beasts held back from murder and violence, and chafing against the restraint.

There was little trouble during the nineteenth and twentieth centuries, except when wars were being waged by the British Empire in Afghanistan. Although the British, attempting to crush and defuse a nationalist current demanding independence, had imposed military rule and were administering heavy punishments for trivial offenses in the frontier province, the largest movement during the twentieth century was explicitly peaceful. Ghaffar Khan and Dr. Khan Sahib, two brothers from a landed family in Charsadda, decided to launch a political, nonviolent struggle against the British in 1930. The Redshirt movement, as it became known (because of the color of the shirts worn by its supporters rather than any other affinities; their inspiration was Gandhi not Lenin), spread rapidly throughout the region. Ghaffar Khan and his volunteers visited every single village to organize the peasants against the empire and branches of the movement emerged even in the remotest village.

The British authorities, stung by the growth of support for this organization, were determined it should be "nipped in the bud." This led to the notorious massacre in the Qissa Khwani (Storytellers) bazaar in 1930, when a thousand or so Redshirts who had gathered to welcome Congress leaders were informed that the authorities had refused to let the leaders enter the province. The Congress held a mass meeting and called for an immediate boycott of British-owned shops. The governor ordered the arrest of Ghaffar Khan and others under Section 144, a legal clause in the public-order ordinance prohibiting the assembly of more than four people in public spaces, a law still much used in South Asia. The demonstrators refused to move, and troops opened fire, killing two hundred activists. More people poured out onto the streets, their numbers compelling the troops to withdraw. Peshawar was under the control of its people for four whole days without any violence prior to the entry of British military reinforcements. The massacre and its aftermath were described by a colonial officer, Sir Herbert

Thompson, as a typical case of "a child astonished by its own tantrum, returning to the security of the nanny's hand."*

Despite the extensive use of policy spies and infiltrated agents, the British could not bring forward a single charge of violence against Ghaffar Khan and his supporters, but this did not prevent them from continually harassing, imprisoning, and maltreating the leaders and activists. The Qissa Khwani massacre increased support for the Redshirts, and because, despite his Muslim beliefs, Ghaffar Khan believed in a unified and secular India, he came to the attention of Mahatma Gandhi and Jawaharlal Nehru. The Redshirts formally applied to join the Congress Party and were admitted. The result was a Congress presence in the province that led to the party winning successive elections from 1937 onward. Nehru would later write in his autobiography:

> It was surprising how this Pathan accepted the idea of non-violence, far more so in theory than many of us. And it was because he believed in it that he managed to impress his people with the importance of remaining peaceful in spite of provocation. . . . [T]he self-discipline that the frontier people showed in 1930 and subsequent years has been something amazing.

This area with a large Muslim majority preferred to remain aloof from the Muslim League and the idea of Pakistan, though the League would acquire a base in the province with the help of the imperial bureaucracy and police force and a combination of chicanery and violence. The British, who had assiduously encouraged the division between the Hindu and Muslim communities, were confused and irritated by the Redshirts. In the work of another British colonial officer, Sir Olaf Caroe, this was expressed in the form of a reactionary mysticism. Caroe's generally interesting history of the Pashtun (Pathan to the colonists) people contains oddities such as "It is hard to see how the

---

*Quoted in *The Pathan Unarmed* by Mukulika Banerjee (Oxford, 2000). This work by an Indian scholar, the most comprehensive history of the Redshirt movement and its leaders, is ignored by most Pakistani historians and social anthropologists because it contradicts the founding myths of the country.

Pathan tradition could reconcile itself for long to Hindu leadership, by so many regarded as smooth-faced, pharisaical and double-dealing. . . . How then could he have associated himself with a party under Indian, even Brahmin, inspiration . . ." There is more nonsense along similar lines. Those Pashtuns who were not prepared to fall into line with the British were dealt with brutally.

A U.S. journalist who witnessed the conflict interviewed Mahatma Gandhi. "What," he asked the Indian leader, "do you think of Western civilization?" The old fox smiled. "It would be a good idea," he replied, the treatment of Pashtun nationalists foremost in his mind. British agents would bribe the tribes while their propagandists spread rumors that Ghaffar Khan, a pious Muslim, was a secret Brahman. Congress leaders were barred from visiting the province while all doors were opened for the pro-British Muslim League. That this special benevolence on the part of the British was repeatedly rejected by a majority of the Pashtuns is an indication of the strength of Ghaffar Khan's movement. His ideas of nonviolence and a unified, independent India went deep. It would take decades of bribery and repression (including after the birth of Pakistan) to wrench them out of the soil, with disastrous consequences.

An imperial stereotype of the "childlike" but "noble savage" Pathan pervades much of colonial literature, including Kipling's short stories and his repressed homoerotic novel *Kim*. Having convinced themselves that these ancient warrior tribes were incapable of rational thought and needed to be spoon-fed forever, the British were genuinely surprised when this turned out not to be the case. In colonial historiography, violence and Pashtun could never be opposites.

The tensions and violent undercurrents that mark Peshawar today have little to do with previous centuries, but are a direct result of the continuing wars in neighboring Afghanistan, whose impact on Pakistan, China, and the United States/European Union is discussed in a subsequent chapter. Pakistan's North-West Frontier Province (NWFP) is the only province named geographically and thus denied its ethnic Pashtun identity.

Since October 2002, the MMA, a united front consisting of the Jamaat-e-Islami (JI) and the Jamiat-Ulema-e-Islam (JUI), together with four minor religious sects, has governed here, though losing badly in 2008. Though it has at times dominated the NWFP, the Islamist coalition won only 15 percent of the national vote in 2002, their highest ever, but still far removed from winning power nationally through the ballot box. The two parties are different in character. Of the two parties, the JI was more rigid in its interpretation of religion. It had been founded in Lahore in 1941 as a riposte to the Muslim League and the Pakistan Resolution and was viewed by its founder, Abul Ala Maududi (1903–79), as a "counter-League." Maududi was highly regarded as a theologian, and his links with the Wahhabis of Saudi Arabia predated the formation of Pakistan. The JUI was based in the North-West Frontier and Baluchistan. Its leader, Mufti Mahmud (1919–80), was a wily political operator, capable of alliances with secular nationalists to further his aims. The origins of this group lay in the Deoband seminary that was regarded as the home of Sunni orthodoxy in prepartition India. Both parties saw the birth of Pakistan as a secular nationalist conspiracy against the "real truths of Islam."

The JI is probably the best-organized political grouping in the country. Its internal structure was modeled on that of traditional Communist parties, and it retains a cell structure in every major city to this day. The JUI was more traditional, confined to the border provinces, and dependent on kinship structures. During the Cold War the JI, through its close links with Saudi Arabia, was firmly committed to the West, while the JUI flirted with the pro-Soviet groups in Pakistan. Today both claim to be hostile to Washington, but the differences are largely tactical and local. Both parties would probably be prepared for a serious deal with Washington and, like the Muslim Brotherhood in Egypt, view how the pro-NATO Islamists run Turkey as a possible model for future relations. The notion that these are hard-core Islamists hell-bent on imposing a caliphate is frivolous. Prevented from any real autonomy in the socioeconomic sphere, they have chosen to assert their Islamist identity by agitating for the Sharia laws, targeting coeducational institutions such as the University of Peshawar (where gender relations have been relatively relaxed since the foundation of the country), painting out women on advertising billboards, threatening video shops, etc.

During a sixty-minute debate with a JI ideologue on CNBC (Pakistan) a few years ago, I asked why they were so obsessed with women. Why not leave them alone? Why try and obliterate their images? His reply was reminiscent of that of a radical feminist from the seventies (when campaigns against pornography and sex parlors were much in vogue): "We do not like women being treated as sex objects. Do you?" I admitted I didn't either, but surely painting over them was hardly a solution. And what about men? I inquired politely. Were they not sex objects as well? At this point the host of the show hurriedly moved on to safer territory. He assumed I was referring to male homosexuality, forbidden by the Koran, which is widespread throughout the country and has strong roots in the Frontier regions, which some trace back to Alexander's invasion and the Greeks that stayed behind. There are other and more mundane reasons. However, I was not merely referring to homosexuality but men as sex objects for women. Why should this be tolerated? I was hoping to move on and discuss the mushrooming of sex videos and porn since the MMA electoral triumph, but there was no more time.

The general disgust with traditional politics has created a moral vacuum, which is filled by pornography and religiosity of various sorts. In some areas religion and pornography go together: the highest sales of porn videos are in Peshawar and Quetta, strongholds of the religious parties. Taliban leaders in Pakistan target video shops, but the dealers merely go underground. Nor should it be imagined that the bulk of the porn comes from the West. There is a thriving clandestine industry in Pakistan, with its own local stars, male and female. Sexual frustration has the country in thrall.

To DISCUSS THE state of the NWFP, I met with a group of local intellectuals, journalists, and secular nationalist politicians, some of them heirs of the old Redshirt tradition even though the shirts are now somewhat soiled. Ghaffar Khan's son and grandson were infected with the disease that afflicts traditional Pakistani politicians, being bereft of principle or program, cutting deals with the military and the Muslim League to further Awami National Party (ANP) interests. We were meeting at the Ghaffar Khan Centre, which is both party headquarters and a library and meeting place. The discussion centered on the MMA, the Taliban, and the U.S./EU occupation of Afghanistan. The view here was that the MMA had only won because they were backed by the military and had equated a vote for them with a vote for the Koran. This was no doubt partially true, but left the tarnished record of the ANP's period in office out of the equation. Understandable enough given the location and circumstances, but something that needs to be addressed if they are to move forward again. This is the only secular force in the region with a sprinkling of cadres who are still capable of seeing the larger picture. They realize they need a strategic plan, and that continually shifting positions and political somersaults spell disaster. The written program of the party has not changed much over the years—land reforms, social justice, etc.—but the remoteness of all this from its practice has led to a great deal of cynicism. In addition, the party has now abandoned its anti-imperialist rhetoric and, like the Bhutto family's Pakistan Peoples Party (PPP), is banking its hopes on a prolonged U.S. presence in the region to get rid of its religious opponents.

Some of the key problems confronting the Frontier Province relate to neighboring Afghanistan. Afrasiab Khattak, the most intelligent leader of the ANP, believes that the worst period in the region's history began during General Zia's dictatorship, when the country was awash with heroin, Western and Mossad agents, and unlimited weaponry and cash to fight the Soviet troops then encamped in Afghanistan. This is true, but some of the principal leaders of the ANP, including Ajmal Khattak, wholeheartedly backed the Soviet intervention and settled down in Afghanistan for the duration. This was, alas, a common view of much of what passed for the left in Pakistan at that time. Some well-known Pakistani commentators who supported the U.S./NATO occupation in 2001 had reacted with a similar enthusiasm when Soviet troops moved southward across the Oxus in 1979.

THE FAILURE OF the NATO occupation has revived the Taliban as well as the trade in heroin and destabilized northwestern Pakistan. The indiscriminate bombing raids by U.S. drones have killed too many innocent civilians, and the culture of revenge remains strong in the region. The corruption and cronyism that are the hallmarks of the NATO-installed Karzai government have grown like an untreated tumor and alienated many Afghans who had welcomed the toppling of Mullah Omar and hoped for better times. Instead they have witnessed landgrabs and the construction of luxury villas by Karzai's colleagues. Western funds designed to aid some reconstruction were rapidly siphoned off to build fancy homes for the native enforcers. In year two of the occupation there was a gigantic housing scandal. Cabinet ministers awarded themselves and favored cronies prime real estate in Kabul, where land prices reached a high point after the occupation since the occupiers and their camp followers had to live in the style to which they had become accustomed. Karzai's colleagues built their large villas, protected by NATO troops, in full view of the poor.

Not all the Pashtun tribes in Pakistan and Afghanistan have recognized the Durand Line imposed by the British. And so, when anti-NATO guerrillas flee to the tribal areas under Pakistani control, they are not handed over to Islamabad, but are fed and clothed till they go back or are protected like the Al Qaeda leaders. This is what the fighting in South Waziristan is largely about. Washington wants to see more bodies and feels that Musharraf's deals with tribal elders border on capitulation to the Taliban. This makes the Americans angry because Pakistan's military actions are paid for directly by CENTCOM (United States Central Command) and they feel they are not getting value for their money. This is not to mention the $10 billion Pakistan has received since 9/11 for signing up for the "war on terror."

The problem is that some elements within Pakistani military intelligence feel that they can take Afghanistan back once Operation Enduring Freedom has come to an end. For this reason they refuse to give up their links with some of the guerrilla leaders. They even think that the United States might ultimately favor such an action, and as is known, Karzai has put out serious feelers to the Taliban. I doubt whether this is possible since other players are in the region. Iranian influence is strong in Herat and western Afghanistan. The Northern Alliance receives Russian weapons. India is the largest regional power. The only lasting settlement would be a regional guarantee of Afghan stability and the formation of a national government after a NATO withdrawal.

Even if Washington accepted a cleansed version of the Taliban, the others will not, and a new set of civil conflicts could only lead to disintegration this time. Were this to happen, the Pashtuns on both sides of the Durand Line might opt to create their own state and further bifurcate Pakistan. It sounds extremely far-fetched today, but what if the confederation of tribes that is Afghanistan were to split up into little statelets, each under the protection of a larger power?

BACK IN THE heart of Pakistan the most difficult and explosive issue remains social and economic inequality. This is not unrelated to the increase in the number of madrassas. If there were a half-decent state education system, poor families might not feel the need to hand over a son or daughter to the clerics in the hope that at least one child will be clothed, fed, and educated. Were there even the semblance of a health system, many would be saved from illnesses contracted as a result of fatigue and poverty. No government since 1947 has done much to reduce inequality. The notion that the late Benazir Bhutto, perched on Musharraf's shoulder, equaled progress is as risible as Nawaz Sharif's imagining that millions of people would turn out to receive him when he arrived at Islamabad airport in July 2007. The outlook is bleak. There is no serious political alternative to military rule.

I spent my last day in Karachi with fishermen in a village near Korangi Creek. The government has signed away the mangroves where shellfish and lobsters flourish, and land is being reclaimed to build Diamond City, Sugar City, and other monstrosities on the Gulf model. The fishermen have been campaigning against these encroachments, but with little success. "We need a tsunami," one of them half joked. We talked about their living conditions. "All we dream of is schools for our children, medicines and clinics in our villages, clean water and electricity in our homes," one woman said. "Is that too much to ask for?" Nobody even mentioned religion.

And religion was barely mentioned in the elections that took place in February 2008. It had been generally assumed that these would be royally rigged, but Musharraf's successor at GHQ, General Ashfaq Kayani, instructed the ISI and its notorious "election cell" not to interfere with the process. This had a dramatic impact. Despite the boycott by some parties and the generally low turnout (40 percent or less), those who did vote treated the polls as a referendum on Musharraf and voted against his faction of the Muslim League. The joint victors were the Sharif brothers and, as the BBC reported, the "widower Bhutto," preferring this to his proper name. Musharraf should have resigned, but insisted on hanging on to power, helped by the U.S. ambassador, who summoned the widower to remind him of the deal done with his late wife. There is little doubt that the dynastic politicians, both the widower and the grandson of Ghaffar Khan, will do Washington's bidding, if what is demanded is not completely irrational.

2

REWINDING PAKISTAN

Birth of Tragedy

IT STARTED BADLY. FOR THREE HELLISH MONTHS A MULTIFORM, irrational mood gripped parts of India. There was a great deal of bloodshed as Hindus, Muslims, and Sikhs in northern and eastern India—Punjab and Bengal—slaughtered each other in preparation for the big day: August 14, 1947, when India would hurriedly be partitioned by a collapsing empire. There was little joy as people on both sides in northern and eastern India, still in a daze, counted their dead and thought of the homes they had left behind. A flood of refugees swamped cities on both sides of the divide. Some Muslims from Delhi and elsewhere who had fled to Pakistan were already disappointed and wanted to go back, only to find their homes and shops had been occupied by others. Old railway stations in new Pakistan were packed with men and women dead to the world, lying on the ground, their makeshift bedding often dyed with blood, soiled with urine and excrement. All were hungry. Some had contracted cholera. Others were desperate for water. There were not enough refugee camps, let alone other facilities. Those who made the decisions had not foreseen the scale of the disaster. It was difficult to predict what might happen next.

It was the same on the other side. Most Sikhs and Hindus from what was now Western Pakistan had fled to India. Mass rapes were common. Men from all three communities regularly targeted young girls between the ages of ten and sixteen. How many died? How many children disappeared? How many women were abducted? The estimates of the dead vary between a million and 2 million. Nobody knows. One grave can contain a whole family, and cremations conceal the numbers. These days they would call it ethnic cleansing or genocide. In 1947–48 they spoke of "an outbreak of communal violence."

Partitions along ethnic or religious lines usually result in mutually inflicted violence, but the politicians of that time had no understanding of the magnitude of what they had prepared. Astonishingly, given the shrewd and effective barrister that he was, Mohammed Ali Jinnah, or the Quaid-i-Azam,* the leader of the new country, seemed unaware of the logic of his own arguments. As late as May 1946, Jinnah had not believed that the creation of a Muslim state separated from India would lead to the partition of Bengal or the Punjab, where the three communities lived in roughly equal numbers, with Muslims more predominant in western Punjab. He had argued that splitting these two provinces "would lead to disastrous results." This was certainly true, but it was pure fantasy to imagine that this could be avoided once a partition along religious lines had been agreed to. The Great Leader thought of Pakistan as a smaller version of India with one small difference: the Muslims would be a majority. He had not thought of asking himself why Hindus and Sikhs should now accept what he had refused to countenance: living under a majority composed of another religious group.

Confronted with a mass influx of refugees, a panic-stricken Muslim League leadership in Karachi now told Indian Muslims that the new state was not intended for all Muslims but only those from east Punjab. The Muslims in Delhi and Uttar Pradesh (UP) should stay where they were. This was bluntly asserted by Pakistan's first prime minister, Liaquat Ali Khan, himself a scion of the UP gentry. What he really meant was that there was no place for middle- and lower-middle-class Muslims from the named regions. Nobody paid any attention. Muslim refugees from Delhi and other areas continued to pour into the new country. The creation of a "separate homeland" for India's

---

*"Great Leader" in English (imagine it in German)—the honorific bestowed on Jinnah by his followers.

Muslims had been taken seriously by the lower orders. They had no idea that it was a state for landlords alone. It's not that many Muslims wished to leave their ancestral villages and towns in search of an uncertain future. The pogroms, real and threatened, left them no alternative.

The Muslim League, a creation of Muslim conservatives, was founded in 1906 when a Muslim delegation sought and obtained a meeting with the British viceroy, Lord Minto. They pledged loyalty to the empire and demanded job quotas and separate electorates for Muslims. Underlying it all was the fear of Muslim professionals that they would lose out badly to the Hindu majority unless the British agreed to positive discrimination. The League's politics varied as did its social composition, and not until 1940 did it pass the Lahore Resolution, demanding a separate state for Indian Muslims, but clearly not all Muslims, since this was not considered feasible.

A conflict of myriad wills sometimes results in the creation of something that nobody willed. At best it can be an approximation of what was desired. At worst a meaningless by-product. So it came about that on the morning of August 14, 1947, a group of surprised men woke to find themselves at the helm of a new Muslim state—Pakistan. They were gathered in Karachi, its then capital. Once a small Sindhi fishing village, it had grown to house parts of the Royal Indian Navy and its population had accordingly increased. Few of them had believed that this would ever come about. In private they whispered to each other that the idea of Pakistan had largely been a bargaining ploy to win institutional safeguards for the large Muslim minority in postindependence India.

Events took another course. Now they had a country. They were, in the main, bandwagon careerists from landed Muslim families who had eagerly collaborated with the British Empire and only lately joined the Muslim League. Their brain cells had become rusty from lack of use. In the old days the "great" imperial bureaucracy had done most of the thinking for them. Their task was to convey orders or transmit ideas received from above to their subordinates. Confronted with actual independence, their lack of substance became apparent. In years to come most of them would dispense with reason altogether, resort to force, and back ambition-soaked generals desperate for power, while bemoaning the fickleness of democracy, which had, in reality, never been given a chance. The reason was never hidden. A structural contradiction lay at the heart of the new country. Religious affinity was the only rationale for uniting West Pakistan and its Muslim-majority provinces—Punjab, Sind, Baluchistan and North-West Frontier—with East Pakistan, which was the Muslim-majority slice of Bengal. The result was one sovereign state consisting of two territorial units separated not only by geographical distance but by linguistic, cultural, social, and ethnic differences that had no commonality other than religion and the state airline. Across this artificial structure, where the center of "national" power was separated from the majority of the population by over one thousand miles of hostile Indian territory, there lay the army and the civil service, both of which treated the Bengali majority as if they were colonial subjects. The absurd attempt to impose Urdu as the lingua franca of the new state had to be abandoned when angry Bengali crowds rioted as they confronted Jinnah on his first and last visit to Dhaka in 1948. The Bengalis, unlike the Punjabis, refused to permit any downgrading of their language. The formative years of Pakistan witnessed a squalid attempt by the new rulers to prevent a majority of citizens in the country from playing a part in determining its future. The Bengalis had to be kept under control, and this became the guiding principle of Jinnah's heirs. For this reason they delayed the adoption of a new constitution for almost a decade, fearing that franchise would give the Bengali majority an advantage.

By this time another "great thing" had come into play: the United States of America was slowly taking over the role of the British Empire. Its needs were different, its method of functioning favored indirect rule via pliant politicians or generals, and as time progressed it would become equally demanding. It was never to be a question of objectively evaluating Pakistan's real needs. As in the case of its British predecessor, U.S. interests were paramount.

Looking back on this period now, it's clear that even though an influential section of the imperial bureaucracy in India was citing the idea of "Muslim civilization versus Hindu civilization" to promote separation on the familiar lines of "two distinct nations," it was, in fact, the Second World War that proved to be decisive in the partitioning of the subcontinent. During the war, when the hub of the British Empire was fighting for its existence, the Congress Party of Mahatma Gandhi and Jawaharlal Nehru demanded immediate independence so that a free India could determine whether it should participate in the war effort. The British were angered by the request and refused. The Congress contemptuously broke off relations with the British and boycotted its institutions. The colonial power was even less pleased when after the fall of Singapore to the Japanese in February 1942 Gandhi proposed and launched a "Quit India" movement in August. An offer from the British cabinet pledging independence at the end of the war was rejected with a biting phrase—"a blank cheque from a failing bank," retorted Gandhi, who was convinced the British would lose in Asia and independence might have to be negotiated with the Japanese.

In polar contrast, the Muslim League had always remained on the British side. It was firmly supportive of the war effort. The British responded in kind. Pakistan was, in effect, a big thank-you present to the Muslim League. Had the Congress Party adopted a similar strategy, the result might well have been different. It is an intriguing counterfactual notion. Once the idea of a division had been agreed on, all movements that became an obstruction were gently discouraged. One of the least discussed aspects of the twenty months preceding partition was a wave of strikes that swept India, putting class above separatism. In the Punjab, Muslim peasants were ranged against Muslim landlords. The most important of these strikes was the naval mutiny in February 1946 that had paralyzed the Royal Indian Navy, evoking the specter of the naval mutinies that had heralded the 1917 Russian Revolution and the triumph of Lenin's Bolshevik Party. Ships were occupied and the strike spread from Bombay to Karachi and Madras. Rear Admiral Godfrey threatened to bomb his own battleships, but his was impotent rage. The Strike Committee comprised Hindus, Muslims, and Sikhs. All were united. Then the politicians stepped in and both the Congress Party and the Muslim League backed the British and helped defuse the strike. Nehru was unhappy. "The choice was a difficult one," he said of his decision.

Jinnah's appeal to the naval ratings was also straightforwardly communal: "I call upon the Muslims to stop and create no further trouble until we are in a position to handle this very difficult situation." A general strike in solidarity with the sailors paralyzed Bombay and crippled industry. British-led troops and police opened fire, killing five hundred people. The politicians were shamefaced, but muted in their criticisms. The poet Sahir Ludhianvi asked, "O leaders of our nation tell us / Whose blood is this? / Who died?"*

In addition to the naval uprising, three hundred sepoys mutinied in Jabalpur, and in March that same year the Gurkha soldiers raised the flag of revolt at Dehra Dun. In April, ten thousand policemen went on strike. Gandhi now became nervous and referred to the united Hindu-Muslim strikes as "an unholy combination." To support them, he argued, meant "delivering India to the rabble. I would not wish to live up to 125 to witness that consummation. I would rather perish in flames."† The acclivity of class tensions helped determine the fate of the subcontinent. Everyone was in a hurry now lest the situation become uncontrollable for all three sides—the British, the Congress Party, and the Muslim League. The deal was done in a hurry.

A sprinkling of lawyers and a clutch of clever businessmen (more interested in influence and increasing their assets than achieving greatness) had provided the Muslim League with brains and cash, but they were never in control of the organization. The principal leaders were all men of a conservative temperament, though modern in outlook.‡ Few had ever been involved in the civil disobedience movements or helped organize peasants or trade unions. Aware that their nationalist credentials were limited, they had staged a few token protests, such as Direct Action Day a few months before the British left. As a result they were able to spend a few hours in prison, about which they would talk for the rest of their lives.

In London, on the eve of partition, an emergency Labour cabinet

---

*It has always struck me as odd that no Indian filmmaker, inspired by Eisenstein's classic *Battleship Potemkin,* has put this most dramatic mutiny on the screen, whereas there have been several movies about the 1857 uprising against the British.

†*Harijan,* April 7, 1946.

‡Jinnah himself had no truck with religion as such, but like Ben-Gurion and the Zionist leadership in Palestine, he used it to carve out a state. Unlike his Israeli counterparts, he did not permit religious laws to govern the private lives of the citizens.

assembled in a somber mood at 10 Downing Street. Presided over by Prime Minister Clement Attlee, it was devoted exclusively to the growing crisis in India. The secretary of state for India was despondent. The search for a last-minute way to stem the flow of blood resulting from the amputation had proved unsuccessful. The minutes reported, "Mr Jinnah was very bitter and determined. He seemed to the Secretary of State like a man who knew that he was going to be killed and therefore insisted on committing suicide to avoid it." Surely he was not alone. The refusal of Congress Party leaders to accept a number of proposals that might have preserved the unity of the subcontinent had left him with no other alternative.

As late as March 1946, Jinnah had been prepared for an honorable compromise, but the visionless and arrogant Congress Party leaders (Gandhi, an honorable exception in this case, had suggested that Jinnah become the first prime minister of a united India) had prevaricated and then the opportunity was lost forever. Had Jinnah been able to peer a few years ahead, he might well have abandoned the experiment. The dust never settled on the state he had created. Jinnah was surrounded by a swarm of excited young men who were in the habit of talking of a "new spirit" without ever being able to explain what it meant. It is too late to turn the clock back now, but it certainly needs to be readjusted to South Asian time.

THE BIRTH OF Pakistan was considered, by most of its supporters, as a great achievement, but the danger of embracing "great achievements" is only understood when the greatness, if ever it really existed, lies buried in the past. It takes decades for most modern states to acquire an identity. Pakistan's rulers, attempting to stamp one by force, downgraded the existing identities of the regions comprised within the new state. Punjabis, Pashtuns, Bengalis, Sindhis, and Baluchis were, in the main, Muslims, but religion, while important culturally, was but one aspect of their overall identity. It was not strong enough to override all else. Historically, for most of these nationalities, Islam was essentially a set of rituals. It appealed to emotions, it made people feel part of a wider history. For the peasants, the interpreters of the true faith were not mullahs, but the great mystic poets whose verses were sung and celebrated in each region. In the early decades of the new state, religion was never ideological except for a handful of clerics and the two small political parties discussed in the previous chapter, the orthodox Jamaat-e-Islami (JI, or the Islam Party) and Jamiat-Ulema-e-Islam (JUI, or Party of Islamic Scholars). Even these organizations and others had espoused universalism and had opposed the creation of a separate Muslim state, referring to Jinnah as Kafir-i-Azam (the Great Infidel), which reportedly amused him a great deal. Pushed by the turn of events, both groups rapidly reconciled themselves to the new reality, and the former became a stern guardian of the "ideology of Pakistan" against secularists, Communists, liberals, and anyone who felt that things were going seriously wrong.

THE HORRORS OF partition could not be addressed by those responsible for the division. It was left to poets and novelists to express the suffering of the many. Three of them produced work that has remained peerless. One was Faiz Ahmed Faiz (1911–84), who together with Pablo Neruda and Nazim Hikmet formed the much celebrated triumvirate of radical twentieth-century poets who shared a common experience of imprisonment and exile. Faiz was one of the greatest South Asian poets of the modern period. A Punjabi by birth, he wrote mainly in Urdu. "The Dawn of Freedom," composed soon after the massacres of August 1947, reflected a widespread sadness, despair, and anger:

> This pockmarked daybreak,
> Dawn gripped by night,
> This is not that much-awaited light
> For which friends set out filled with hope
> That somewhere in the desert of the sky
> The stars would reach a final destination,
> The ship of grief would weigh anchor. . . .

> Our leaders' style is changing,
> Sexual pleasures permitted, sadness for separation forbidden,

This cure does not help the fevered liver, heartburn or the
    unsettled eye.
That sweet morning breeze
Where did it come from?
Where did it disappear?
The roadside lamp has no news;
The heavy night weighs the same
The heart and eye await deliverance;
Forward, we have not yet reached our goal. . . .

Saadat Hasan Manto (1912–55), one of the most gifted Urdu short-story writers produced by the subcontinent, took an even more detached view of the killings. Like Faiz, he too was able to turn painful events into great literature. He took no sides. He wrote with a passionate detachment, depicting the summer of 1947 as a state of utter madness. For Manto, it was a crisis of human nature, a sharp decline in moral conduct and behavior, and this shaped the structure of his stories about partition. The fear that gripped northern India in the months leading up to partition profoundly affected most people.* Manto's stories help us understand how and why.

Manto died in Lahore when I was eleven years old. I never met him and have always wished I had. In later photographs his melancholy is striking. He appears exhausted, the consequence of unhappiness and a ravaged liver; but earlier portraits reveal an intelligent and mischievous face, sparkling eyes, and an impudence almost bursting through the thick glass of his spectacles, mocking the custodians of morality, the practitioners of confessional politics, or the commissariat of the Progressive Writers. "Do your worst," he appears to be telling them. "I

---

*My mother, for instance, an active member of the Communist Party at the time and proud of her correspondence with Jawaharlal Nehru, would often recall how in April 1947, heavily pregnant with my sister and alone at home, she was disturbed by a loud knock on the front door. As she opened the door, she was overcome by panic. She thought she was about to be murdered. In front of her stood the giant figure of a Sikh. He saw the fear on her face, understood, and spoke to her in a soft, reassuring voice. All he wanted was the exact location of a particular house on a nearby road. My mother gave him the directions. He thanked her warmly and left. She was overpowered by shame. How could she of all people, without a trace of communal prejudice, have reacted in that fashion? She was not alone.

don't care." He could never write to please or produce formulaic literature in the name of "socialist realism."

Manto wrote "Toba Tek Singh" immediately after partition. The
setting is the Lahore *pagalkhana* (lunatic asylum). When whole cities
are being ethnically cleansed, how can the asylums escape? Bureaucrats
organizing the transfer of power tell the Hindu and Sikh lunatics that
they will be forcibly transferred to institutions in India. The inmates
rebel. They embrace each other, weeping. They will not be willingly
parted and have to be forced onto the trucks carrying them to new asylums. One of them, a Sikh, is so overcome by rage that he dies on the
demarcation line that now divides Pakistan from India. Confronted by
so much insanity in the real world, Manto found normality in the asylum. The city he loved was Bombay, but he was forced to move to
Lahore. He would later write:

> My heart is heavy with grief today. A strange listlessness has enveloped
> me. More than four years ago when I said farewell to my other home,
> Bombay, I experienced the same kind of sadness. There was a strange
> listlessness in the air much like that created by the forlorn cries of kites
> flying purposelessly in the skies of early summer. Even the slogans of
> "Long Live Pakistan" and "Long Live Quaid-e-Azam" fell on the ear
> with a melancholy thud.
>
> The airwaves carried the poetry of Iqbal on their shoulders, as
> it were, night and day and felt bored and exhausted by the weight
> of their burden. The feature programs had weird themes: how to
> make shoes . . . how to propagate poultry . . . how many refugees
> had come to the camps and how many were still there.

Faiz belonged to the region that became Pakistan. Manto migrated
from India. Amrita Pritam, a Sikh by birth (1919–2005), was younger
than both of them. She was born in Gujranwala, a small Punjabi town,
but was educated in Lahore. Her father was a schoolteacher who also
wrote poetry. Amrita wrote in Punjabi (the divine language of the
Sikhs) and published an acclaimed first collection when she was seven-
teen. She did not want to leave Lahore and her many Muslim friends,
but was swept across the new border by the merciless tide of history.

Traumatized by the partition, which would mark much of her work, she invoked Waris Shah (1706–98), the great mystical love poet of the Punjab, whose epic *Heer and Ranjha,* a ballad of impossible love, parental tyranny, and forced marriage, remains a great favorite on both sides of the Punjabi divide and is performed as regularly as Shakespeare. Pritam described the division of the Punjab as a poison that had destroyed a common culture:

> *I ask Waris Shah today:*
> *"Speak up from your grave,*
> *From your Book of Love unfurl*
> *A new and different page.*
> *One daughter of the Punjab did scream*
> *You covered our walls with your laments."*
> *Millions of daughters weep today*
> *And call out to Waris Shah:*
> *"Arise you chronicler of our inner pain*
> *And look now at your Punjab;*
> *The forests are littered with corpses*
> *And blood flows down the Chenab."*
> *Our five rivers lie poisoned*
> *Their waters irrigate the earth. . . .*

Poets and writers stirred the dissatisfaction that stalked Pakistan. They shattered the self-image of the leadership, but to no avail. The Muslim League confiscated the heritage of the late Muhammad Iqbal (1877–1938), a great poet from a preceding generation, educated at Heidelberg and heavily influenced by German philosophy, which explains his later attraction to metaphysics. Iqbal wrote much about Islam and was a believer but never pious and, in the tradition of the Sufi poets of the Punjab, was contemptuous of mullahs. When he was alive, the preachers villified him as an "apostate," "heretic," and "infi-del." After his death they mummified him into an icon of the new state, a cultural equivalent of the Great Leader, and thus considerably reduced the impact of his poetry by presenting him as a crude revival-ist. Some of us who came of age in the first decades of Pakistan were alienated by this image. Only later did the radical literary critic Sibte Hassan rebuke us for our philistinism and teach us to appreciate Iqbal's poetry and his "hidden" poems. One such remains apposite, though written about an earlier kind of globalization than the one we live in today:

> *Monarchy, you know, is coercion*
> *Trade, is coercion too*
> *The shopkeepers stall integral to throne and crown;*
> *Profit from trade, tribute from occupation,*
> *The world-conqueror is also a merchant*
> *Killing without war a strategy;*
> *In the rotation of his machines lurks death.*

Alongside the hidden or explicit critiques of the poets, the new country faced serious problems. How would it function in the absence of the imperial parent? What were its global priorities, and, most important, where was the cash coming from? Unsurprisingly, India had claimed the giant's share of the combined state's assets. There was also the question of personnel. Who would run the army and the civil service, two crucial bequests of the British Empire? Some of Jinnah's colleagues were fond of recounting a popular anecdote from the Mogul period, considered the high point of Muslim rule despite the fact that virtually all the Mogul rulers, much addicted to the pleasures of wine, women, and hashish, could hardly be described as model Muslims. A Mogul emperor is said to have summoned a highly respected scholar to the audience chamber in the palace and informed him, "I wish to make you the *qadi* [a chief justice with wide-ranging administrative powers] of this city." The learned man responded, "Your majesty, I am not fit for this post." A surprised ruler asked why this should be the case. The scholar replied, "Consider whether what I have just said is true or false. If it is true, then accept it. If it is a lie, then reflect whether it is permissible to make a liar the chief justice of this fair city."

But few people in the new state confessed to not being fit for the positions on offer. This state had been created, after all, to make it easier for them to get all the jobs without competition from Hindus and

Sikhs. It now became their unflinching duty to keep permanent vigil and ensure that the lower classes of the Muslim population never received an education that might lead them to challenge their monopoly of power. This continuity has been carefully maintained.

Even in those trying times, during the first months after independence, most of the people at the top were mainly thinking about themselves. Young Pakistanis should have no illusions. The situation has worsened considerably, but there never was a golden age.

Take the Great Leader, Jinnah. A revealing portrait of his priorities emerges from a confidential report by Paul H. Alling, the Connecticut Yankee sent as the first U.S. ambassador to the new country. While presenting his credentials, Alling informed his hosts that the United States was "appreciative of the difficulties which beset a new nation" and was "deeply sympathetic with the many problems which face Pakistan." Clearly this sympathy had its limits: the Joint Chiefs of Staff had contemptuously rejected an earlier request from the Pakistan government asking Washington for $2 billion to modernize the army.

Nonetheless the ambassador was invited to a picnic with Jinnah and his sister, Fatima. Assuming that important matters of state might be discussed, Alling prepared himself as best he could and joined the siblings on the governor-general's launch close to their beach cottage on Sandspit. The discussion centered on nation building of a special variety. Jinnah was widely regarded as a fop, a somewhat prim and very proper Edwardian gentleman, far removed from the world of vulgar commerce and the mass struggles for independence. Decorum mattered a great deal to him. This was less true of Fatima, a thin woman with a drawn, careworn face who knew that her brother did not have long to live and the future needed to be secured. Given the refusal of his estranged daughter to leave Bombay, Fatima ran the household. As turbaned waiters were serving tea and cucumber sandwiches, Jinnah wanted to know how the ambassador was getting on with the acquisition of property for the new embassy and staff. Alling explained that they had a tentative program and everything was under control:

Both he and his sister then inquired whether we were interested in their house "Flagstaff" which he had told me a few days previously was available for purchase. I explained that our negotiations for the purchase of an Ambassador's residence at No 1 Bonus Road had progressed so far—before we had knowledge that "Flagstaff" was available—that it had proved impossible to withdraw.

He then asked if "Flagstaff" would not be suitable for the use of other personnel of the Embassy. In reply I said that we had, of course, explored that possibility but that our building expert felt he could not justify the purchase of such an extensive property for any of the subordinate personnel. I added that actually we were interested only in purchasing a few small houses or flats whereupon he said he would send us details of one or two such properties. I could sense, however, that Mr Jinnah and his sister were disappointed that we had been unable to purchase "Flagstaff."*

The Father of the Nation died soon after in September 1948. Alling had left for another posting a few months earlier. Several weeks before his departure, a thoughtful State Department sent Jinnah a small gift as a token of their esteem. Four ceiling fans, twelve inches in diameter, arrived at Flagstaff and were accepted. The embassy surveyors' work had not been entirely in vain.

It was not an auspicious beginning either for the country or its relations with Washington. In the years that followed, "Flagstaffing" would reach epidemic proportions, with politicians and senior armed services personnel competing with each other for unearned income. Meanwhile the ruling elite would sigh with relief and happiness at being accepted as servitors in a Washington heaven, their country now a U.S. satrapy in a continent racked, for most of the twentieth century, by colonial wars and revolutions. Milton's Satan was convinced that it was "better to reign in hell than serve in heaven." Pakistan's rulers proved it was possible to do both.

Jinnah had become the governor-general of Pakistan without having ever created a substantial party organization, let alone one of a mass

*The Ambassador in Karachi (Paul H. Alling) to the Secretary of State (Marshall), March 22, 1948, 845F.00/3–2248, cited in M. S. Venkataramani, *The American Role in Pakistan* (Lahore: 1984).

character. The United Provinces in India, one of the main regions of the Muslim middle classes for whom he spoke, was not included in the new state. Largely a stranger to the present provinces of West Pakistan, he simply confirmed the provincial landlords and feudalists in power as the representatives of his party there. The result was that the ruling elite in Pakistan never possessed a reliable political party capable of controlling the masses. The Muslim League soon became a clutch of corrupt and quarrelsome caciques who discredited it permanently. Pakistan was thus, from the outset, firmly dominated by its civilian bureaucracy and the army, both of which had faithfully served the British. The top echelons of each were composed of an exclusive English-educated elite, handpicked and trained for their tasks by the British Empire. In the first decade after partition, the civilian bureaucracy exercised political paramountcy in Pakistan. The CSP—Civil Service of Pakistan—comprised a closed oligarchy of five hundred functionaries commanding the state. Indeed, the two masterful heads of state of this period, Ghulam Mohammad (1951–55) and Iskander Mirza (1955–58), were co-opted directly from its ranks. They manipulated the token parliamentarism of the time, until it became so discredited that in 1958 a military coup was engineered, which brought General Ayub Khan to the presidency.

Given that Pakistan had been created in the name of religion, new questions arose. What would be the nature of the new state? Could a state created for one religious community be nonreligious? Jinnah was staunchly secular. In a memorable address to the Pakistan Constituent Assembly on August 11, 1947, he left no room whatsoever for any doubt:

> . . . every one of you, no matter to what community he belongs, no matter what relations he had with you in the past, no matter what his colour, caste or creed, is first, second and last a citizen of this State with equal rights, privileges and obligations. . . . I cannot emphasise it too much. We should begin to work in that spirit and in course of time all these angularities of the majority and minority communities—the Hindu community and the Muslim community—because even as regards Muslims you have Pathans, Punjabis, Shias, Sunnis and so on—will vanish . . . you are free; you are free

to go to your temples, you are free to go to your mosques or to any other places of worship in this State of Pakistan . . . you will find that in course of time Hindus would cease to be Hindus and Muslims would cease to be Muslims, not in the religious sense, because that is the personal faith of each individual, but in the political sense as citizens of the state.

This attempt to institutionalize a Muslim nationalism dissociated from religion was analogous to Zionism. Ben-Gurion, Golda Meir, Moshe Dayan, and all the other implacable and ironhearted creators of a Jewish state were not religious. The same was, more or less, true of a number of Muslim League leaders. This was one reason why the more serious Islamist organizations in India, the Jamaat-e-Islami, led by Maulana Maududi, and the Majlis-i-Ahrar, had both opposed the demand for Pakistan to be "un-Islamic." The Majlis had been set up in 1929 and was linked to the Congress Party. Its key founder, Maulana Abul Kalam Azad, refused to accept Pakistan and became a leader of the Indian Congress Party and a close friend of Nehru's. The Ahraris believed in a composite nationalism and had been long aligned with the Congress Party, but key figures split with Azad and decided to shift to Pakistan. Like Maududi, they loathed Jinnah. He was trying to steal their flock. For them the idea of a secular nationalist Muslim state was "a creature of the devil." They migrated to Pakistan and gave battle.

The headquarters of the Islamist groups had been in what was now India. Had they been consistent in their beliefs, they would have stayed there propagating the idea of a world Islamic caliphate. It was not as if India were ever going to be denuded of Muslims, however hard the Hindu fundamentalists might try to bring this about. Some venerated Muslim leaders such as Maulana Abul Kalam Azad were members of the new Indian government. Azad had reduced the Muslims of Delhi to tears with his famous address pleading with them to stay on: "How can you bear to leave this our city, our Chandni Chowk, all that our forebears helped to build. . . ." But Maududi and the Ahraris chose Pakistan. Having done so, they were determined to purify it of all un-Islamic influences, and of these there were many, starting with the Great Leader himself. So began a long battle for the soul of the new state. The terrain chosen by the Islamists was faith. They ignored non-Muslims since they were unbelievers and should be treated as such without any nonsense of equal citizenship. None of the Islamist groups, however, could agree on what constituted an Islamic state, though Saudi Arabia came close to being a model for many orthodox Sunni Muslims. Shia divines would hark back to the form of government during the Prophet's lifetime, but there was never any agreement on the precise functions of the state or the composition of those who controlled it. What the followers of Maududi and the Ahrar leadership and smaller groups did agree on was that the Muslim League was led by a bunch of infidels, and that the country's first foreign minister, Zafarullah Khan, was an apostate who deserved death. Why? Because, they argued, he belonged to the heretical Ahmediyya sect, which had no place in the Islamic community. Having opposed the creation of Pakistan, these worthies were now determined to prove their loyalty to the new state by sprinkling hydrochloric acid on the impure.

A campaign against the Ahmediyya community began with the birth of Pakistan and was the first episode in the long duel between Islamists and the state for control of the country. Islamic history is replete with "heretical sects" and reform movements from the earliest days after the death of the Prophet Muhammad. During the nineteenth century a self-proclaimed Mahdi (a controversial notion in Islam, a redeemer who will make himself known before the Day of Judgment) emerged in the Sudan at the head of a giant mass movement, created a guerrilla army, and defeated the British at Khartoum in 1885. Poor General Charles Gordon was martyred in the process.

Mirza Ghulam Ahmed (MGA), the founder of the Ahmediyya sect, was far removed from any notion of an armed struggle against British imperialism. He was born in Qadian in 1835, the grandson of a Muslim general who had fought under the legendary Sikh ruler Maharaja Ranjit Singh. In a subcontinent riven with religious controversy and Islam under attack by Christian missionaries as well as Arya Samajists (a Hindu reform movement), Mirza Ghulam Ahmed became a religious scholar, mired himself in Persian and Arabic manuscripts and books on early Islam, and developed an interesting synthesis in a lengthy four-volume defense of his faith and dozens of other works, including one on Muslim philosophy that greatly impressed the Russian novelist Tolstoy. Unsurprisingly, the gifted scholar acquired a large following. No Elmer Gantry was he. His view that Islam in India had become obsessed with rituals and forgotten the content was close to the mark.

Had he confined himself to scholarship, Mirza G. undoubtably would have become a popular figure among Indian Muslims, but an overimmersion in any faith can sometimes have a hallucinatory impact, as Joan of Arc and Teresa of Ávila have demonstrated in the past. In 1882, MGA told his followers that he had received a divine revelation entrusting him with a special mission. This was dangerous territory and challenged Islamic tradition, according to which only the founder of the faith could be so blessed. MGA persisted, however, and as the recipient of divine messages he demanded recognition from his followers of this new status.

According to Ahmed, the revelation he'd received went like this: Jesus, son of Mary, had not died on the cross, had not ascended to heaven, but had rather been rescued off the cross by an intrepid band of disciples, cured of his wounds, and helped to escape from Palestine. He reached Kashmir, where he lived a long and happy life and died a natural death. This is strong stuff, but the revelation ended on a truly surreal note.

The rescue of Jesus and his asylum in Kashmir negated any idea of a literal Resurrection. What it meant was that someone else with all the attributes of Jesus would one day appear among the followers of the Prophet of Islam. This had now come to pass. Mirza Ghulam Ahmed, he announced, was none other than that person and should accordingly be greeted and treated as the Messiah, whose arrival had been foretold. He also declared himself a Mahdi. Ahmed declared he would wage the jihad of reason and defeat the opponents of Islam through argument and not violence.

Mainstream Islam responded to this with a shower of fatwas, but the Ahmediyya sect continued to win adherents over the years and was in 1901 registered as a separate Muslim sect. The founder died in 1908 and was succeeded by another scholar as the caliph. On the latter's death Mirza G.'s son, Mirza Bashir-ud-din, became the head of the organization. This, as is so often the case with sects, led to a split. A group that accepted the teaching but rejected the claims of prophet-hood seceded and set up their own group in Lahore.

In 1947, according to their own estimates, there were over two hun-dred thousand Ahmediyyas in both factions. They became known for their missionary zeal abroad, and Ahmediyya missions were active in East and South Africa, where they achieved some success. Like the Baha'is in neighboring Iran, they looked after their own, had a much higher level of education than the rest of the country, and made sure that none of their number was ever in serious need of food or shelter. They were represented in virtually every sphere of public life. Their phil-anthropy was appreciated by many people who were far removed from their interpretation of Islam. The poet Iqbal, who understood Islamic philosophy and history better than most, was certainly impressed by Ahmediyya scholarship and worked with them in some areas.

The Islamist groups began a violent campaign against them, attack-ing their meetings, killing an Ahmediyya army major, demanding the sacking of the foreign minister, and insisting that the sect be declared non-Muslim. This could easily have been stopped, but sections of the Muslim League leadership in the Punjab, reeking of opportunism, jumped on the bandwagon, including the oily-tongued, Oxford-educated Mian Mumtaz Daultana, who had flirted mildly with Com-munism during his youth. Daultana effectively prevented the police from providing protection to the besieged Ahmediyya community. In 1953, serious riots broke out, Ahmediyya shops were looted and mosques attacked, and some members of the community lost their lives. As a nine-year-old it was my first encounter with irrationality. Just below our apartment in Lahore was a Bata shoe store, owned by an Ahmediyya, whose son was at school with me. Returning from school one day, I saw it being attacked by armed hoodlums. Nobody was hurt, but it was a frightening experience.

An angry provincial governor called on the army to intervene. Mar-tial law was declared in Lahore. General Azam gave orders to shoot riot-ers on sight. Within twenty-four hours the crisis was over. Maulana Maududi and others were tried for treason, and Maududi was sen-tenced to death, which was later commuted.

A court of inquiry was established to inquire into the cause of the disturbances. It was presided over by Justice Munir and Justice Kayani. The published report, I have often argued, is a classic of its type, a modern masterpiece of political literature. It should become part of the national curriculum if a serious state education system is ever established. The two judges began to question Muslim clerics from rival schools, and different factions testified as to what they thought constituted a Muslim state and their definition of a Muslim. With each new reply the judges found it difficult to conceal their incredulity, some of which was reflected in their report. All the groups concurred in the view that a secular state was impermissible and that non-Muslims could not be treated as equal citizens. This raised a new problem:

> The question, therefore, whether a person is or is not a Muslim will be of fundamental importance, and it was for this reason that we asked most of the leading ulama [religious scholars] to give their definition of a Muslim, the point being that if the ulama of the various sects believed the Ahmadis to be *kafirs* [unbelievers], they must have been quite clear in their minds not only about the grounds of such belief but also about the definition of a Muslim because the claim that a certain person or community is not within the pale of Islam implies an exact conception of what a Muslim is. The result of this part of the inquiry, however, has been anything but satisfactory, and if considerable confusion exists in the mind of our ulama on such a simple matter, one can easily imagine what the differences on more complicated matters will be. . . .
>
> Keeping in view the several definitions given by the ulama, need we make any comment except that no two learned divines are agreed on this fundamental. If we attempt our own definition as each learned divine has done and that definition differs from that given by all others, we unanimously go out of the fold of Islam. And if we adopt the definition given by any one of the ulama, we remain Muslims according to the view of that alim, but kafirs according to the definition of everyone else.*

Report of the Court of Inquiry on the Punjab Disturbances of 1953 (Lahore: 1954).

The demand to declare the Ahmediyyas infidels faded from public view. No government took it seriously, and threats to the community receded. Ironically, it was Prime Minister Zulfiqar Ali Bhutto, under political siege by a combined opposition in 1976, who thought he would outflank the Islamist parties by implementing three of their old demands: a ban on alcohol, Friday and not Sunday as the official holiday, and, more serious, declaring the Ahmediyyas a non-Muslim sect. This craven capitulation could only strengthen those who had first proposed these measures. Ahmediyyas remain Muslims in India, Britain, France, Germany, East Africa, but not in Pakistan. The late Pakistani physicist Dr. Abdus Salam was the only Muslim scientist to win the Nobel Prize. That he was an Ahmedi would make the preceding sentence inaccurate in Pakistan.

The Pakistan envisaged by Jinnah never took off. The geographical entity died on the killing fields of East Pakistan. Over 70 percent of Pakistanis were born after the debacle of 1971. Amnesia prevails. Few have any idea what took place or even that there was once another country. The country's name was the brainchild of Chaudhry Rahmat Ali, an Indian Muslim studying in London during the thirties and evidently with time on his hands. He played around with the initials of Muslim majority areas in India: *P* represented the Punjab, *A* was for Afghanistan, *K* was Kashmir, *S* represented Sind. Unfortunately, *pak* also means "pure" but, more interesting, there was no *B* for Bengal or Baluchistan. Could a nuclear Pakistan dominated by the military fragment still further, and if so, what might be the consequences for the region as a whole? Whose interests would another division serve? Those without knowledge or understanding of their own history are fated to repeat it. What follows is an attempt to explain the past and the present in the hope of a better future.

3

THE WASHINGTON QUARTET

The Man Who Would Be
Field Marshal

IN OCTOBER 1958, A DECADE AFTER THE GREAT LEADER'S DEATH, the political system he had set in place received its first shock. The Pakistan Army, backed by Washington, decided on a preemptive strike against democracy and declared martial law. Some months later at a public poetry reading, most of the participants confined themselves to reciting love poems. When it was his turn, the Punjabi poet Ustad Daman began to recite a poem about birds twittering. Some of us shouted from the audience, "For Allah's sake, say something!" This unseemly provocation elicited an extemporized couplet:

Now each day is sweet and balmy,
Wherever you look, the army.

Cheered by the large crowd, he was then picked up by the police a few hours later and held in custody for a week or so. Pakistan had changed.

How and why did this happen? Within a year of the country's founding, the Great Leader was dead, leaving behind a set of notables—mainly landed gentry sometimes doubling as hereditary religious leaders (Pirs, Makhdooms, etc.)—who sometimes wondered how they were going to muddle through. The new rulers were soon confronted with two contradictions, one of them serious.

The first of these concerned the political geography of the new country. It was divided in two parts, East and West, separated from each other by a thousand miles of India and having little in common except religion, and sometimes not even that. If Islam constituted a nationality (as the Muslim League insisted but as orthodox Islamists initially resisted), this was always going to be its big test. Sixty percent of the population was in East Pakistan, with their own language, tradition, culture, diet, and time zone. The overwhelming bulk of the bureaucracy and army was from or based in West Pakistan. The reason was simple. The Punjab had been the "sword arm" of the raj especially after the conclusion of the Sikh Wars of the nineteenth century. A large share of the native soldiery came from the most economically backward parts of the subcontinent; the army was considered a step up by poor peasant families groaning under the yoke of native landlords. The British virtually restricted recruitment to the countryside. They were suspicious of the urban petit bourgeois and saw the Bengalis as the epitome of this layer, loquacious and unreliable, who had to be kept out.

In 1933, General Sir George MacMunn (1869–1952), a doughty warrior from the Scottish lowlands, wrote a quaint tract entitled *The Martial Races of India,* replete with imperial justifications for the pattern of recruitment to the British Indian army:

> The staunch old yeoman who came into the Indian commissioned ranks via the rank and file, or the young Indian landowner made the Indian officer as we know him. . . . The clever young men of the Universities were quite unfitted for military work . . . the army officers had long realised that the Indian intelligentsia would never make officers.

This rule was relaxed during the Second World War when expediency dictated the entry of educated officers, and a number of undesirables (including even Communists after Hitler's invasion of the Soviet Union) were hastily recruited to assist the war effort in India and Britain.

Postwar pruning got rid of most of this layer. Others left voluntarily. Staunch yeomen and younger sons of the landed gentry remained.

The British Indian army was shaken during the war. The fall of Singapore to the Japanese had pierced the myth of British invulnerability. There was no fail-safe inoculation against the nationalist disease, and a number of officers and soldiers (some of them from the "martial races") captured by the Japanese defected and set up the Indian National Army, which fought alongside their captors against the British on the basis of wrongheaded nationalist logic according to which "the enemy of my enemy is my friend," something that is almost always never the case. Empires old and new have no friends. They only have interests. The civil conflicts during partition also colored the thinking of Indian officers in the north. They had witnessed appalling massacres that they were helpless to prevent, largely because the imperial power feared that divided loyalties would lead to chaos if there was a breakup of the army along communal lines. For that reason the military was not encouraged to intervene in order to stop the massacres. At best, the army offered some limited protection to refugees on both sides.

This army itself was partitioned along communal lines, creating two different command structures, each temporarily under the control of a British general. Consequently, the new Pakistan army maintained most of the old colonial traditions with continuity preserved in the first instance by the appointment of General Sir Frank Messervy and subsequently Sir Douglas Gracey, a colonial veteran, as its first two commanders in chief. In addition, over five hundred other British officers stayed behind to give the new fighting force a much-needed boost. This created some resentment. In 1950, a small group of more nationalist-minded officers (including a general, Akbar Khan), together with an even tinier collection of Communist intellectuals, discussed a possible coup d'état to topple the pro-West government. The half-baked plot was uncovered, and the participants (including the poet Faiz Ahmed Faiz and the literary critics Sibte Hassan and Sajjad Zaheer) were sent to prison, and the infinitesimal Pakistan Communist Party was banned.

In contrast to Hindu and Sikh detachments, no all-Muslim units had been allowed in the colonial army, a decision dating back to the 1857 anti-British uprising for which the imperial power wrongly held the old Muslim aristocracy exclusively responsible. In fact, it was a proto-nationalist rebellion by Indians of every stripe against the new conquerors. The old recruitment policy persisted till well after partition. Few Bengalis were recruited to the Pakistan army. The policy was changed much later with the partially successful, if politically disastrous, Islamization during the late seventies and eighties that is discussed in a subsequent chapter and whose effects are still present.

The first Pakistani military chief met all MacMunn's criteria. General Ayub Khan was tall, mustachioed, and well built. He was from tried and tested stock, the son of a risaldar major (a noncommissioned officer), and regarded by his superiors as an obedient and trustworthy soldier. He was to fully justify that trust, remaining loyal first to the British and later to the United States throughout his years in military politics. He reached the top effortlessly, helped by fate: General Iftikhar, due to succeed Gracey and generally regarded as a sharper and more independent-minded officer, perished in an air crash in 1949. It would be unfair to single out Ayub Khan as the only native conservative-minded and submissive, pro-British senior officer in the new Pakistan army. Few of his well-trained contemporaries were any different. The same could be said about their Indian counterparts. Reading through the prolix and self-serving memoirs of postindependence generals on both sides of the Indo-Pak divide is tedious and unrewarding. The books are revealing, however, in that they provide an insight to the psychology of the generals. The golden age, for most of them, lies firmly in the past, with gimlets (gin cocktails) at lunchtime or a post-sunset whiskey with their pink-skinned superiors. That they had not been allowed membership in exclusive whites-only clubs till after independence did not bother them unduly. They had got used to the social apartheid. At their happiest fighting alongside and working under British officers, they would treasure those times for the rest of their lives. Ayub Khan, for instance, had been among an early batch of young native cadets sent to Sandhurst when the "Indianization" of the army had become necessary. He would later proudly recall that he was "the first foreign cadet to be promoted Corporal and given two stripes."

A majority of ruling Pakistani politicians too had grown up serving the British. Like their old mentors, they regarded the ordinary people with a mixture of repugnance and fear. Small wonder that senior civil servants and military officers, true heirs of the departed colonial power, treated the politicians with contempt. On this front, the difference with India could not have been more pronounced. In India the political leadership had been forged over three decades of continuous nationalist struggles and long periods of imprisonment. No general or civil servant would have had the nerve to challenge a first-generation Congress leader. Had he lived longer, Jinnah might possibly have stamped his authority on the two institutions—the army and the civil service—that dwarfed the Muslim League on every level, but his deputy, Liaquat Ali Khan, prime minister and Leader of the Nation (Quaid-i-Millat) and himself a refugee, lacked the same authority over his own party and the country. The Punjabi landlords who dominated the Muslim League and were desperate to gain total control viewed the prime minister as an unnecessary impediment to their own rise, and there is little doubt that it was they who had him assassinated while he was addressing a large crowd in the municipal park in Rawalpindi in October 1951. His assassin, Said Akbar, was immediately shot dead by the police on the orders of Najaf Khan, a senior police officer and factotum of the then inspector general of police, Khan Qurban Ali Khan, who in turn was a close friend of senior Punjabi landlord-politicians.

Liaquat's assassination symbolized the deep-rooted antagonisms that had developed between the local gentry and the refugee "interlopers" who had crossed the river Jumna and made their way to the Muslim homeland. Some of the wealthier refugees would later regret their decision to come to Pakistan, but the less privileged had no alternative. They were driven out of their villages and towns. That the refugees tended to be more cultured and better educated than their unwilling hosts soon became another point of contention. They were strongly embedded in the civil service of Pakistan, and this created resentments. Their linguistic affectations and mannerisms were constantly caricatured, and they in turn found it difficult to conceal their contempt for the wooden-headed and uncouth Sindhi and Punjabi politicians. The cold-blooded decision to bump off Liaquat was partly intended as a shot across the bows of his fellow migrants. The message was simple: you are here on sufferance and don't forget that this country belongs to us. So much for "the homeland of Islam in the subcontinent." Worse was yet to come.

General Ayub Khan was in London when Liaquat was assassinated, and later described, somewhat disingenuously, his shock on meeting the new prime minister, Khwaja Nazimudin, and cabinet: "Not one of them mentioned Liaquat Ali's name, nor did I hear a word of sympathy or regret from any one of them. Governor-General Ghulam Mohammad seemed equally unaware of the fact that the country had lost an eminent and capable Prime Minister. . . . I wondered how callous, cold-blooded and selfish people could be. . . . I got the distinct impression that they were all feeling relieved that the only person who might have kept them under control had disappeared from the scene."

That the country's senior politicians did not copiously weep was to their credit. Having approved the removal of their colleague, it would have been gross hypocrisy on their part to do so. But it seems unlikely that General Ayub's intelligence chiefs had not informed him of who was behind the assassination. This being so, why did he not act at the time and insist that the rogues responsible organize an immediate general election? He was, of course, preoccupied elsewhere, engaged in political intrigues of his own with the defense secretary, Iskander Mirza, a former general turned senior bureaucrat. Mirza was an astute manipulator. He took advantage of the weakness of the political leadership, ousted a mentally decaying, foulmouthed fellow bureaucrat, Ghulam Mohammad, and took over as governor-general, the country's head of state.

Mirza ruled with a heavy hand, and when the Bengalis toppled a Muslim League government after provincial polls in 1954, the governor-general removed the elected government and imposed Governor's Rule throughout East Pakistan. It was the first step toward the disintegration of the country and the militarization of its political culture. It is a sad story that I have written about in some detail elsewhere.* Here it is sufficient to stress that the alienation of the eastern half of the country began early and got worse each consecutive year. The prejudice of Pun-

---

*Pakistan: Military Rule or People's Power? (London and New York: 1970).

jabi officers and civil servants against the Bengalis mirrored British prej-
udices during the colonial period.

As with others who would follow him, Mirza's overconfidence
brought about his political demise. He had presided over the intro-
duction of a new constitution in 1956 declaring Pakistan an Islamic
republic and himself as its first president. Mirza and Ayub together
institutionalized Pakistan's role as a U.S. satrapy by joining a network
of Cold War security arrangements known as the Baghdad Pact and
the Southeast Asia Treaty Organization (SEATO), designed to defend
U.S. interests in both regions. Ayub had negotiated directly with Washington to secure the military aid program of 1953–54 and Pakistan
admittance to the "free world" together with South Korea, South Vietnam, and Thailand.

The writer Saadat Hasan Manto, bemused by what was taking
place, wrote a set of nine satirical "Letters to Uncle Sam." The fourth
was written on February 21, 1954, a year before his death:

Dear Uncle:

I wrote to you only a few days ago and here I am writing
again. My admiration and respect for you are going up at the
same rate as your progress towards a decision to grant military aid
to Pakistan. I tell you I feel like writing a letter a day to you.

Regardless of India and the fuss it is making, you must sign a
military pact with Pakistan because you are seriously concerned
about the stability of the world's largest Islamic state since our
mullah is the best antidote to Russian communism. Once military
aid starts flowing you should arm these mullahs. They would also
need American-made rosaries and prayer-mats, not to forget small
stones that they use to soak up the after-drops following nature's
call. . . . I think the only purpose of military aid is to arm these
mullahs. I am your Pakistani nephew and I know your moves.
Everyone can now become a smartass thanks to your style of
playing politics.

If this gang of mullahs is armed in the American style, the
Soviet Union that hawks communism and socialism in our
country will have to shut shop. I can visualise the mullahs, their

hair trimmed with American scissors and their pyjamas stitched by American machines in strict conformity with the *Sharia*. The stones they use for their after-drops [of urine] will also be American, untouched by human hand, and their prayer-mats, too, will be American. Everyone will then become your camp-follower, owing allegiance to you and none else.*

Pakistan's servile leaders were supportive of the Anglo-French-Israeli invasion of Egypt in 1956. This was totally unnecessary, and one can only assume that they thought the United States would, however reluctantly, fall in line behind the adventure, which it did not. Their support for the war on Nasser's Egypt inflamed public opinion and created a wave of anger that led to mass demonstrations throughout the country. Interestingly, the Jamaat-e-Islami played no part in these mobilizations. Political parties now began to demand an exit from the security pacts and a neutral foreign policy. These demands were popular. Mirza and Ayub were apprehensive that the country's first general election, scheduled for April 1959, might produce a coalition that would take Pakistan out of the security pacts and toward a nonaligned foreign policy, like neighboring India. The United States was even more nervous over such a prospect and encouraged a military takeover.

Mirza, ever arrogant, thought he could run the show with Ayub as his loyal sidekick. He underestimated the autonomy of the army. Simply because General Ayub had, until then, supported every measure he had proposed, the president assumed he would be able to maintain complete control. On Mirza's initiative, the Pakistan army seized power on October 7, 1958. A cabinet dominated by generals was appointed together with a few nonparty civilians. These included Mohammed Shoaib, a veteran U.S. agent, as finance minister; a brilliant lawyer, Manzur Qadir, as foreign minister; and an unknown young Sindhi, Zulfiqar Ali Bhutto, as minister for commerce. The response of the West was supportive, and the *New York Times,* while deploring the suspension of the constitution, was nonetheless hopeful:

---

*"Letters to Uncle Sam," translated into English by Khalid Hassan, the letters were first published by Alhamra Press, Islamabad, a few weeks before 9/11.

"In Pakistan both President Mirza and the army's head General Ayub Khan have stated clearly that what they propose and wish to do is to establish in due course a fine, honest, and democratic government. There is no reason to doubt their sincerity."*

A few weeks later three generals called on the president and read out to him his political obituary. A shaken Iskander Mirza left the country forever and became an exile in London, where he later died.

General Ayub Khan became Pakistan's first military dictator. Within six months all political parties and trade unions had been banned, and the largest chain of opposition newspapers, Progressive Papers Limited, was taken over by the government without a whimper of opposition from the tame Pakistani press or its Western counterparts. A secret Ministry of Education directive was issued in August 1959. Its aim was to "stop the infiltration of communist literature into the country and to prohibit its publication and circulation within the country." All educational institutions were instructed to "undertake a survey of books in university and college/school libraries to ensure that all objectionable materials are withdrawn." The delighted Islamists cheered the announcement. As a dictatorship, Pakistan became an even stauncher member of the free world. General Ayub told the first meeting of his cabinet, "As far as you are concerned, there is only one embassy that matters in this country: the American embassy." The United States reciprocated with a statement endorsed unanimously by the National Security Council (NSC) that noted "the presence of important U.S. security facilities in Pakistan" and gave full backing to the military takeover of the country:

The political instability which was characteristic of previous governments and seriously impeded the effectiveness of U.S. efforts in Pakistan has been replaced by a relatively stable martial law regime. . . . The present political situation should be conducive to the furtherance of U.S. objectives. . . . In view of the present stability, even though achieved by fiat, the problem has changed from one

_____
* *New York Times,* editorial, October 12, 1958.

of short-term urgency, requiring us to reckon with individual politicians in one crisis after another, to one which allows us to take a longer-range view of Pakistan's potential. . . . We give special emphasis to assuring the Pakistan government of our sympathetic interest in and support for its proposed economic and social reforms.

This was simply a case of putting immediate U.S. interests above all else—an imperial failing since ancient times. The NSC statement supporting the military dictatorship ran counter to an extremely astute analysis that was also on the table. A top-secret report from the Office of Intelligence and Research Analysis of the State Department written in December 1958 bluntly stated the consequences of backing the military dictatorship:

> . . . a prolonged period of military rule, which Ayub apparently contemplates, could intensify provincial and class tensions. It would probably disillusion the intellectuals, teachers, journalists, lawyers and the broad run of the middle class whose deepest political desire has been to see Pakistan match India's record of democracy and avoid degenerating to the level of a Middle Eastern or Latin American dictatorship.
> . . . only under a democratic system would East Pakistan, with its greater population, appear to be able to match the greater military and bureaucratic weight of West Pakistan. . . . The prospect of prolonged suppression of political freedom under military domination would intensify the risk of such an increase in tension and discontent in East Pakistan as perhaps to jeopardize the unity of the two wings of the country.

Those who made similar arguments inside Pakistan were denounced as "pro-Indian traitors" or "Communist agents." Ayub Khan, who soon promoted himself to field marshal, differed on this assessment of democracy and came up with a novel explanation. In an early radio broadcast to the nation, the military dictator informed his bewildered "fellow countrymen" that "we must understand that democracy cannot work in a hot climate. To have democracy we must have a cold climate like Britain." Few doubted his sincerity on this matter.

Remarks of this sort did little to diminish Ayub's popularity in the West. He became a great favorite of the press in Britain and the United States. His bluff exterior charmed the notorious showgirl Christine Keeler (they splashed together in the pool at Cliveden during a Commonwealth Prime Ministers' Conference in 1961), and the saintly Kingsley Martin of the *New Statesman* published a groveling interview. Meanwhile opposition voices were silenced and political prisoners were tortured.

In 1962, Ayub decided that the time had come to widen his appeal. He took off his uniform, dressed in native gear, and, addressing a forced gathering of peasants assembled by their landlords, announced that there would soon be presidential elections and he hoped people would support him. The bureaucracy organized a political party, the Convention Muslim League, and careerists flocked to join it. The election took place in 1965, and the polls had to be rigged to ensure the field marshal's triumph. His opponent, Fatima Jinnah (the aged sister of the Great Leader), fought a spirited campaign but to no avail; family links did not count for as much in those days. The handful of bureaucrats who refused to help "adjust" the election results were offered early retirement.

Meanwhile, Western backing for the regime continued apace. The arguments used in its support related principally to the "economic development" taking place, which was supposedly transforming Pakistan from a rural to an urban economy and paving the way for the modernization of the country. This was certainly the view of Finance Minister Mohammed Shoaib, who was so close to Washington that it sometimes received the minutes of cabinet meetings, together with Shoaib's assessments, before they were even seen by its own members. Shoaib was given strong backing by many visiting stars from the U.S. academe. Gustav Papanek from Harvard fully approved the state establishment of enterprises that could then be turned over to private entrepreneurs and wrote in praise of the "free market economy" that "through a combination of incentives and obstacles produced an environment in which success was likely only for the ruthless individual . . .

whose economic behaviour was not too different from their robber baron counterparts of 19th century Western industrialisation."* Robber barons they certainly were, but unlike their European counterparts they enjoyed the support of a fiscal and economic system that diverted the productive wealth produced by agriculture via a network of subsidies into manufacturing.

The resulting redistribution was at the expense of the peasantry, but few cared. The U.S. economic advisers echoed Papanek's view that "great inequalities were necessary in order to create industry and industrialists," and that the growth generated in this fashion would lead to a "real improvement for the lower income groups." This is what later, in the era of globalization, became known as the trickle-down effect. It did not work then as it does not work now. The upper-income groups in the towns paid no taxes and illegally moved their money abroad. Little was invested in the productive nonagricultural sector. Even the official planning commission set up by the government bewailed the bad habits of the city elite in West Pakistan. Keith B. Griffin, an Oxford economist well versed in the economic problems confronting the country, produced a report showing that between 63 percent and 83 percent of savings transferred from agriculture were wasted in nonproductive extravagances, i.e., the sumptuous style cultivated by the nouveaux riches. Griffin went on to point out that in West Pakistan "the potential surplus of these savings units was used to consume more, to buy more ornaments, jewellery and consumer durables and to bid up the prices of real estate and farm lands, helping their owners to disinvest. Often such surplus was devoted to luxury house construction or to open up one more retail store in the already crowded streets and bazaars."[†]

The greater inequalities accepted by the Neanderthal Harvard Group were creating new divisions in the country as a whole. In the West wing of the country the elite flaunted its new wealth without shame. There was no shortage of critical comment, but few of the crit-

---

*Gustav F. Papanek, *Pakistan's Development: Social Goals and Private Incentives* (Cambridge, MA: 1967).

[†]Keith B. Griffin, "Financing Development Plans in Pakistan," *Pakistan Development Review,* Winter 1965.

ics took the imbalance this was creating with the East wing very seriously. The Bengalis, naturally, were not pleased with this state of affairs.
In addition to being punished politically simply because they were a
majority, they now saw moneys accrued by jute production in their
region, the export of which had provided a balance of payments surplus during the boom created by the Korean War, disappearing into the
coffers of West Pakistan. The stark contrast between the West and East
wings of the country created the basis of the national movement in
Bengal. The demands of the nationalist Awami League were a local version of "no taxation without representation."

As the tenth anniversary of the field marshal's reign approached, a
sycophantic intelligentsia and a myopic bureaucracy began to prepare
the celebrations, known as the Decade of Development. The Ministry
of Information decided on a trumpet call in the shape of a book. It was
thought that Pakistan's soldier-statesman would be further legitimized
on the world stage by the publication of his memoirs. Ayub Khan's
Friends Not Masters: A Political Autobiography was published by Oxford
University Press in 1967 to great acclaim in the Western press and
nothing short of sycophantic hysteria in the government-controlled
media at home.*

The biography's publication was linked to the dictator's growing
unpopularity. A military adventure against India in 1965 had ended in
disaster. Ayub, always cautious in these matters, was reluctant to authorize a strike against India. Bhutto and a number of senior generals convinced him that a preemptive strike would take the Indians by surprise
and that Operation Grand Slam would liberate Kashmir, the disputed
and divided province claimed by both sides after 1947. Ayub finally

---

*Ayub's information secretary, Altaf Gauhar, a crafty, cynical courtier, had ghosted a truly
awful book: stodgy, crude, verbose, and full of half-truths. It backfired badly and was soon
being viciously satirized in clandestine pamphlets on university campuses. Ayub had in
Chairman Mao mode suggested that Pakistanis "should study this book, understand and act
upon it. . . . It contains material which is for the good of the people." But in China there
was universal literacy so people could read the wretched *Little Red Book.* In Pakistan over 75
percent of the population was illiterate, and of the rest only a tiny elite could read English.
An Urdu edition was produced but bought only by government employees. It was not considered necessary to waste money on a Bengali edition, the only sensible decision of the
period.

agreed. India was taken by surprise and Pakistani forces came close to achieving their strategic objectives, but serious operational and organizational failures halted the advance, giving India time to move its troops forward and push Pakistan back, but only after the largest tank battle since the Second World War. Sixty Pakistani tanks were captured intact after the Indian victory.

Ayub was forced to travel to Tashkent, where the Soviet prime minister, Aleksey Kosygin, brokered a cease-fire deal between the two countries. Zulfiqar Ali Bhutto, by this time a mercurial foreign minister, resigned soon afterward, alleging that secret protocols attached to the Tashkent Treaty amounted to a betrayal of the Kashmiri people's right to self-determination. This turned out not to have been the case, but it had become a useful weapon at mass meetings. When, a year later, I asked Bhutto why he had pushed Ayub to wage an unwinnable war, his reply took me aback: "It was the only way to weaken the bloody dictatorship. The regime will crack wide open fairly soon." Bhutto had by this time decided to organize his own political grouping, and the Pakistan Peoples Party (PPP) was founded in 1966.* From the beginning the party line was to destroy the Ayub regime. In 1967, Bhutto began to address a series of large meetings throughout the country and was arrested. His confidence was high. Knowing full well that his cell was bugged, he would, during meetings with his lawyer, Mahmud Ali Kasuri, provoke the military. "General Musa's days as governor of West Pakistan are numbered. We'll dress him in a skirt and make him dance on the streets like a monkey," was one of the few insults that were printable.

In response to the growing opposition in the country the regime decided that a distraction was needed. In October 1968 lavish celebrations to commemorate the tenth anniversary of the dictatorship were in progress. The Karachi daily *Dawn* competed with the government press by publishing sixty-nine photographs of the field marshal in a single issue. The citizens were triumphantly informed that in Karachi, a city with only three bottled-milk outlets, the consumer could choose

---

*For an account of my own involvement during an early stage of the new party's manifesto and relations with Bhutto, see *Clash of Fundamentalisms: Crusades, Jihads and Modernity* (London and New York: 2003), 240–44.

among Bubble Up, Canada Dry, Citra Cola, Coca-Cola, Double Cola, Kola Kola, Pepsi-Cola, Perri Cola, Fanta, Hoffman's Mission, and 7UP. In Lahore a reporter from the government newspaper *Pakistan Times* slobbered over a fashion show:

> The mannequins received a big hand from the elegant crowd as they moved up and down the brightly lit catwalk modelling the dresses. Some of the creations which the audience warmly applauded were "Romantica," "Raja's Ransom," "Sea Nymph" and "Hello Officer." . . . The Eleganza '69 look was defined as a blend of the soft and the severe.

But the bread and circuses became a public relations disaster. On November 7, 1968, students in Rawalpindi and Dhaka surprised the government and themselves by marching out onto the streets. They demanded freedom and the restoration of democracy, recalling the words of the Martinican poet Aimé Césaire:

> *It was an evening in November . . .*
> *And suddenly shouts lit up the silence;*
> *We had attacked, we the slaves; we, the*
> *Dung-underfoot, we the animals with patient hooves . . .*

Soon student action committees were springing up across both parts of the country. This was the "unfashionable" 1968, far removed from the glamour of Europe and the United States. It was also different in character. The gap between the actions of the Pakistani students and workers and the actual conquest of state power was much narrower than in France or Italy, let alone the United States or Britain. No democratic institutions existed in Pakistan. Political parties were relatively weak. The movement was stronger than them.

The scale of the uprising was breathtaking: during five months of continuous struggles that began on November 7, 1968, and ended on March 26, 1969, some 10–15 million people had participated in the struggle across East and West Pakistan. The state responded with its customary brutality. There were mass arrests and the dictatorship ordered the police to "kill rioters" on sight. Several students died during the first few weeks. In the two months that followed, workers, lawyers, small shopkeepers, prostitutes, and government clerks joined the protests. Stray dogs with *Ayub* painted on their back became a special target for armed police.

But here too the two halves of the country saw a marked disparity in the degree of repression. A few hundred died in West Pakistan. Nearly two thousand perished in Bengal. More than in the Punjab, Sind, North-West Frontier, and Baluchistan put together. One of the most moving aspects of this insurrection was the unity it imposed from below. When students died in the West, barefoot women students of Dhaka in the East marched in silence in a show of respect and solidarity. These six months were the only period in the history of united Pakistan where ordinary people on both sides of the country genuinely felt close to each other. I know this from personal experience. For three months, from March to May 1969, I traveled extensively in both parts of Pakistan, addressing meetings large and small and talking to student leaders and antidictatorship politicians, poets, and trade union leaders. The mood was joyous. The country had never been so full of hope before or since.

In those few months, the Pakistani people spoke freely. All that they had kept repressed since 1947 poured out. And the movement was not without humor. For hundreds of years the Punjabi word *chamcha* (spoon) has been used to denote a stooge. The origins of this are obscure. Some argue that it goes back to the arrival of the British. Local potentates who had hitherto subscribed to the art of eating delicately with their fingers had abandoned tradition and begun to use spoons and forks. Whatever the truth, the demonstrators started greeting pro-regime civil servants and politicians with spoons, the size depending on the self-importance that the dignitary attached to himself and popular estimates (usually accurate) of the degree of his sucking up to power at home or in Washington. When Ayub or his ministers arrived, they were greeted by gigantic homemade spoons as well as hundreds of the normal variety bought in the bazaar and used as cymbals to enliven proceedings.

The meetings I attended in East Bengal were particularly heated. I could see before my eyes the large gulf that separated the two wings of Pakistan. I argued that a voluntary socialist and democratic federation was the only thing that could save the country. This view sounds utopian today, but in those heady days everything seemed possible.

On a hot and humid afternoon in April 1969 I was taken to address the students of Dhaka University under the *amtala* tree on the campus. Many a political movement had been born in this symbolic space. Here, the students had, after a spate of fiery speeches, decided to fight the dictatorship. They would not let me speak in Urdu and voted, by an overwhelming majority (which included Nicholas Tomalin of the *Sunday Times*), that I speak in English, suggesting wryly that I learn Bengali for the next time. It is a beautiful language and I promised I would, even though I half knew that there never would be a next time. Every political instinct told me that Bengali national aspirations were about to be crushed by the army, that it would rather destroy Pakistan than permit any meaningful autonomy, let alone accept a confedera-tion. I made this point forcefully to the students that day. This being the case, I told them, why not go for complete independence? Take over your country. Done quickly, it might avoid the bloodshed to come. There was a hush. The audience looked at me in amazement. Someone from the other side, a Punjabi to boot, had mentioned the word *independence*. Then they cheered and chanted slogans, before car-rying me on their shoulders back to my car.

The "Lal salaams" (red salutes) were still ringing in my ears when I was taken that same day to meet Sheikh Mujibur Rahman, the leader of the nationalist, but still staunchly parliamentarian, Awami League. In March 1965, the Awami League, in the person of the sheikh, had dropped a bombshell with what became the famous Six Point plan for regional autonomy (discussed in the following chapter). The opposi-tion West Pakistani leaders were so shocked that they accused the Ayub regime's most Machiavellian civil servant, Altaf Gauhar, of having drafted the plan to split the anti-Ayub opposition.

This marked the beginning of the gulf between Bengali national-ism and the West Pakistani opposition parties. The abyss widened over the years, and the united struggle against the dictatorship was just a passing phase. Sheikh Mujibur Rahman knew my own sympathies were on the left and that I was closer to the Bengali peasant leader Maulana Bhashani, who had taken me on a tour of the villages and small towns of the Eastern province a few weeks previously. Bhashani had told me then of his meetings in China with Chou En-lai, who had pleaded with him not to weaken Ayub Khan since he was a friend of China's. The majority of Pakistani Maoists had loyally followed this advice, but Bhashani had realized that to support Ayub meant political suicide. He had joined the movement, but it was already too late.

Sheikh Mujib now reminded me that I had recently referred to him as "Chiang Kai-Sheikh" and muttered something about Mao backing Ayub Khan. Nonetheless he greeted me warmly and came straight to the point.

"Is it true that you said what they told me you said today?"

I nodded.

"You are sure they will use force. How sure?"

I explained that my certainty did not come from any hard information from those in power or even through understanding their psychology, but from one hard fact. The primary export commodities of East Bengal were vital to the economy of West Pakistan. Autonomy would mean the loss of financial control for the West. Sheikh Mujib listened attentively, but did not seem fully convinced. Perhaps he thought he could maneuver his way to power via a deal with the military chiefs. His party was pro-West and had, only recently, stressed its closeness to Washington and security pacts. He may have believed that Washington would compel the Pakistani military to play ball. Later when Nixon and Kissinger "tilted toward" Islamabad, it was a bitter cup for him to swallow. Mujib felt he had been badly betrayed.

The movement in 1968 was overwhelmingly secular, nationalist, and anti-imperialist. The student wing of the Jamaat-e-Islami would sometimes try to disrupt meetings, including two of mine in Rawalpindi and Multan, occasionally by force, but were swept aside by waves of students chanting various versions of "Socialism is on its way" and "Death to Maududi," the latter a reference to the leader and principal theologian of the Islamists, patronized by the Saudi royal family and a committed supporter of the United States.

The war in Vietnam had struck a deep chord among Pakistanis of virtually all social classes, and the poet Habib Jalib was wildly cheered on platforms we shared that year when he recited:

Global defenders of human rights,
Why the silence?
Where are you?
Speak!
Humanity is on the rack
Vietnam is on fire,
Vietnam is on fire

Jalib would then turn on the rulers of Pakistan and warn them that if they carried on as before, the Vietnamese fire might spread to "where you are" and "clouds filled with dynamite will pour down on you."

A detailed survey of the casualties revealed the scale of the mobilizations. November 1968: 4 deaths and over 1,000 arrests; December 1968: 11 deaths, 1,530 arrests; January 1969: 57 deaths, 4,710 arrests, and 1,424 injured; February 1969: 47 deaths, 100 arrests, and 12 injured; March 1969: 90 deaths, 356 arrests, and 40 injured. These figures were based on press releases from the government and were generally regarded as a considerable underestimation. It had by now become obvious to the military high command that blanket repression was not deterring the crowds. They had lost their fear of death. When this happens, revolution becomes a possibility.

Railway workers in the Punjab had begun to sabotage rail tracks to prevent troop movements, and in East Bengal police stations were attacked and armories raided. A week later, the generals in GHQ called on their field marshal with sad faces but firm instructions. Ayub did not hesitate. He surrendered. His resignation was announced that same day. His successor, General Yahya (a particular pronunciation means "fuck-fuck" in Punjabi) Khan, took over and immediately announced that the country's first-ever general election would be held in December 1970. A euphoric fever gripped the country. Clashing cymbals, cheering crowds, and loud drumbeats marked the fall of Ayub Khan, who had, as Bhutto later recalled, been considering elevating himself to an even higher position than field marshal:

During the "golden era" of Ayub Khan an earnest proposal was made to him by an eminent personality to declare a hereditary monarchy in Pakistan and to make himself the first monarch. Ayub Khan took the proposal seriously. He formed a two-man Supreme Council of Nawab of Kalabagh and myself to examine it. We returned the proposal together with its blue-print to Ayub Khan within a week with the recommendations that he should forget it altogether. Ayub Khan's observations were "bhehtar sallah" (good advice). He added however, "It is not all that senseless."*

This jovial Sandhurst-trained officer, secular in outlook, fond of the odd drink, and used to obeying orders, had, alas, been overpromoted. Now he was gone. His overdependence on Washington and his own Svengalis had brought him down.

What lay ahead? Just three years previously, Karl von Vorys, a political science professor at the University of Pennsylvania, had concluded a 341-page book on Pakistan with these words:

"Just six years ago Mohammad Ayub Khan took the helm of the State of Pakistan. Since then he has many accomplishments to his credit. The disintegration of the country, an acute threat in 1958, seems rather remote now."† At least one sentence was accurate.

---

*Zulfiqar Ali Bhutto, *If I Am Assassinated* (New Delhi: 1979).

†Karl von Vorys, *Political Development in Pakistan* (Princeton: 1965).

4

THE WASHINGTON QUARTET

The General
Who Lost a Country

THE PAKISTAN ARMY PRIDES ITSELF ON BEING A UNIFYING FORCE, without which Pakistan would disappear. The history about to be recounted suggests that the opposite is the truth. In March 1969, Ayub passed control of the country to General Yahya Khan, who promised a free election within a year and, fearing the revival of the mass movement, kept his word. Before returning to the twisted narrative of Pakistani history, a pen portrait summarizing the place and function of the army might be helpful to the reader.

The army's oft-repeated claim that it is independent of "vested interests" had finally been exposed. Ayub Khan had played politics and enrolled the landed gentry in his Muslim League. His son had utilized the military umbrella to become a businessman and had amassed a small fortune. Indeed, the whole historical role of the military and bureaucratic state apparatus that Pakistan "inherited" from British rule in India had now emerged into the light of day for many Pakistanis of the '68 generation. This role was in many ways a peculiarly central and concentrated one in Pakistan, setting it off from the military regimes that exist in various Asian and African countries today.

The Japanese invasion and occupation of Southeast Asia during the

Second World War temporarily smashed the old colonial apparatuses of government—which had anyway never had a large indigenous quotient—in Burma, Indonesia, and elsewhere. After the war, there was little chance for the imperial powers to reconstitute these, and considerable sections of the armed forces and civil services that emerged in the postindependence period had participated in a national liberation struggle against either Japanese or European oppressors.

In Africa, on the other hand, the colonial administrations were usually staffed so thoroughly by the colonizing power itself that the civilian bureaucracy and—above all—the army had to build up virtually from scratch after independence was granted. On the Indian subcontinent, however, neither of these patterns prevailed. Here, a large and locally recruited civil service was an absolute necessity, since the British could not hope to staff themselves the bulk of the administrative system necessary to control such an immense population. The same situation obliged them simultaneously to create an extremely large Indian army, whose junior and some senior officers were recruited from the feudal aristocracy of the subcontinent. Lord Curzon's Memorandum on Army Commissions for Indians stated in 1900 that indigenous officers "should be confined to the small class of nobility or gentry . . . [and] should rest upon aristocracy of birth." Such an officer corps would serve "to gratify legitimate ambitions, and to attach the higher ranks of Indian society, and more especially the old aristocratic families, to the British Government by closer and more cordial ties."*

On the whole the scheme worked pretty well until the end of the Second World War. Indian troops performed sterling service for their imperialist masters in both world wars, and in relentless domestic repression at home. No other colonial power could boast of such a capacious sepoy force. A precondition of its success was, of course, the ethnic heterogeneity of India, which allowed the British to recruit their mercenary army from selected "martial races"—mainly Punjabis, Sikhs, Pathans, Rajputs, Jats, and Dogras—who could be relied on to keep down the other subject nationalities of the empire.

---

*See C. H. Phillips, ed., *Select Documents on the History of India and Pakistan* (London: 1962), 4: 518–20.

However, in India the Congress Party had led a strong independence movement from the 1920s onward that built a mass organization in the countryside and succeeded in levering Britain out of its imperial suzerainty after it had been fatally weakened by the Second World War. The Congress was then able itself to knit the state together and dominate a parliamentary system that has survived ever since.

The scenario in Pakistan was very different. The Muslim League was always an extremely weak organization by comparison. Originally created by Islamic princes and nobles in 1906 "to foster a sense of loyalty to the British government among the Muslims of India" (to cite from its statement of aims), it was captured by the educated Muslim middle class led by Jinnah in the 1930s and for a brief period was in alliance with the Congress Party. However, its main thrust was always anti-Hindu rather than anti-British. It collaborated with the raj during the Second World War and received a separate state from it in 1947, without having seriously struggled for independence. This change was itself stage-managed by the bureaucracy, which initially wielded most of the real power. However, once in the saddle, Ayub surrounded himself with a clique of cronies and increasingly made his regime into a personal dictatorship, rather than institutionalizing corporate military rule. A decade later Ayub's regime had become so immensely unpopular that it provoked the largest social upheaval in the history of the country. It was henceforward useless to the ruling class. Thus, in the emergency of early 1969, with masses on the streets in Rawalpindi, Lahore, Karachi, Dhaka, and Chittagong, and continuous strikes and riots in both East and West, the army dislodged Ayub and finally assumed direct political command.

The Yahya interregnum represented the end of a slow shift in the intrastate complex of power from the civilian to the military apparatus. Naturally, the civil service remained influential within the government: key civilian bureaucrats still concerned themselves with those manifold problems of running the state machine and the economy that were beyond the competence of the army officers. But the military were now the senior partner.

Already in 1971, the Pakistan army constituted a force of three hundred thousand troops, mostly recruited from those sections of the

Punjabi and Pathan peasantry who traditionally provided infantry for the British. Seventy thousand of them were deployed in Bengal. The officer corps, from the critical rank of lieutenant colonel upward, was a select elite screened with the utmost care for its class background and political outlook. The generals, brigadiers, and colonels of the Pakistan army are scions (usually younger sons) of the feudal aristocracy and gentry of Punjab and the North-West Frontier, with a sprinkling of wealthy immigrants from Gujarat and Hyderabad. The impeccable social credentials and accents of this group, which so entrance Western journalists, reveal their past. They were trained as imperial recruits in Sandhurst or Dehra Dun. The Punjabi regiments engaged in repression in Bengal thus included units who once practiced their trade under General Gracey in Vietnam. General Tikka Khan, who later became known as the butcher of Dhaka, was a veteran of Montgomery's army in the North African campaign. General "Tiger" Niazi, who signed the act of surrender to India in December 1971, later wrote with pride in his memoirs that the nickname Tiger "was given to me by Brigadier Warren, Commander, 161 Infantry Brigade, for my exploits in Burma during World War Two."* This was the situation at the time of the military offensive against the Eastern portion of Pakistan by its own army.

MEANWHILE, THE ignominious departure of Ayub Khan had shifted the struggle from the streets to electoral campaigning. Two political parties dominated the scene. In the West, the Peoples Party, led by Zulfiqar Ali Bhutto, had absorbed some of the most courageous and intelligent leaders and activists of the 1968–69 movement. They were aware that the country's mood of unfocused euphoria could not go on. It required a political outcome. For this a party was essential, and all the other parties were either discredited or irrelevant in the larger scheme

---

*A. A. K. Niazi, *The Betrayal of East Pakistan* (Karachi: 1999). What this and other self-serving memoirs of the period reveal is that most of the Pakistani generals involved in this tragedy have learned nothing and forgotten nothing. All they can contemplate is their own navels. Everyone else is to blame but them. There were no war crimes, no massacres. If anything, the military and its Bengali Razakar units (collaborators) were the victims.

of things. Bhutto had sown the seeds and he would reap the rewards. In the East, the bulk of the Maoist left that had supported Ayub Khan because of his links with China collapsed. The weaknesses of the traditional pro-Moscow left, strong in the media, weak on the streets, left the field wide-open to the Awami League. This party had defended Bengali autonomy and won over the movement to this cause. It became the voice of Bengali nationalism and was politically prepared for the onslaught that was being planned in Islamabad.

In 1947, the predominantly Hindu trader and landlord class of East Bengal migrated to West Bengal, which was and is a part of India, leaving their businesses and lands behind them. From the start this vacuum was filled by Bihari Muslim refugees from the United Provinces of India and non-Bengali businessmen from the Western portion of Pakistan. The economic exploitation of East Bengal, which began immediately after partition, led to an annual extraction of some 3 billion rupees (approximately $300 million) from the East by West Pakistani capital. The most important foreign-exchange earner was jute, a crop produced in East Pakistan that accounted for over 50 percent of exports. This money was spent on private consumption and capital investment in West Pakistan. The sums granted for development projects by the central government offer an interesting case study of discrimination. Between 1948 and 1951, $130 million were sanctioned for development. Of this, only 22 percent went to East Pakistan. From 1948 to 1969 the value of the resources transferred from the East amounted to $2.6 billion. The West Pakistan economy was heavily dependent on East Bengal, partly as a field for investment, but above all as a mine of subsidies and as a captive market. The Six Points demanded by the Awami League included both political and economic autonomy and directly threatened the immediate business interests of West Pakistani capitalists and their supporters embedded in the military and the civil service. The Six Points were:

1. A federal system of government, parliamentary in nature and based on adult franchise.
2. Federal government to deal only with defense and foreign affairs. All other subjects to be dealt with by the federating states.

3. Either two separate, but freely convertible, currencies for the two parts of the country or one currency for the whole country. In this case effective constitutional measures to be taken to prevent flight of capital from East to West Pakistan.
4. Power of taxation and revenue collection to be vested in the federating units and not at the center.
5. Separate accounts for foreign-exchange earnings of the two parts of the country under control of the respective governments.
6. The setting up of a militia or paramilitary force for East Pakistan.

These demands were both a response to the exploitation cited above and a serious attempt to maintain the unity of Pakistan via a new constitutional arrangement. When reproached by foreign correspondents for being "unreasonable," Sheikh Mujibur Rahman would become extremely irritated: "Is the West Pakistan government not aware that I am the only one able to save East Pakistan from communism? If they make the decision to fight, I shall be pushed out of power and the Naxalite types [Maoists] will intervene in my name. If I make too many concessions, I shall lose my authority. I am in a very difficult situation."*

The Six Points represented the charter of the aspirant Bengali bourgeoisie; it articulated their desire to create their own regional state apparatus and to have an equal share of the capitalist cake. But this was precisely the reason why the dominant bloc in West Pakistan was opposed to them. The Pakistan army was organically hostile to the prospect of a Bengali civilian government because of the danger that it would reduce the lavish military apparatus that had been a built-in feature of the Islamabad regime since Ayub seized power in October 1958. Some idea of the enormous stake the Pakistani officer corps had in retaining the status quo is reflected in that military expenditures over the preceding decade (1958–68) had absorbed no less than 60 percent of the total state budget. In the fiscal year of 1970 alone, some $625 million were allocated for the armed forces. The shortsighted West Pakistani political leaders who failed to appreciate this would soon become

---

*Le Monde (Paris), March 31, 1971. The interview had been conducted some weeks earlier by an Agence France-Presse correspondent.

the victims of the same machine, for the army was not seriously in favor of any government that might challenge the imbalance between social and military expenditure.

To their credit the Awami League politicians had repeatedly denounced these colossal outlays on a military machine that was over-whelmingly non-Bengali and saturated from top to bottom with racist and religious chauvinism against the Bengalis, who had traditionally been regarded as dark, weak, and infected with Hinduism. For its part, the Pakistani business class had its own material reasons for resisting the Six Points. Business interests in the West no longer regarded the East as an optimal field of investment. Bengal remained of vital importance to them, both as a captive market and as a source of foreign exchange. In the late sixties, between 40 percent and 50 percent of West Pakistan's exports were taken by the East at monopoly prices. Where else could West Pakistani capitalism have disposed of its high-cost manufactures?

The Awami League won widespread political support in East Bengal for two important reasons. First, it grasped the importance of the national question: it saw clearly the subcolonial status of East Pakistan. Second, political parties of the extreme left, which gave opportunistic support to the Ayub dictatorship because of the latter's "friendship" with China, failed. The Maoist wing of the National Awami Party (NAP) insisted, with Chinese backing, that the Ayub regime had "certain anti-imperialist features" and was therefore in some ways to be pre-ferred to bourgeois democracy.

Thus the Awami League could present itself as the only meaningful opposition force in the province. It constantly carried out propaganda in favor of its Six Points; it called for free elections, and it organized demonstrations against the Ayub dictatorship. Some of its leaders, including Mujibur Rahman, were consequently arrested, which only increased their popularity. When the anti-Ayub upsurge resulted in the fall of the dictator and his replacement by the Yahya junta in early 1969, it was hardly surprising that the Awami League reaped the benefits. Yet it could still not disavow its heritage. In the weeks before the army per-suaded Ayub to retire, the Awami League eagerly participated in the "constitutional" talks at the Round Table Conferences called by Ayub to reach a compromise. It had fueled the mass movement and witnessed the anger of Bengali peasants and workers; even so it remained tied to its parliamentarist past.

THE YAHYA MILITARY regime, unable to quell the mass upheaval in both parts of the country, was forced to promise a general election on the basis of adult franchise. Its advisers evidently believed it could concede this as a diversionary tactic. They were confident that the bureaucracy, from long experience in such matters, would be able to manipulate the results satisfactorily. To give the latter some time to prepare itself, the elections were postponed—ostensibly because of the cyclone disaster in late 1970, which claimed two hundred thousand Bengali lives. But the failure of the army to provide any adequate flood relief only intensified the deep anger of the Bengali people. When the different Maoist factions in East Bengal decided to boycott the elections, which were finally held in December 1970, the Awami League was given a free hand and won a tidal victory. Of the 169 seats allocated to East Pakistan in the National Assembly, the League won 167. It also gained 291 out of the 343 seats in the provincial parliament. Its bloc in the National Assembly gave it an overall majority throughout the country and entitled it to form the central government. Such a prospect traumatized the West Pakistani ruling oligarchy. Given that the Awami League had fought the elections on the basis of the Six Points and had indeed on occasion surpassed them in its electoral rhetoric, it was clear that the army would try to prevent a meeting of the National Assembly. In this they were greatly helped, if not led, by Zulfiqar Ali Bhutto, who refused to countenance a Pakistan government led by the majority party.

Bhutto's Pakistan Peoples Party had triumphed in the western portion of the country and should have negotiated a settlement with the victors. Instead Bhutto sulked and told his party to boycott a meeting of the new parliament that had been called in Dhaka, the capital of East Pakistan, and thus provided the army with breathing space to prepare a military assault. He coined the slogan "Idhar Hum, Udhar Tum" (Here It's Us, There It's You), making it clear that, like the military, he was not interested in sharing power. This made a split inevitable. Bengal now went into noncooperation mode. A wave of strikes paralyzed the province. Even in the army cantonments the tension was deeply felt. For instance, when the Awami League decided on noncooperation, all the Bengali cooks, servants, and laundrymen left the cantonments; in the food markets the vendors refused to sell soldiers any food, and Bengali cars visiting cantonments had their numbers published in the *People* newspaper. At one stage the situation became so desperate that special nourishment for the officers had to be flown out from West Pakistan.

EVEN BEFORE THE formal invasion took place on March 25, 1971, hundreds of Bengali lives had been lost at the hands of what was seen as an oppressor army dispatched by West Pakistan. Some of the generals involved at the time have subsequently written that Mujib, frightened of his own people, asked the army to crush the movement, but that this, in reality, was a trap to make them even more unpopular. What a tangled web they weave, those who practice to deceive.

These earlier demonstrations of the army's brute power should have convinced the Awami League politicians of what was likely to follow unless they prepared the Bengali people for a protracted struggle. This they refused to do, despite the evident desire of the masses, expressed in thunderous slogans at Awami League meetings, for a total break with Pakistan. The rising tide of popular political consciousness was already clear in the enormous meetings that took place throughout the province both before and after the general election of 1970. At every stage the citizens assimilated the lessons of the past much more rapidly than their parliamentarist leaders and showed their willingness to fight the colonial state in East Bengal. At every stage they were again and again checked by the visceral constitutionalism of the Awami League leadership. This conflict between the mass movement and the tame reformism of its official guides was all the more tragic in that the existing organizations of the left were localized or discredited and thus not in a position to influence the course of the struggle decisively.

Ranajit Roy, a respected Indian press commentator, candidly noted a common element of Indo-Pakistani establishment politics in expressing his sympathy for Sheikh Mujibur Rahman: "The Awami League leadership in many ways corresponds to the leadership of our own Congress—a leadership which, with the backing of peaceful agitation, sought to arrive and ultimately succeeded in arriving at compromises with our colonialist masters. Our independence was the result of an understanding with the British masters. Sheikh Mujibur hoped to pull off a comparable deal with Islamabad. Like the Congress Party in India, the Awami League does not have the stomach for the type of war circumstances have forced Bangla Desh to wage."

These musings, of course, unwittingly pointed to an important difference between British and Pakistani colonialism in the subcontinent. British imperialism was able to grant a political decolonization because it nowhere meant the abandonment of its real economic empire, whose central segments were Malayan rubber and tin, Middle Eastern oil and South African gold, and Indian plantations. But the loss of political control of East Bengal affected the vital interests of the impoverished and wretched subcolonialism of Islamabad directly. For the weaker a colonial power, the more dependent it is on formal political possession of its subject territories. The history of the twentieth century has a striking lesson for us in this respect.

The European imperialism that waged the longest and most stubborn war for the retention of its overseas possessions was not industrialized England, France, or even Belgium. It was the small, backward, and predominantly agrarian society of Portugal. Lisbon fought a ferocious and unremitting campaign in Africa to keep Angola, Mozambique, and Guinea because of the enormous economic and ideological importance of these colonies. The subcolonialism of Portugal, whose own economy had been deeply penetrated by the capital investment of the advanced powers, furnished an instructive comparison with that of Pakistan. Neither had much politico-economic room for maneuvering; both were in their different ways consequently driven to extreme and unmediated measures of repression.

These led to a massive crisis for both countries: the breakup of one as documented in this book and a serious split in the army of the other. Portuguese majors and colonels were in the vanguard of the popular movement that toppled Salazar's Estado Novo in the democratic revolution of 1974.

Any objective assessment of the Awami League, which is still a major party in Bangladesh, would conclude that it has been a secular, but conservative party since its birth. Its formative years, like those of its West Pakistani siblings, were dominated by parliamentary maneuver and intrigue. Its main social roots have always been in the functionaries, teachers, petty traders, and shopkeepers who proliferate in East Bengali society. Its founder, H. S. Suhrawardy, who for a short time succeeded in becoming Pakistan's prime minister, distinguished himself in 1956 by supporting the Anglo-French-Israeli invasion of Egypt. He became one of the most articulate defenders of imperialist interests in Pakistan and American policy in Asia as a whole. Left-wing parties and organizations in East Pakistan who opposed these policies were physically attacked by Awami League "volunteers" and had their meetings broken up with monotonous regularity. Suhrawardy's other notable achievement was to supervise the fusion of the provinces of Baluchistan, Sind, and the North-West Frontier into a single territorial unit dominated completely by Punjab. In this way he showed his respect for the "autonomy" of the West Pakistani provinces.

After 1958, Suhrawardy played a dissident role during the early years of the Ayub dictatorship and was imprisoned for a short time as a result; but his opposition was always limited to the bourgeois constitutionalist framework. Suhrawardy's undoubted talents—he was a proficient lawyer, an artful political manipulator, and a glib conversationalist—placed him head and shoulders above the rest of the Awami League leadership. His ambitions were, however, far removed from Bengali independence: his aim was to make the Awami League an all-Pakistan electoral machine, capable of winning power as a "national" party and thus catapulting H. S. Suhrawardy into the highest-possible office. His untimely death in 1963 put an end to this dream.

It is essential to recall this early history to understand the later attitudes of the Awami League. It continued to play an oppositional role during the remaining years of the Ayub dictatorship. Ayub himself more than once considered the idea of reaching some compromise with its leaders and incorporating them into the central government, but the gangster politicians from the East Pakistani underworld, on whom Ayub had relied for so long to maintain "law and order" in Bengal, constantly and successfully sabotaged this plan, as it would have meant the end of their own political careers.

The Awami League was thus offered no choice but to continue as an oppositional force. It joined a multiparty alliance (Combined Opposition Parties) in 1964 to field a candidate against Ayub, but the elections were rigged by the army and the civil service and the field marshal was returned with a comfortable majority. As a result the country suffered an inner breakdown, but nobody in power noticed. From now on the Awami League, however reluctantly, would be pushed in a different direction, leaving it with few options but to challenge the military head-on. The hopes of the transatlantic press rested on a military dictator. Some weeks before the military was unleashed against 75 million Bengalis, the *Economist* was representative of this mainstream opinion and approved of General Yahya: "It is also likely that the President will do his best to stay the army's hand. So far he has proved a model soldier in politics, remaining aloof from the electioneering and releasing all political prisoners after the election."

Jinnah's Pakistan died on March 26, 1971, with East Bengal drowned in blood. Two senior West Pakistanis had, to their credit, resigned in protest against what was about to happen. Admiral Ahsan and General Yaqub left the province after their appeals to Islamabad had been rejected. Both men had strongly opposed a military solution. Bhutto, on the other hand, backed the invasion. "Thank God, Pakistan has been saved," he declared, aligning himself with the disaster that lay ahead. Rahman was arrested and several hundred nationalist and left-wing intellectuals, activists, and students were killed in a carefully organized massacre. The lists of victims had been prepared with the help of local Islamist vigilantes, whose party, the Jamaat-e-Islami, had lost badly in the elections. Soldiers were told that Bengalis were relatively recent converts to Islam and hence not "proper Muslims"—their genes needed improving. This was the justification for the campaign of mass rape.

In Dhaka, Mujibur Rahman waited at home to be arrested. Many of his colleagues went underground. The military shelled Dhaka University. Artillery units flattened working-class districts; trade-union and newspaper offices were burned to the ground. Soldiers invaded the women's hostel on the university campus, raping and killing many res-

idents. With the help of the intelligence agencies and local collaborators, mainly Islamist activists, lists of nationalist and Communist intellectuals had been prepared (as in Indonesia in 1965), and they were
now picked up and killed. Some had been close friends of mine. I was
both sad and angry. I had predicted this tragedy, while hoping it might
be avoided. Immediately after the December 1970 general election I
wrote, "Will the Pakistan Army and the capitalist barons of West Pakistan allow these demands to go through? The answer is quite clearly
no. What will probably happen is that in the short-term Mujibur
Rehman will be allowed to increase East Pakistan's percentage of
import and export licenses and will be allocated a larger share of foreign capital investment. These are the 'concessions' which the Army
will be prepared to make in the coming few months. If Rehman accepts
them, he will be allowed to stay in power. If not, it will be back to business as usual in the shape of the Army. Of course there is no doubt that
in the event of another military coup there will be no holding back the
immense grievances of Bengal and the desire for an independent Bengal will increase a hundredfold."*

The Bengali political leaders had not prepared the people for this
onslaught. Had they done so, many lives might have been saved. Bengali policemen and soldiers had been waiting for the word from above
to desert with their weapons and defend their people. It was the death
knell of Jinnah's Pakistan. Bangladesh (Bengali nation) was about to be
born. The struggle that now erupted between the Bengali liberation
forces and the armed might of West Pakistani capital represented both
a continuation of the mass movement that erupted in 1968–69 and a
qualitative break.

There were two distinguishing features of politics in East Bengal
from the beginning of 1971: on the one hand, the enthusiastic participation of the people in every level of an escalating social and
national struggle; and on the other, the political deficiencies of the petit
bourgeois notabilities of the Awami League, whose whole tradition of
compromise and maneuver rendered them incapable of providing lead-

---

*"Pakistan: After the December Elections, What Next?" *Red Mole,* January 1, 1971, 10.

ership in a real independence movement. Mujib had addressed a mass meeting of nearly a million people on March 7, 1971, where he had fulminated against the delays and intrigues but refused to declare independence. Ordinary Bengalis paid the price for his prevarications.

Operation Searchlight was brutal, but ineffective. Killing students and intellectuals did not lead to the quick and clear victory sought by the Pakistani generals. Once the initial attack had failed, the military with the help of local Islamist volunteers (members of the Jamaat-e-Islami) began to kill Hindus—there were 10 million of them in East Pakistan—and burn their homes. Tens of thousands were exterminated. These were war crimes according to any international law.*

All this was taking place while most pro-Yahya Western governments averted their eyes and hoped for the best. As news of the offensive spread, the predominantly Bengali East Pakistan Rifles mutinied. Much was made in later propaganda by Islamabad about how the West Pakistan commander Colonel Janjua was woken up by a Bengali subordinate, taken to his office in his pajamas, sat down in the commanding officer's chair, and executed by his batman. It was ugly, but what civil war is not? Few asked how had it come about that the only Bengali company in the country had a non-Bengali commander? It was part of the problem.

Guerrilla units emerged in different parts of the province, representing different political factions but united in the struggle for independence. The strongest of these was the Mukti Bahini (Liberation

---

*The Nuremberg Principles, as formulated by the International Law Commission, left no room for doubt. They defined war crimes as:

Violations of the laws or customs of war which include, but are not limited to, murder, ill-treatment or deportation to slave-labor or for any other purpose of civilian population of or in occupied territory, murder or ill-treatment of prisoners of war, or persons on the seas, killing of hostages, plunder of public or private property, wanton destruction of cities, towns, or villages, or devastation not justified by military necessity.

Crimes against humanity were:

Murder, extermination, enslavement, deportation and other inhuman acts done against any civilian population, or persecutions on political, racial or religious grounds, when such acts are done or such persecutions are carried on in execution of or in connection with any crime against peace or any war crime.

Army), led largely by Awami League nationalists, but others operated locally, including groups inspired by Che Guevara and led by Tipu Biswas and Abdul Matin. These militants had been left with no other choice. The ruling elites in both India and Pakistan wanted a rapid conclusion to the struggle. This did not happen. Supreme power in Islamabad at this stage was exercised by a small circle of military officers, flanked by a few civilian advisers and accomplices. Yahya Khan himself had become a dim and slothful figurehead. Reports would later emerge of how late one night while intoxicated, he had rushed out stark naked onto the streets of Peshawar roaring with laughter, chased by his favorite mistress (widely known as "General" Rani), and had to be escorted back indoors by his unsurprised guards. This was at the height of the war. None of this would have mattered if he had been successful, but failure stared the army in the face.

The clique that ruled behind him and was conducting the war included five senior generals and a few civil servants, none of whom were distinguished for their competence. In his memoirs, General Gul Hassan, a senior officer at the time, recounts the chaos in GHQ during the war: dispatches full of lies, cover-ups designed to conceal military failures, the overextension of military units that left Dhaka vulnerable, and so on. Viewed coldly as a military operation, it was a disaster. General "Tiger" Niazi, commandant of East Pakistan, had boasted that he would crush the rebellion within weeks, but this braggadocio was to no avail. Gul Hassan could barely conceal his contempt for Niazi, who he felt was no more than "company commander material." Hassan himself was not a great strategic thinker and came up with a madcap scheme to open a second front. This entailed a strategic thrust against India on its western frontiers. He argued that the best way to save East Pakistan now was via a full-scale war that would lead to a UN/U.S./China intervention to impose a global cease-fire. The risk here was that if, as was likely, this did not happen, then West Pakistan too might go up in smoke. His more friendly superiors patted him on the back for clever thinking but rejected the idea.* They were not totally stupid. The com-

---

*Memoirs of Gul Hassan Khan (Karachi: 1993).

plete control of the state by the army now raised more fundamental questions.

The Pakistan army and civil bureaucracy have always enjoyed a relative autonomy from the landlords and businessmen of West Pakistan. But the converse does not hold. The latter were heavily dependent on the military-bureaucratic complex that dominated the state. This process had been accelerated by the mass upsurge of 1968–69. The oligarchy in the West became more and more acutely aware of its dependence on the continued strength of the military and civilian state machine. The army and its cohesion was thus needed as a political rallying point over and above its purely repressive functions. The Six Points of March 1971 had struck at the heart of oligarchic rule in the West. This explains the frenzied refusal to compromise with the Awami League, the ferocity of the action against the East, and the remarkable degree of unanimity in West Pakistani ruling circles in immediately supporting the coup of March 25. It also explains the fidelity of the United States and its British adjutants to the military regime, despite the fact that it had jeopardized "stability" in Bengal.

The United States did try to inflect the Pakistani dictatorship toward "moderation," while shoring it up otherwise. Critical voices in Washington were annoyed by the threat posed to their global interests by the narrow national egoism of the Pakistan army. They were also nervous that the debacle in the East might destabilize the hitherto solid command structure of the Pakistani military.

Steeped in British conventions, the senior officers had hitherto always respected strict hierarchy of rank. Both Ayub and Yahya, when they assumed power in 1958 and 1969 respectively, were commander in chief of the army and formally acted in an ex officio capacity. A Middle Eastern– or Latin American–style putsch by radical younger generals or colonels would have represented a sharp rupture with this whole tradition. Such an eventuality was avoided in the nick of time after the crushing defeat of December 1971, when the domestic situation had already greatly deteriorated and the junior ranks were restive because of the ineptitude of the high command.

The war in Bangladesh had badly shaken the Pakistani economy, which had been depressed anyway since 1968. Foreign exchange had drastically dwindled, while prices and unemployment rose in tandem. Jute exports had naturally collapsed, precipitating steep falls on the Karachi stock exchange. This grave economic crisis was, of course, caused by the cost of the expeditionary force in Bengal. Press estimates calculated this at something like $2 million a day (the equivalent of $40 million today), a massive burden when added to West Pakistan's chronic import deficit of $140 million dollars ($2.8 billion today) a month. The Islamabad regime was thus faced with a domestic squeeze it had not bargained for when it embarked on its genocidal operations in March. It unilaterally suspended payments on its foreign debts and needed further large infusions of U.S. aid to ward off total bankruptcy.

New dangers loomed on other fronts. It soon became clear to the Indian government, led by Indira Gandhi, that a protracted struggle in East Bengal could have critical repercussions inside India in West Bengal. The latter province had been in the throes of a profound social crisis for three years now. Peasant uprisings and generalized social unrest had made the border province a powder keg. The Indian ruling elite, although far stronger than its Pakistani counterpart, was well aware of this and nervous that the infection might spread. Many reading this account today will be surprised by the thought that anyone in power ever feared a "Red revolution," but they did. The strength of the Communist Party (Marxist) and Maoist groups to its left worried successive Indian governments.

This was one of the main reasons that Mrs. Gandhi was quick in her demagogic response to the events in East Bengal. Every opposition party in India had been urging New Delhi to intervene more forcefully. However, Indira Gandhi's policy was to prop up the Awami League, while repeatedly disarming guerrillas crossing the border and instituting strict political control over the so-called "training camps" set up on Indian soil. Although it enjoyed great military superiority, the Indian government was initially daunted by the prospect of an intervention in East Bengal. It would anger the United States and China and might plunge the whole region into a turmoil that New Delhi feared it might not be able to control. Indeed, even if the Awami League succeeded in establishing what Indira Gandhi referred to as a "secular and democratic state" in East Bengal, the weakness of the indigenous elite and the virtual absence of a developed state apparatus would have posed the question of some sort of a revolutionary solution with great rapidity.

THE MOST EFFECTIVE political force in West Bengal itself at that time (as today) was undoubtedly the Communist Party of India (Marxist), or CPI(M), with its tens of thousands of militants and millions of supporters. The centrist inclinations of this party were in full view even then as it formed a coalition state government in the province, though once governor's rule was imposed and the center took charge, it allowed itself more revolutionary rhetoric. Its leaders stated that Indira Gandhi and Yahya Khan represented equally reactionary social and political forces, which was a bit unfair. They argued that just as East Bengal was specially exploited by West Pakistan, so "West Bengal was especially exploited by the Indian Centre." The logical conclusion to this view was to develop a strategy for a United Socialist Bengal. But to think in such terms necessitated a break with the past, and this the CPI(M) could not do. Perhaps it was a utopian notion, and perhaps it was the strong utopian streak in me that led me later, and quite independently of the CPI(M), to raise the demand for a United Socialist Bengali Republic. I found myself being denounced as an "ultraleft adventurist," a criticism that, on thinking back, possibly contained a germ of truth. At the time it seemed a reasonable enough response to military dictators, compromised politicians, and ignoble businessmen.

It was as an "ultraleft adventurer" that I arrived on a pitch-dark night in Calcutta in 1971, disguised as a Hindu trader. My aim was to meet up with a courier from the war zone and cross the border with him into East Pakistan and establish direct contact with the Bengali resistance. I had shaved off my mustache for the first and last time and barely recognized myself. I was traveling on a fake British passport that had once belonged to a man called Muttabir Thakur, a Bengali trader from Brick Lane in the East End of London. I had no idea who he was, but he had volunteered to surrender his passport to help the Bengali struggle. I was at that time still a Pakistani citizen and was aware that then, as now, a Pakistani passport did not facilitate a quick entry into most countries and especially not India.

For some unfathomable reason, Sophie, the French militant who had dyed my hair in Paris, had given it and my eyebrows a reddish tint so that when I looked in the mirror, I saw someone resembling a Hollywood serial killer. I was carrying a revolver gifted indirectly by the IRA for this journey, which I had packed in my suitcase together with some ammunition.

At Bombay airport the immigration officer asked me a routine question: "What is your father's name?" I had memorized Thakur's address in Calcutta, but had stupidly not foreseen this question. I panicked, blurting out, "Mohammed." The immigration officer was shocked, but before he could say anything, an elderly, ample-girthed Parsi lady queuing up behind me, evidently touched that a Hindu boy's father had been named Mohammed, defused the situation by exclaiming, "How sweet!" Everyone smiled, my papers were stamped, and Customs did not bother to open my suitcase.

I had arrived determined to cross the border and establish contact with the guerrilla band of Abdul Matin and Tipu Biswas, who represented the most sympathetic, Guevarist wing of the Bengali left. One of their supporters had translated Che Guevara's *Guerrilla Warfare* into Bengali, and it was now being read by soldiers in the Mukti Bahini, the official liberation army, which included former Bengali soldiers and officers of the Pakistan army. Matin and Biswas's irregulars were said to be operating in Pabna, in the heart of the province between the Ganges and the Brahmaputra rivers, as well as in the northeast of the province, in the region of Sylhet and Mymensingh. This last had been the epicenter of the great Tebhaga peasant uprising for rent reductions in 1945–47, the most militant social revolt of the rural poor in the subcontinent to that date. The tradition had certainly not disappeared. A courier from the Bengali maquis met me in Calcutta. He must have been only eighteen years old, but his composure and authority belied his youth. He impressed me greatly. He told me that the resistance was growing and maturing every day and had succeeded in paralyzing the port towns of Chittagong and Khulna, thus reducing interzonal trade to a trickle. "Soon we will take Santa Clara and then Havana," he said with a smile, the closest he came to revealing his political identity. In those days, given the diversity of groups engaged in the resistance, it was better not to pry too deeply into political affiliations, especially if one was a Punjabi from West Pakistan.

His instructions were to take me across the border, from where others would be responsible for my transportation. He insisted that we could not travel with any weapons in case we were stopped and searched by the Indian border police. So, reluctantly, I left the revolver behind. As we moved in the direction of the border, we began to encounter roadblocks and signs of heavy Indian troop movements and tanks. The border was obviously being sealed off. We were warned by activists en route that border crossings were virtually impossible. There was no option but to abort the mission. The courier kept his cool. He left me at a safe location in Calcutta and returned. I never discovered his real name. Some years later a Bengali friend told me that he was dead.

Over breakfast one morning at the Great Eastern, a dilapidated but atmospheric relic of the raj in central Calcutta, I was chatting with friends when an English journalist, Peter Hazelhurst of the *Times*, walked over and stared at me. I looked up, gave no sign of recognition, and turned away. We all fell quiet and buried our faces in newsprint. Hazelhurst hovered around, then returned to our table. He said something to me but I ignored him. He now insisted that he had recognized my voice, congratulated me on the effectiveness otherwise of my disguise, and threatened to expose my presence unless I gave him an exclusive interview as to what I was doing there. I was trapped and agreed. Afterward he gave me twenty-four hours to get out and helped to throw pursuers off the scent by writing I was heavily bearded and heading for Delhi. In fact I went to the airport and hopped on the first flight to London. In the interview I had raised the desirability of a United Red Bengal, a beacon for the whole region, a spark that would set the prairie on fire. Words came easily in those days. Hazelhurst agreed that a Red Bengal would alarm Delhi even more than Islamabad and reported me accurately, a rare enough occurrence at the time. These stray reflections stirred a hornet's nest. The Maoist groups, in particular, saw this as a "petty-bourgeois nationalist deviation." The prospect of a united Bengal was viewed with equal alarm by Washington, which perceived it as a stepping-stone to the possible Vietnamization of South Asia. This became clear when, astonishingly but to my immense delight, the following editorial appeared in the *New York Times*:

> Mr. Ali's radical vision of chaos on the Indian subcontinent cannot be taken lightly. . . .
>
> A prolonged guerrilla conflict in East Pakistan would have profound repercussions in the neighboring violence-prone Indian state of West Bengal, already shaken by the influx of more than three million refugees from the Pakistani Army's campaign of terror. Prime Minister Indira Gandhi is under mounting pressure to intervene to try to check this threat to India's own internal peace and integrity.
>
> It is obviously in nobody's interest to allow the Bengali "spark" to explode into a major international conflict, one which might speedily involve the major powers. Nor is it wise to permit the situation in East Pakistan to continue to fester, inviting the gradual political disintegration of the entire subcontinent.
>
> To deprive Tariq Ali and his like of their "big opportunity" it is essential that Pakistan's President Yahya Khan come to terms speedily with the more moderate Sheik Mujibur Rahman and his Awami League, which won an overwhelming popular mandate in last December's national and state elections. Such an accommodation with East Pakistan's elected representatives should be a prerequisite for the resumption of U.S. aid, except for relief assistance, to Pakistan.*

But Yahya Khan was out of it by now. It was Mrs. Gandhi, the Indian prime minister, who would deprive us of our "big opportunity." It had become obvious to New Delhi that the Pakistan army could not hold the province for long, and if the guerrilla war persisted, the Awami League leadership might be bypassed by more radical elements. Accordingly, on December 3, 1971, the Indian army crossed the East Bengal border, were greeted as liberators, were helped by the local population, and advanced toward the capital, Dhaka. Within a

---

*"Bengal Is the Spark," editorial, *New York Times*, June 2, 1971.

fortnight they had compelled "Tiger" Niazi to surrender himself and the rest of his command. Pakistan lost half its navy, a quarter of its air force, and just under a third of its army. The rout was complete. Within weeks Sheikh Mujibur Rahman had been released from a West Pakistani prison and flown to Dhaka via London. Washington, fearing chaos in his absence, had pressured Islamabad for his swift release. A defeated leadership had little choice but to oblige. East Bengal now became Bangladesh, a country of 70 million people. Within several weeks the Indian army had left, leaving the new state to construct its own apparatus.

The ferocious cyclone that had struck East Bengal in 1970, a year before the Pakistan army, had claimed two hundred thousand lives. Nature was kinder than the war. Sheikh Mujibur Rahman insisted that 3 million Bengalis had been killed in the war. The Pakistan army disputed these figures without supplying their own. A senior State Department mandarin, presumably relying on U.S. intelligence reports, wrote that "one million people were killed in Bengal between March and December [1971]. Some four million families—up to 20 million people—appear to have fled their homes, nearly half of them to refuge in India. Between one and two million houses were destroyed."* These are shocking figures, dwarfing the massacres at the time of partition and even the appalling Bengal famine of 1943. General A. O. Mitha, with the help of the U.S. military, had created the Special Services Group (SSG) in the sixties. Its purpose was to carry out specialist missions behind enemy lines (India), and its commandos had been sent to East Pakistan long before March 1971. In his memoirs, Mitha describes being stationed in Calcutta as a young officer and witnessing the heartrending plight of the famine victims. The same general, this time part of the war machine, exonerated the military commanders and blamed the politicians for the bloodbath.

Back in Islamabad, General Hameed, the man responsible for the prosecution of the war and on behalf of the high command, addressed all the officers in GHQ to explain why they had surrendered and lost

---

*Phillips Talbot, "The Subcontinent: Ménage à Trois," *Foreign Affairs* 50, no. 4 (July 1972), 698–710.

half the country. Thirty years later, Mitha, who had thought the meeting was a bad idea but had to attend, described the scene when Hameed invited questions:

> All hell broke loose. Majors, Lt. Colonels, Brigadiers screamed and shouted at him and called him and Yahya filthy names. The gist of what they shouted was that the reason for the defeat was that all senior officers were interested in was getting more and more plots and more and more land. . . . Hameed tried to calm them down but nobody would listen to him now, so he walked out.*

General Gul Hassan, who was at the same meeting, wrote in his memoirs, "One incessant demand I vaguely recall was that all officers' messes should be declared dry." He was convinced that a group of conspirators in the army were planning to use the SSG to either arrest or kill Bhutto when he returned to Islamabad from New York, where he had been addressing the United Nations Security Council. Gul Hassan noted:

> I do not know what role was contemplated for the SSG in Rawalpindi, but I can state categorically that the one purpose it was not intended for was to furnish a guard of honour to Bhutto at the airport. Had this drama been staged, it would have smacked of a re-enactment of our military action in Dhaka. Whether the President [Yahya Khan] was a party to this design, I am in no position to say. General Mitha, with his potent credentials, was the obvious choice to set this plot in train. . . . The discipline of the Army was on the verge of snapping and the repugnant odour of anarchy was in the air. . . . The induction of a company of the SSG, by no stretch of imagination for a Samaritan role, was a move so reckless that, had it materialised, it could have dispatched the country into oblivion.†

---

*Major General A. O. Mitha, *Unlikely Beginnings: A Soldier's Life* (Karachi: 2003).

†*Memoirs of Lt. Gen. Gul Hassan Khan* (Karachi: Oxford University Press, 1993).

In his memoirs, General Mitha denied the charge and accused Gul Hassan of pandering to Bhutto and "lying." What none of them could deny was that their fun-loving president, General Yahya Khan, had presided over a monumental political and military disaster. Having successfully liquidated the old state, he was now asked to relinquish power. His reign had lasted less than three years. The debate as to the inevitability of this loss continues to this day within the military elite, and a hard-line view of the conflict insists that it was all an Indian plot and Pakistan will have its revenge in Kashmir provided it is permitted "strategic depth" in Afghanistan. Action based on half-baked ideas of this variety might, on the contrary, lead to a repeat performance of 1971 and further dent, if not destroy, the state.

What would happen to a remaindered Pakistan? The overwhelming electoral success of the Awami League had stunned Bhutto. It utterly upset his plans for taking power. He had emerged as the most vociferous defender of the traditional hegemony of West Pakistan, had hysterically denounced the Six Points, and after confabulations with top army generals had whipped up an intensely chauvinistic atmosphere in Punjab to prepare his supporters for war.

In the 1970 elections in West Pakistan, Bhutto's Pakistan Peoples Party (PPP) had emerged as the largest Western party in the new constituent assembly. But smaller parties had also emerged with significant regional bases in Baluchistan and the North-West Frontier, and Bhutto knew that at best he would be a junior partner in any coalition government at the center. If the Awami League chose to govern alone, he would be acknowledged only as the leader of West Pakistan. Bhutto had won the elections in Punjab and Sind after his party had campaigned on a radical platform promising massive land reforms, extensive nationalization, food, clothing, and shelter for all, universal education, and an end to the economic power of the twenty-two families who, according to the Planning Commission, controlled 70 percent of the country's industrial capital, 80 percent of banking, and 90 percent of the insurance industry. These were improbable promises. Because of the virtual eclipse of the left, he was able, for a while, to don the socialist mantle. People close to him at the time, experienced veterans of the caliber of Meraj Mohammad Khan, Mukhtar Rana, Dr. Mubashir Hassan (the first finance minister in the PPP government), would later reveal that the radical rhetoric was little more than a mask designed to win and retain power. It was never meant seriously, and Bhutto would often laugh at the early descriptions of him in the Western press as an Asian Fidel Castro. It undoubtedly tickled his vanity, but his ideas and plans were far removed from any revolution. If anything, he believed in a form of social autocracy on the Lee Kuan Yew pattern in Singapore. A city-state could not, however, provide a model for even the new, reduced Pakistan.

Bhutto's party organization was an improvised assemblage of feudalists, racketeers, lawyers, and bandwagon petit bourgeois together with some of the most dedicated student activists who had helped topple the dictatorship. Its electoral success owed a great deal to Bhutto's deals with powerful landlord cliques in the provinces (his pact with leading Sindhi feudalists, of which he was one, was particularly notorious). However, the PPP also reflected, captured, and confiscated the genuine popular aspirations for social transformation of towns and villages. He made his party the only possible conduit for change and had destroyed the stranglehold of traditional landlord politics in the Punjab. For the first time peasants defied their patrons and voted for Bhutto.

According to the wits in Lahore's teahouses, "even a rabid dog on the PPP ticket" would have won that year. This was proved by the election of Ahmed Raza Kasuri, one of Bhutto's early and more eccentric supporters, who would later be a turncoat and accuse his former leader of murder. I remember well, in 1969, Bhutto arriving at a wedding in Lahore, preceded by Ahmed Raza in butler mode announcing, "Everyone, please rise for Chairman Bhutto, who is about to arrive," a remark that caused much merriment and was greeted with ribaldry.

So great was the enthusiasm and so deep the desire for social change that in those early months a great deal could have been accomplished. That the chairman of the Peoples Party was no visionary was revealed by his attitude to East Pakistan. Serious class tensions within Bhutto's electoral bloc and the hollowness of its party organization meant that the only cement to hold it together was a popular national chauvinism as embodied in the language and style of its leader.

The generals who had lost the war and some of their junior officers hated references to themselves by critics of every hue as "wine-soaked generals and bloodthirsty colonels." Nor were they alone. West Pakistani bureaucrats, state television executives, and numerous others who had been caught up in the euphoria unleashed by the chauvinism were now afflicted with a deep melancholy. Instead of calmly evaluating what had happened, they retreated into a fantasy world, occasionally quoting the poetry of Faiz to enliven otherwise dull and dreadful memoirs. They were careful never to mention the three grief-stricken poems Faiz wrote about blood-soaked East Bengal after 1971, the voice of a nation that had lost its tongue. The second of these was a bittersweet plea for truth and forgiveness:

> This is how my sorrow became visible:
> Its dust, piling up for years in my heart,
> finally reached my eyes,
>
> the bitterness now so clear that
> I had to listen when my friend
> told me to wash my eyes with blood.
>
> Everything at once was tangled in blood—
> each face, each idol, red everywhere.
> Blood swept over the sun, washing away its gold.
>
> The moon erupted with blood, its silver extinguished.
> The sky promised a morning of blood,
> and the night wept only blood.
>
> The trees hardened into crimson pillars.
> All flowers filled their eyes with blood.
> and every glance was an arrow,
>
> each pierced image blood. This blood
> —a river crying out for martyrs—
> flows on in longing. And in sorrow, in rage, in love.

*

Let it flow. Should it be dammed up,
there will only be hatred cloaked in colours of death.
Don't let this happen, friends,
bring all my tears back instead,
a flood to purify my dust-filled eyes,
to wash this blood forever from my eyes.

Finally realizing the scale of the disaster they had brought on themselves, a battered army leadership now turned to a patrician political leader, Zulfiqar Ali Bhutto, to manage the rump state and help them out of their mess. At this point the "relative autonomy" of the military had ceased to exist. That they would ever return to power seemed unimaginable. It is not often in history that a political leader is given a chance to look ahead and stamp a vision, a new imprint, on the future of his country. History offered Bhutto that chance. Would he take it?

5

THE WASHINGTON QUARTET

The Soldier of Islam

THE HEADLINES IN THE YEAR 1972 WERE GRABBED BY EAST PAKistan becoming Bangladesh. But the impact of the disintegration of the old state on West Pakistan should not be underestimated. The three minority provinces—Baluchistan, Frontier, and Sind—felt orphaned and began to resent the center. The presence of Bengal in Pakistan had provided them with a protective umbrella in the sense that they always felt that if they combined with Bengal, they could outvote the Punjab. Now they were alone. Nor should it be imagined that everyone in the Punjab was happy with what had taken place. The enthusiasm for Bhutto demonstrated in the 1970 elections never entirely disappeared, but it began to wane. The passionate social and political atmosphere I had experienced immediately after the fall of the dictatorship in 1969 had become polluted by the knowledge of the atrocities in East Pakistan. The racism directed against the darker-skinned Bengalis was much stronger among sections of the English-educated elite. The common people were troubled. Their living conditions were no different from those of their former compatriots in East Pakistan.

The war had diminished the revolutionary ardor of the students, workers, and urban poor. They had demonstrated that the power of a military dictatorship and its capacity to resist popular pressures had been greatly overrated. It was they who had sacrificed lives to wrest the instruments of power from the dictatorship, only to experience their own leaders collaborating with the generals to crush an insurgent population of East Pakistan, with disastrous results. The effect of this was twofold. It created enormous political confusion and led to the disappearance of the mass spontaneity that had characterized the uprising of 1968–69.

The PPP's politics too had become tangled up in the blood of Bengal. However it was justified to their supporters, it still did not seem right. But despite the change in mood, their supporters still expected something positive from the PPP. The longing for social change, for freer intellectual and political life and space to breathe, would never disappear.

In 1972, Bhutto was the unchallengeable leader of a truncated Pakistan. He knew that the only way to rekindle the movement and enthuse his supporters was by implementing the reforms that had been promised in the election manifesto of the Peoples Party, the demands that had been summarized in a popular chant against the Jamaat-e-Islami. When Islamist sloganeers asked, "What does Pakistan mean?" their activists would reply in unison, "There is only one Allah and he is Allah." The response of PPP militants to the same question was less abstract: "Food, clothing, and shelter." This had become the electoral battle cry of Bhutto's party, had won him the majority in West Pakistan, had left the Islamists fuming but impotent. In his first address to the new Pakistan, Bhutto pledged, "My dear countrymen, my dear friends, my dear students, laborers, peasants . . . all those of you who fought for Pakistan. . . . We are facing the worst crisis in our country's life, a deadly crisis. We have to pick up the pieces, very small pieces, but we will make a new Pakistan, a prosperous and progressive Pakistan."

How would this deadly crisis be resolved? Everything favored Bhutto and the Pakistan Peoples Party. The military high command was totally discredited, the right-wing parties isolated, and the two provinces not under PPP control—Frontier and Baluchistan—were governed by a coalition of secular nationalists led by the National Awami Party (now the Awami National Party—ANP) and the JUI, which were both committed to social reforms and an independent foreign policy. The JUI was not at that time making the implementation of the Sharia (Islamic laws) a precondition for anything.

Despite the promises and the propitious circumstances for honoring them, little was actually delivered to the majority of citizens. The country became oversaturated with PPP propaganda, the cult of the leader, and dehydrated ideas. Change was purely cosmetic, as symbolized by Bhutto's decision to design special military-style uniforms for party leaders and members of the government that were compulsory for official occasions. The sight of some overweight ministers ridiculously garbed created a great deal of amusement. Few were aware that the inspiration for this artificial grandeur came from Benito Mussolini rather than local bandleaders. The nub of the matter was that Bhutto was a man of few convictions. His opinions were never firm and settled. What he lacked in this department was overcompensated for by his sharp wit and intelligence, but that was never enough.

The balance sheet of Bhutto's five years in office is not edifying. From January to April 1972, he ruled the country as chief martial law administrator, and in that capacity he issued the Economic Reform Order on January 3, 1972, under which the banks, insurance companies, and seventy other industrial enterprises, large and small, were nationalized by the government. These included the medium-size steel foundry in Lahore owned by the Sharif family, which made them Bhutto's enemies for the rest of his life. Simultaneously, trade unions were given more rights than ever before and encouraged to keep a watch on industry. This was undoubtedly radical and broke the power of the twenty-two families that had dominated the country's economy, but was it effective without more generalized reforms in other spheres of life?

In domestic politics, two key issues mattered most to people at the time. A majority of the population was rural, and the stranglehold of landlords in the countryside stifled agriculture. The land ceiling (amount of land permitted to large landowners) was reduced, but in such a way as to make the change ineffective, and the usual allowances were made exempting orchards, stud farms, stock rearing, and *shikar-gahs* (hunting grounds) from the new assessments.* Even staunchly pro-PPP commentators in the press expressed their disappointment. They had hoped that, if nothing else, Bhutto would free Pakistan (as Nehru had done in India) from the multifarious survivors of feudalism that impeded the country's modernization.

Why did he not do so? The size of his own landholdings was not a deterrent. His cousin Mumtaz Bhutto was the big landowner in the family. He was a leader of the PPP and at the time favored radical reforms. What held Bhutto back was political opportunism. He had defeated the Punjabi landlords electorally. The loyalty of this social layer was to itself and its property. Many of them happily jumped ship and clambered aboard Bhutto's shiny, new vessel. Within six months some of the largest landlords in the country had aligned themselves with Bhutto. To keep them in line, the threat of land reform was used as the sword of Damocles. It was one of Bhutto's more serious errors. It had been taken for granted that health care, child care, and education would improve under the new dispensation. The statistics suggested otherwise. The infant mortality rate in 1972, one of the highest on the continent, was 120 per 1,000 live births. The figures were exactly the same in 1977. There was a marginal rise in literacy, but the elite structure of education remained unchanged.

In the absence of change, the indiscriminate nationalizations antagonized capitalists large and small without bringing any real improvement to the lives of urban dwellers. It resulted in increasing the weight of the state bureaucracy, encouraged cronyism and massive corruption, and scared off the industrialists, who fled with their capital to the Gulf, East Africa, London, and New York. Some would never return. Industrial output declined. This suggested that piecemeal reform would not work. Selective nationalizations of public utilities together with a stringent tax regime and tough regulation might have been more beneficial.

The second issue related to the army. The army's political role was never that of a lobby trying to influence government, as is the case, for

---

*See Tariq Ali, *Can Pakistan Survive?* (London: 1983), pp. 102–4, for a more detailed critique.

instance, in the United States, but a permanent conspiracy trying to replace the government. Bhutto knew this better than most. Yet he did little to change the existing structures, instead setting up his own para-military organization, the Federal Security Force, a praetorian guard led by ex-general and fantasist Akbar Khan, who had been imprisoned for planning a coup in league with Communist intellectuals in the fifties. This antagonized the military high command while leaving it intact. There were purges, with a thousand officers prematurely retired from the army and several hundred civil servants sacked for "corruption." Recognition that the two institutions needed reform was not enough. Its overall impact was to subordinate the civilian bureaucracy to exec-utive power, which made things worse, not better.

A new constitution was drafted by one of the country's most distin-guished lawyers, Mian Mahmud Ali Kasuri, who, as minister of law, was one of the few people capable of resisting Bhutto. Kasuri strongly opposed a presidential system and pressed for a federal parliamentary solution that made the executive accountable to parliament. Bhutto finally accepted this but insisted on provisions that made it virtually impossible for the National Assembly to remove a prime minister, a task assumed happily later on by the army. The new constitution came into force in August 1973. Despite the recent experience of losing Bengal, the Peoples Party leadership backed Bhutto when he dismissed the elected governments in Frontier and Baluchistan, accusing the National Awami Party leaders of "treason," and had them arrested and tried on spurious charges. They were accused of being involved in a plot with the Soviet Union and Iraq to break up Pakistan and Iran. The only plot that existed had been hatched by the Iranian and Pakistani intelligence services to crush the autonomous governments in Pakistan because the Shah of Iran regarded them as "subversive."

Bhutto's fatal flaw was a refusal to share power within his party and without. Had he done so with Sheikh Mujibur Rahman, it would have made it difficult, if not impossible, for the army to invade Bengal and destroy the old state. Had he been more farsighted he would have brought the provincial leaders of the National Awami Party into the central government. His refusal to surrender a monopoly of power would be his undoing. Its immediate consequences were disastrous.

The two elected leaders of Baluchistan, Ghaus Bux Bizenjo and Ataullah Mengal, the governor and chief minister of their province, were in prison. I knew both of them well, and during a lengthy conversation with Mengal in 1981, he described the problems that had confronted them:

> When I was in Mach jail in Baluchistan, our situation was brought home to me very vividly. A prison warder is the lowest-paid government employee. There were one hundred twenty warders in this prison, but only eleven of them were Baluch. If anyone had stated this, he would have been denounced as a traitor. When we took office in 1972, there was a total of twelve thousand government employees in twenty-two grades. Only three thousand were Baluch. There are only a few hundred Baluch in the entire Pakistan army. The Baluch regiment has no Baluch in it! The Kalat Scouts was a paramilitary force raised during the Ayub dictatorship. There were only two people from Kalat recruited to its ranks. . . . If you land at Quetta airport today and visit the city, you will soon realize that ninety-five percent of the police constables have been brought from the outside. When we tried to correct the balance, Bhutto and his Punjabi aide Khar organized a police strike against our government. This merely added fuel to the fire of nationalism. The students, in particular, wanted to go the whole way. Bizenjo and I told them, "These are temporary phases. We don't have another alternative." Governments, military regimes, have come and gone, but they have shared one attitude in common. They have mistreated and oppressed the Baluch.

The Baluch resented the overthrow of their government in 1973 and within weeks several hundred students and activists had fled to the mountains. The more radical nationalists among them led by the Marxist-Leninist-Guevarist leaders of the Marri tribe organized the Baluch Peoples Liberation Front (BPLF) and fought back by unleashing an insurgency that lasted four years. Bhutto sent in the predominantly Punjabi army, thus revealing his own incapacity to deal with a political crisis for which he was responsible. The rehabilitation of the discredited military that this represented was another serious error. To achieve victory the army required help, which came in the shape of HueyCobra helicopter gunships supplied by the Shah of Iran and flown by Iranian pilots. In the nineteenth century the British had imposed national boundaries dividing Baluchistan into Iranian, Afghan, and British Indian segments, disrupting the easygoing tribal nomadism of the region. The Shah was fearful that the rebellion would cross borders and disrupt his kingdom. The West backed Bhutto because it feared an autonomous Baluchistan might come under Soviet influence and the Soviet navy might use the port at Gwadar to further its global ambitions. The army finally succeeded in crushing the rebellion, but at some cost. The brutality of the campaign left the province smoldering with resentment.*

THE CRISIS IN Baluchistan dented Bhutto's standing in the country. Through this inability to cope with the real problems of the new Pakistan, the PPP demonstrated its futility. Many felt that the tragic lessons of Bengal had not been learned. It was back to business as usual, but this time under a civilian autocrat. State television projected Bhutto as it had Field Marshal Ayub. The print media was kept under strict surveillance, and internal debates and discussion were being actively discouraged inside the Peoples Party. The word of the leader was sufficient. This led to some resignations and, later, police repression against PPP dissidents. It was a confession of political bankruptcy. Had inner-party democracy prevailed, Bhutto as well as his party and the country would have benefited greatly. Instead the intelligence agencies were strengthened and given free range to spy and report back on the activities of rival political parties.

Bhutto had derived all his nightmares and fears from his experience

---

*A small group of middle-class Punjabi socialists defended the honor of their province by joining the Baluch resistance. One of them, Johnny Das, the son of a senior air force officer of Hindu origin, was captured, tortured, and killed. The others survived. They included the brothers Asad and Rashid Rehman (the former was the legendary guerrilla leader Chakar Khan), Najam Sethi (currently editor of the *Daily Times*), and the journalist Ahmed Rashid. This was undoubtedly their finest hour.

as a cabinet minister in Field Marshal Ayub's government. He was aware of how the intelligence agencies tortured opponents and, on rare occasions, killed political prisoners. He had observed firsthand the ironfisted feudal and backward Nawab of Kalabagh, Ayub's governor in West Pakistan, treating the province as a fiefdom. In his own villages, Kalabagh did not permit schools lest the peasants get ideas above their station. Bhutto feared but also respected his authoritarian style.

Instead of making a clean break with this past, Bhutto molded it to serve his own political needs. He did so not out of a conscious desire to mimic Ayub or Kalabagh, but because he feared the rise of a new opposition. Deeply insecure psychologically, he saw imaginary enemies everywhere. Self-defense, self-love, self-preservation, and sycophancy became the overpowering characteristics of his administration. None of this was necessary. Not even his enemies disputed that he was the most gifted political leader that the country had ever produced. Intellectually he was light-years ahead of any general or politician. His grasp of world politics was based on a deep reading of history. He had studied international law under Hans Kelsen at Berkeley, and both in California and at Oxford his precociousness left a mark on his tutors. The tragedy was in his imagining that his intellectual superiority made him infallible, and this made him his own worst enemy. The majority of his supporters were poor. What they wanted, above all, was an equality of opportunity for their children. Even if this craving was difficult to satisfy immediately, a start could have been made and the foundations laid for modernizing the country. There was to be no beginning, and so when the end came, all that people remembered was a courageous individual who had spoken on their behalf against their traditional oppressors. They understood that this was important, but also knew that it was not enough. On one occasion in Larkana, his hometown in Sind, peasant leaders and activists came to speak with him. For a whole hour they poured out their bitterness about promises he had made and not kept and how PPP landlords were not interested in implementing any reforms. Bhutto heard them out and then asked, "Now tell me this and be completely honest. Can you think of any other prime minister who would have met you and sat quietly listening to your complaints?" The peasant leaders laughed and cheered and the meeting came to an end.

They deserved better. The generation that had propelled Bhutto to power contained enormous reserves: it was rich in political passion, generous, idealistic, and this allowed it to visualize a better future for everyone. Morally exhausted now by the events in Bengal, silencing self-doubts and surfing on the wave of chauvinism promoted from above, the poor still hoped that conditions would change for the better in what was left of their country. They were disappointed. The predicament of Pakistan has never been that of an enlightened leadership marooned in a sea of primitive people. It has usually been the opposite.

What of the defeated army? It was not uncommon in those days to encounter a street wisdom: if only Bhutto had executed six or seven generals, all would have been well. Even if this had been desirable, how could Bhutto have ordered such an act? He had, after all, supported the military intervention in East Pakistan. Had he agreed to participate in the National Assembly after the 1970 elections and had he accepted Mujib as the prime minister of the country, it would have been difficult for the army to intervene. Had they done so, then West Pakistan too might have risen in arms, and that would have created a completely different situation. Soldiers encouraged to rape Bengali women and shoot Bengali civilians might have been more restrained in the Punjab, from where they had come.

The majority view in the Punjab was that drunk and incompetent generals combined with an Indian military intervention had lost them Pakistan. As I have argued, this was a simplistic and chauvinist view that ignored the structural exploitation of East Bengal by a predominantly West Pakistan–based elite. Given his own position on the conflict, Bhutto could not have tried the generals for treason and executed them, but he could certainly have transformed the basic structure of the colonial army by drastically reducing its size and instituting a more democratic command structure. There would have been widespread support for any such change in 1972–73.

Instead, and in keeping with his character, Bhutto tinkered with the army by retiring some senior generals and favoring others. He appointed General Tikka Khan, a "hero" of the war against Bengal, as the new commander in chief, and on his retirement in 1976, he leapfrogged Zia-ul-Haq over the heads of five senior generals and appointed him as army chief. Bhutto regarded him as a loyal simpleton. This was inaccurate, but even if it had been true, it would not have mattered much. To concentrate on the personnel rather than reforming the institution was a fatal error. Bhutto paid for it with his life. The country continues to suffer.

Far from being a useful idiot, Zia always reminded me of Dickens's inspired creation Uriah Heep, the hideous clerk in *David Copperfield*. A hypocrite whose body language stressed his humbleness while masking his ambition. His closest general-in-arms, K. M. Arif, referred to him without irony as "a practicing Muslim, he was a model of humility." General Saeed Qadir, another close colleague, listed "humbleness" as one of his boss's positive attributes and "hypocrisy" as one of his weaknesses, failing to link one to the other. Like many of his more senior colleagues, Zia had come of age in the British Indian army. Born in Jullundhur in 1924 and educated in Delhi, he moved to Pakistan after partition and was fond of stressing his "humble origins" in contrast to those who hailed from the gentry. Nor was he ever hesitant in praising the leader who had entrusted him with command of the army.

After training at Fort Leavenworth in Kansas during the early sixties, Brigadier Zia-ul-Haq was dispatched to Jordan in late 1968 to help train the locals in the art of suppressing popular uprisings. The target in this case were the Palestinians, who comprised a majority of the country's population and were in a turbulent mood after the six-day Israeli blitzkrieg in June 1967 had destroyed the Egyptian and Syrian armies, occupied large tracts of Palestine and Gaza, and delivered a fatal blow to Arab nationalism, which never recovered. The Palestinians realized they had to fight for themselves and correctly perceived Jordan as a weak link. The monarchy had become extremely unpopular after the Israeli triumph, and its overthrow would have provided the Palestinians with a state. It was not to be. In September 1970, Zia led the Jordanian troops to crush the Palestinian uprising. Between five and seven thousand Palestinians were killed. General Moshe Dayan noted that King Hussein "killed more Palestinians in eleven days than Israel could kill in twenty years." The month became known as Black September. Zia was awarded the highest Jordanian honor and returned home in triumph. Soon afterward he was promoted and posted as a corp commander in Kharian, a military city in the Punjab. According to friends, the Black September operation was one aspect of his past that he would never discuss, but clearly it was treated as a routine operation even by Bhutto, who publicly defended the Palestine Liberation Organization (PLO).

The poor may have felt instinctively that Bhutto was on their side (the elite never forgave him for encouraging this view and for the nationalizations), but few measures were ever enacted to justify their confidence. His style of government was authoritarian; his personal vindictiveness was corrosive. Under his watch the Inter-Services Intelligence (ISI) set up the notorious "election cell" to help the government "win" elections by threatening opposition candidates and ensuring that local bureaucrats rigged the ballot in favor of the government. This desperate opportunism created the basis for what followed after him. He attempted to fight the religious opposition by stealing their clothes: he banned the sale of alcohol, made Friday a public holiday, and declared the Ahmediyya sect to be non-Muslim (a long-standing demand of the Jamaat-e-Islami that had, till then, been treated by most politicians with contempt). By accepting the battleground determined by his enemies, he was bound to lose. These measures did not help him, but damaged the country by legitimizing confessional politics.

What a contrast this was to the mood in 1972 when Bhutto had addressed a giant rally in Lahore. He habitually carried a silver flask containing whiskey that he would mix with water and sip at public meetings. On this occasion a well-orchestrated group of Islamist militants strategically placed stood up the minute he mixed his drink and started shouting, "What are you drinking?" Bhutto held up the glass and replied, "Sherbet." The crowd laughed. The indignant hecklers were enraged. "Look, people," they said, "your leader is drinking *sharab* [liquor] not sherbet." An angry Bhutto roared back, "Fine. I am drinking *sharab*. Unlike you sisterfuckers I don't drink the blood of our people." The people rose to their feet and chanted in Punjabi, "Long may our Bhutto live, long may our Bhutto drink."

•   •   •

FEW PAKISTANI politicians were as obsessed with world politics as was Bhutto. All his knowledge was put to the test soon after he came to power in a truncated state crippled by defeat. Bhutto successfully concluded an agreement with Mrs. Gandhi in Simla that led to the release of ninety thousand Pakistan soldiers taken prisoner after the 1971 surrender in Dhaka. Soon after, he organized the Islamic Summit in Lahore, whose main function was to make the recognition of Bangladesh palatable to the army, but this was not enough to silence the self-doubt and fill the vacuum left by the loss of East Bengal. Pakistan's survival as a nation, Bhutto now decided, was dependent on nuclear parity with India.

"We will eat grass for a thousand years," he had shouted at a public meeting in Rawalpindi after India announced its first nuclear test, "but we will make the bomb." He knew perfectly well which section of the population would dine on grass for a millennium, but felt that a new Pakistan required a sense of pride and achievement. Unable to deliver food, clothing, education, health, and shelter, he would work hard at giving the people a bomb. This was to be the cornerstone of a new Pakistani nationalism that had not been possible before the amputation of Bengal. It was a deadly decision.

The plan to acquire a nuclear device could only be carried out nocturnally, under cover of a total information blackout and with Bhutto as the presiding genius. He saw this as a supreme and redeeming act. It was all meant to be a secret, but an early meeting with the country's physicists could not have taken place in a more inappropriate location, of the sort that Bhutto usually favored for clandestine trysts. It was on the estate of Nawab Sadiq Hussain Qureshi, a large landlord in Multan. The city was known for the delicacy and sweetness of its mangoes, a burning-hot wind that blew in the summer months, Sufi shrines, and a tradition of exquisite tile-making that went back to the early Mogul period. Qureshi was a recent supporter of Bhutto's (and a second cousin of mine) and could be relied upon to maintain secrecy.

The country's senior scientists, less than half a dozen men, were incredulous when informed as to why they had been summoned. This was empty talk, they said to each other, a hashish-induced fantasy. Dr. I. H. Usmani, chairman of the Pakistan Atomic Energy Commission, was openly skeptical. He knew that India was two decades ahead of Pakistan and that "Pakistan just didn't have the infrastructure for that kind of programme. I'm not talking about the ability to get 10kg of plutonium. I'm talking of the real infrastructure. Pakistan totally lacked a metallurgy industry. But if you're playing political poker and have no cards, you have to go on betting."

Bhutto was reminded of the low standard of most of the country's science graduates. It was impossible, he was told, he should forget it. Instead Bhutto ignored them and went over their heads to a younger, eager group of physicists, men such as Munir Ahmed Khan, Samar Mubarakmand, and Sultan Bashiruddin Mahmood, who were hungry for success and state patronage. They were only too happy to be lured into the surrealistic enterprise by a political leader whose mind was possessed by the vision of a mushroom cloud over the Pakistani desert. Soon they would be joined by another Muslim nationalist, A. Q. Khan, a postpartition refugee from India filled with hatred for that country. These were the men who built the Pakistani bomb, and in remote Kahuta, Bhutto's nuclear state was born. The nuclear facility remains there to this day.

While the scientists were happily working away, Bhutto's high-handedness in neighboring Islamabad had united all his opponents under the umbrella of the Pakistan National Alliance. An election was eagerly awaited. Despite all his mistakes Bhutto would probably have won the 1977 elections without state interference, though with a much-reduced majority. This is generally agreed. His more sycophantic adherents in the state bureaucracy and the ISI were not prepared to take any risk. The manipulation was so blatant and crude that the opposition came out on the streets, and neither Bhutto's sarcasm nor his wit was enough to allay the crisis. Nor was the United States. Washington had always regarded Bhutto as unreliable and untrustworthy and was unimpressed by the pretensions of his flaccid party or the large crowds that came to hear him. Now it became fearful that he would acquire the bomb. It wanted him out and soon.

In June 1977, on the verge of being toppled by the military, Bhutto told parliament, "I know the bloodhounds are after my blood," and denounced the U.S. secretary of state, Cyrus Vance, for interfering in the internal affairs of Pakistan. In his death-cell memoir, *If I Am Assassinated,* he alleged that Henry Kissinger had warned him, during one of his visits to Pakistan in August 1976, that unless he desisted on the nuclear question, "We will make a horrible example out of you." Both Kissinger and Bhutto could be economical with the truth, but the remark has recently been confirmed. A journalist in the Pakistan financial paper *Business Recorder* cites a senior Pakistani foreign official (on condition of anonymity) present on the occasion:

> . . . Kissinger waited for a while, and said in a cultured tone, "Basically I have come not to advise, but to warn you. USA has numerous reservations about Pakistan's atomic programme; therefore you have no way out, except agreeing to what I say." Bhutto smiled and asked, "Suppose I refuse, then what?" Henry Kissinger became dead serious.
>
> He locked his eyes on Bhutto's and spewed out deliberately, "Then we will make a horrible example of you!" Bhutto's face flushed. He stood up, extended his hand towards Kissinger and said, "Pakistan can live without the US President. Now your people will have to find some other ally in this region." Bhutto then turned and went out.*

If this is accurate, then we have to ask, what happened between February and August 1976? On February 26 that year, while Bhutto was in New York attending the United Nations, a meeting was organized with the secretary of state. The declassified memorandum of conversation offers some interesting insights. Bhutto's attempts to offer ultraloyal advice on how the United States should have dealt with the Cuban intervention in Angola (via a firm military riposte) and related matters clearly irritated Kissinger, who asked if Bhutto had been speaking to Brzezinski. A rambling discussion on world politics and U.S. strategy follows in which the satrap expresses concern that the imperial power is seen as weak by its enemies, which is disorienting for its

---

Business Recorder, January 29, 2008.

friends. Détente is viewed by Bhutto as having gone too far when "pip-squeak countries like Cuba" can score wins with ten thousand troops in Angola. "There were twelve thousand Cubans," corrects Kissinger as he deftly parries each thrust. It's obvious that for him the main reason for the meeting, apart from humoring Bhutto, is the nuclear issue. As the following extract reveals, each side was aware of the other's position, but the tone here is friendly (if occasionally servile on Bhutto's side) and far removed from any threats:

> BHUTTO: Mr. Secretary, I am sure you like the role we played in the Middle East debate.
> THE SECRETARY (KISSINGER): Yes. That was appreciated. If I spoke vehemently on the topic of détente, Angola, and the erosion of central authority, I did so because I believe you were one of the world leaders who understands us.
> BHUTTO: After that remark I don't want to provoke you by mentioning nuclear reactors.
> THE SECRETARY: . . . What concerns us is how reprocessing facilities are used at a certain point. I told you last year that we appreciated that you were forgoing a nuclear capability. This placed us in a good position and gave us arguments to assist you in other ways.

The discussion continues with Kissinger stressing his concern that once a nuclear reprocessing plant was built it could easily develop in another direction, and Bhutto pleading disingenuously that in such a case the West could easily bring pressure to bear that could stop that. Kissinger remains unconvinced. When Bhutto explains that Pakistan had pledged never to misuse the reprocessing facilities, his interlocutor points out that he is not interested in "words, but concerned with realities." The country with the facilities could easily abrogate a binational agreement whenever it wished.

Earlier Bhutto had been informed that the United States was quite happy to provide Iran with nuclear reprocessing plants that could be used by Pakistan and other states in the region. This brilliant idea had matured in the heads of two senior officials in the Ford administration

who would resurface in a later Republican administration: Dick
Cheney, then chief of staff at the White House, and Donald Rumsfeld,
the defense secretary. Cheney is a keen advocate today of bombing
Iran's nuclear energy stations, an idea that has, till now, been vetoed by
the Pentagon. That Cheney and Rumsfeld's plan might not have been
entirely determined by U.S. strategic needs is mentioned in a recent
study, whose authors point out that "the first proposed US nuclear deal
with Iran would have been extremely lucrative for US corporations like
Westinghouse and General Electric, which stood to earn $6.4 billion
from the project."* Cheney and Rumsfeld were never great believers in
self-renunciation. Strategic and business interests could never be separate for them.

Bhutto was not interested in playing second fiddle to Iran and
rejected the idea, but he was also not seriously interested in a reprocessing plant. All he wanted was the bomb. That was the instruction he had
given to Pakistani scientists. Clearly, between the two meetings with
Kissinger the latter was informed by U.S. intelligence of what was really
going on. Kissinger's realization that he was being lied to so blatantly
prompted him to start playing the godfather. His rage was not just
imperial, but also personal. From 1973 onward Kissinger had spear-
headed a campaign to lift the U.S. arms embargo on Pakistan and had
dispatched Henry Byroade as U.S. ambassador to accelerate the process
and control the nuclear ambitions. Byroade later confirmed this in an
interview with historian Niel M. Johnson:

JOHNSON: . . . So you left there in '73 and went to Pakistan.
BYROADE: That's right. I planned to retire, and Henry Kissinger
    talked me into going to Pakistan. I went there for one specific
    purpose, and I planned to stay about eighteen months. We'd
    had an arms embargo on Pakistan for about ten years, growing
    out of the India-Pakistan war. This had worked out in the long
    term to be, I thought, very unfair to Pakistan, because India
    turned to the Soviet Union for their armament needs, primar-

*Adrian Levy and Catherine Scott-Clark, *Deception* (London: 2008). This is the most complete and best-researched account to date of how Pakistan became a nuclear power.

ily, but also to a lot of other countries. . . . Kissinger said, "This
is unfair, and we've got to lift that embargo, but it's not easy with
the India lobby and all of that." So he said, "You go out there
and stay long enough to be credible and come back and talk to
people on the Hill about it, and see if we can lift that thing."

. . . You know, it's very easy to impose these things; India and
Pakistan get into a war, our weapons are involved, so "bingo,
embargo!" It was very proper, but when it came around to lift-
ing it, it's something else. But we did during Bhutto's visit, and
we did get a little flak from the Hill but not very much. So we
lifted that and were able for the first time to start replenishing
some of their equipment. I was then ready to come home, but
Pakistan got involved in the nuclear business, which upset me
no end. I stayed and struggled, trying to keep that from being a
problem between us for two more years. I was there about four
years.

JOHNSON: Four years, and Bhutto was still in power?

BYROADE: Bhutto was in trouble, deep trouble when I left, but he
was still in power.

JOHNSON: General Zia, was he the one that was . . .

BYROADE: When I left, he was chief of staff, with, I think, no idea
of taking over at that point.*

In 1976, Zia had been made chief of staff by Bhutto. It is possible,
but unlikely, that Byroade, whose links with the U.S. military stretched
back to the Second World War, had no idea of DIA/Pentagon contacts
with Zia, which went back to his time in Fort Leavenworth and had
been renewed in Jordan in 1970. Military coups in Pakistan are rarely,
if ever, organized without the tacit or explicit approval of the U.S.
embassy. Bhutto's "treachery" on the nuclear issue was the principal reason why the United States gave the green light for his removal.

On the night of July 4–5, 1977, to preempt an agreement between
Bhutto and the opposition parties that would have entailed new gen-

---

*"Oral History Interview with Henry Byroade," 1988, Truman Library archives.

eral elections, General Zia struck. Having reached an agreement with the United States that Bhutto's rule was intolerable, Zia was not prepared to tolerate a rapprochement between the two rival political groups. He proclaimed martial law, declared himself chief martial law administrator, promised new elections within ninety days, and placed Bhutto "under protective custody." Bhutto was stunned. In January 1977 I had visited Pakistan and on my return written a series of three short articles for the *Guardian* predicting a military takeover. This was considered fantastical and the articles were not published. I had repeated the argument to Benazir Bhutto in Oxford, to which she had replied that her father might well be assassinated, but that there could never be a coup "since Zia was in our pocket." I told her to let her father know that in Pakistan no general was ever in the pocket of a civilian politician.

The army had assumed there would be large public protests and had been prepared to crush them, but was encouraged by the muted response. As a result, Bhutto was released on July 28, 1977. He immediately embarked on a political tour of the country and was greeted by large crowds. In Lahore, half a million people came out to receive him, thus destroying the military's illusions that he was a discredited and spent force. "Two men, one coffin" is what Zia's colleagues now told him. Zia realized that Bhutto would win any election that was not heavily rigged. Were this to happen, Zia's own future would be truncated. This time he made sure that Bhutto would never be free again.

On September 3, 1977, Bhutto was arrested in Lahore and charged with "conspiracy to murder Ahmed Raza Kasuri," a former PPP member who had joined the opposition. In November 1974, a group of gunmen had opened fire on a car carrying Kasuri and his father. The latter died. Kasuri had accused Bhutto of being responsible, but a special inquiry tribunal had looked into the allegations and rejected them. Kasuri then rejoined the Peoples Party and remained a member from April 1976 to April 1977, but was refused a party nomination to contest the ill-fated March 1977 general elections. This rejection went deep. After Zia's coup, Kasuri embarked on a private prosecution of Bhutto, and this was now used by the military as a motive in a case of alleged murder. On September 13, 1977, Bhutto was released on bail by two senior High Court judges—K. Samdani and Mazharul Huq. Four days later he was rearrested in Karachi by commandos under martial law regulations.

The trial for murder began in September 1977 before the Lahore High Court. The two judges who had granted bail were excluded from the bench. The acting chief justice, Maulvi Mushtaq, was a close personal friend of Zia's and his conduct at the trial was a travesty. Even journalists who disliked Bhutto were shocked by Mushtaq's vindictiveness. He had been ordered to insult and humiliate Bhutto, and he did so throughout the trial, which lasted till March 1978. Only hearsay evidence implicated Bhutto. One of the state witnesses was Masood Mahmood, a former boss of the Federal Security Force. He had been promised immunity, but ended up with a new identity, a great deal of money, and a luxury apartment in California, where he died in the late nineties. Foreign observers attending the trial included John Mathew, QC, and Ramsey Clark, former attorney general of the United States. Both agreed that in Britain and the United States such a case would never have come to trial since it was based on the uncorroborated evidence of pardoned accomplices.* Bhutto and four others were sentenced to death on March 18, 1978. An appeal against the judgment was heard in the Supreme Court on May 20, 1978, and continued for several months. Bhutto's appearance before the court shocked observers. He had lost a great deal of weight and looked haggard. His speech lasted three hours. He defended his political honor, refused to take the charge of murder seriously, and pointed the finger at Zia and his generals, who had decided to do away with him. He concluded by looking at the judges with contempt and saying, "Now you can hang me." The Supreme Court rejected the appeal by a 4–3 vote. One judge who was considered unreliable by the military was retired during the trial; a second was denied sick leave and a delay in the trial. He had to withdraw from the bench. Chief Justice Anwarul Haq was in communication with the military dictator every single day. A detailed two-hundred-page

---

*Ramsey Clark, "The Trial of Ali Bhutto and the Future of Pakistan," *Nation,* August 19–26, 1978.

dissenting opinion by Justice Safdar Shah provided a devastating rebuttal of the case brought forward by the state. Shah, with whom I spent many hours in London, revealed that he had been threatened before and during the case and told that his relations in the army would suffer unless he behaved himself. He told me, "I was ashamed to belong to a Supreme Court which did the bidding of the military."

Bhutto was hanged at 2 a.m. on April 4, 1979, in the district jail, Rawalpindi. The day before, he had been visited by his wife, Nusrat, and daughter, Benazir, for the last time. Both women had courageously been campaigning against the dictatorship and had been in and out of prison themselves. He told them how proud he was of his family. Neither woman was allowed to attend his funeral. Some years later the prison where Bhutto was hanged was demolished on Zia's orders.

Zia had the support of the military high command (with only a single general against) and, of course, the United States.* The notion that Zia would have gone through with the hanging had it been opposed by Washington is risible. U.S. operatives in the region (including the "anthropologist" and Afghan expert Louis Dupree) had told a number of senior Pakistani officials that Bhutto was dispensable and would soon be out of the way.

The Pakistani leader's judicial assassination transformed him into a martyr and ensured that his legacy would endure. Washington had assumed that with Bhutto out of the way the Pakistan army would abandon all notions of acquiring a nuclear identity. Here they miscalculated badly. In fact, Bhutto had retained political control of the nuclear facility, keeping the generals at a safe distance. One of Zia's first instructions was to authorize a total military takeover of Kahuta. Since 1971, the military had become obsessed with revenge. In return for the loss of Bangladesh, they were now going to make a determined effort to destabilize and capture Kashmir, a long-disputed territory to which both India and Pakistan laid claim and which is discussed in a subsequent chapter. It was almost as if they believed their own propaganda according to which "Hindus and traitors" had been responsible for the

---

*Ali, *Can Pakistan Survive?*

Bengali defection. The trauma of military defeat had left a permanent scar on the psyche of many officers unaccustomed to thinking for themselves. A debilitated military apparatus was prepared to take risks to restore its pride.

Bhutto's decision to respond to India's nuclear test by securing a "Muslim bomb" strongly appealed to the army as well as those whose financial help would be essential. These included Mu'ammar al-Gadhafi, the eccentric and unpredictable leader of Libya, who would sometimes fly over from Tripoli unannounced, causing havoc for the chief of protocol in Islamabad, to have breakfast with his dear friend Bhutto and find out how work on the bomb was proceeding. Of all the Arab leaders, Gadhafi alone had genuinely intervened to save Bhutto's life. Zia had promised him to commute the sentence, but later said he was overruled by his colleagues.

With Bhutto out of the way, the military could now control the entire nuclear process till success had been achieved. Whether they would have succeeded in hoodwinking Washington indefinitely—had not another major shift occurred in the region—remains an open question. But a geopolitical earthquake, the Soviet occupation of neighboring Afghanistan in December 1979, provided the cover for Pakistani scientists to mimic their Indian counterparts and split the atom. Zia himself was given a whitewash in the West. He was no longer a temporary necessity. From being viewed as a squalid and brutal military dictator, he was transformed into a necessary ally defending the frontiers of the free world against the godless Russians.

Religious affinity had done little to mitigate the hostility of Afghan leaders toward their neighbor to the east. The main reason was the Durand Line, a border imposed on the Afghans by the British Empire in 1893 to mark the frontier between British India and Afghanistan after the British had failed to subjugate the country. This arbitrary line through the mountains had purposefully divided the Pashtun population of the region. It was agreed at the time that, on the Hong Kong model, after a hundred years all of what became the North-West Frontier Province of British India would revert to Afghanistan. But no government in Kabul accepted the Durand Line any more than they accepted British, or, later, Pakistani, control over the territory.

• • •

In July 1977, when Zia seized power, 90 percent of men and 98 percent of women in neighboring Afghanistan were illiterate; 5 percent of landowners (most of whom were also tribal leaders) held 45 percent of the cultivable land, and the country had the lowest per capita income of any in Asia. A majority of the people in the countryside were desperately poor. Comparisons with other countries seem absurd when the classification that matters is between those who eat twice a day, those who eat once, and the hungry. In these conditions it is hardly surprising that fatalism and religion become deep-rooted. The tiny intellectual elite—monarchists, liberals, republicans, Communists—that dominated political life in Kabul were heavily dependent on local traders, businessmen, and tribal leaders. Money from the former helped to bribe the latter. The Afghan rulers had preserved their independence and held the British at bay. For most of the twentieth century geography had dictated neutrality in the Cold War. The rulers were friendly with Moscow and New Delhi. Some Pashtun Hindus had relocated in Kabul rather than flee to India during partition, and the Afghan rulers were much more tolerant in religious matters than their neighbors.

By a strange quirk of history, the same year that Zia seized power, the Parcham (Flag) Communists in Afghanistan, who had backed the 1973 military coup by Prince Daud after which a republic was proclaimed, withdrew their support from Daud and were reunited with other Communist groups to form the People's Democratic Party of Afghanistan (PDPA). Despite its title, the new party was neither popular nor democratic. Its most influential cadres were strategically concentrated in the army and air force.

The regimes in neighboring countries became involved in the brewing crisis that now threatened Daud. The Shah of Iran feared a Communist takeover and, acting as a conduit for Washington, recommended firm action—large-scale arrests, executions, torture—and put units from Savak, his tried-and-tested torture agency, at Daud's disposal. The Shah tried to bribe Daud. If he recognized the Durand Line as a permanent frontier with Pakistan, Iran would give $3 billion to Afghanistan and ensure that Pakistan ceased all hostile actions in the tribal zones. Pakistani intelligence agencies had (even under Bhutto) been arming Afghan exiles while encouraging old-style tribal uprisings aimed at restoring the monarchy. Daud was tempted to accept the Shah's offer, but the Communists in the armed forces, fearing Iranian repression as in Baluchistan, organized a preemptive strike and took power in April 1978. Washington was in a panic. This increased tenfold as it became clear that its long-standing ally, the overconfident Shah, was about to be toppled together with his throne.

General Zia's dictatorship thus became the linchpin of U.S. strategy in the region, which is why Washington green-lighted Bhutto's execution and turned a blind eye to the country's nuclear program. The United States wanted a stable Pakistan, whatever the cost.

Zia understood his role well and instructed General Akhtar Abdul Rahman, his director general at the ISI, "The water in Afghanistan must be made to boil at the right temperature." Rahman, an efficient, bigoted, and cold-blooded officer, set up the Afghan Bureau of the ISI, which worked with U.S. intelligence agencies and was provided with unlimited supplies of funds and weaponry. Its aim was straightforward: to set a "bear trap," in the words of the U.S. national security adviser, Zbigniew Brzezinski, via a simple strategy to destabilize the Afghan government, in the hope that its Soviet protectors would be drawn into the conflict.

Plans of this sort often go awry (as in Cuba over five decades), but they succeeded in Afghanistan, primarily because of the weaknesses of the Afghan Communists: they had come to power through a military coup that hadn't involved any mobilization outside Kabul, yet they pretended this was a national revolution; their Stalinist political formation made them allergic to any form of accountability, and such ideas as drafting a charter of democratic rights or holding free elections to a constituent assembly never entered their heads. Ferocious factional struggles led, in September 1979, to a Mafia-style shoot-out at the Presidential Palace in Kabul, during which the prime minister, Hafizullah Amin, shot President Taraki dead. Amin claimed that 98 percent of the population supported his reforms but the 2 percent who opposed them had to be liquidated. The photographs of the victims were proudly published in the government press. Repression on this scale and of this

variety had never before been experienced in the country. Mutinies in
the army and uprisings in a number of towns resulted, and this time
they had nothing to do with Washington or General Zia, but reflected
genuine revulsion against the regime. Islamabad, of course, incited and
armed the religious opposition. One of the ideological weapons used
was a campaign against the PDPA's decision to make literacy compulsory for all Afghan women. This was publicized as a ferocious assault
on Islam and Afghan traditions.

FINALLY, AFTER TWO unanimous politburo decisions against intervention, the Soviet Union changed its mind, saying that it had "new
documentation." This is still classified, but it would not be surprising
in the least if the evidence consisted of forgeries suggesting that Amin
(who was educated at Columbia University in the United States) was a
CIA agent. Whatever it was, the politburo, with Yuri Andropov, then
head of the KGB, voting against, now decided to send troops into
Afghanistan. Its aim (not unlike that of the United States in 2001) was
to get rid of a discredited regime and replace it with a marginally less
repulsive one. The bear trap had worked. On Christmas Day in 1979,
a hundred thousand Soviet troops crossed the Oxus and rumbled into
Kabul. President Carter referred to the event as "the greatest threat to
peace since World War Two" and warned the Soviet leader, Leonid
Brezhnev, to "either withdraw or face serious consequences."

Given that Afghanistan, thanks to the Russians, had now become
fundamental to civilization, it was crucial for it to acquire a heroic
political history. This required outside help on various levels. Knights
in shining armor were dispatched to the region. Washington alerted
researchers and advisers from different agencies and think tanks. The
Rand Corporation reacted swiftly and decided that one of its more pre-
cocious staff members, a twenty-eight-year-old Japanese-American,
should be parachuted into Pakistan on a rapid reconnaissance mission.

Francis Fukuyama spent ten days in the country from May 25 to
June 5, 1980, as the guest of the director of military intelligence and
was provided with access to generals and senior civil servants. Pakistan
had earlier turned down a $400 million aid package offered by the

White House's national security adviser, Zbigniew Brzezinski, on the grounds that "it was peanuts" and informed Washington that it was looking forward to subsidies that, at the least, were on a scale similar to what was being provided to Egypt and Turkey. Why should Pakistan accept anything less? It was now a frontline state, and in pleasant anticipation of what this new status entailed, a number of senior members of the elite had opened bank accounts in far-flung tax havens.

The military top brass confided their innermost fears to Fukuyama. The Soviet Union might cross the Durand Line and detach a salient of their North-West Frontier Province. A carefully orchestrated Indo-Soviet-Afghan pincer movement with the aim of further fragmenting Pakistan "along ethnic lines" was always a possibility. The guilty conscience on Baluchistan was beginning to affect the brass.

Fukuyama accepted much of what he was told, since it tied in neatly with U.S. interests. In any case, he knew that history is never written by any particular authors but often emerges from the periphery to surprise the center. The Vietnamese victory of 1975 still haunted U.S. policy makers. This new history being made in the awesome environment of the Hindu Kush just needed occasional help to proceed along similar lines. Muddling through was not an option. Fukuyama summed up the pros and cons of a tighter U.S.-Pakistan embrace. The advantages were obvious:

(1) denial of Pakistani territory to the Soviet Union.
(2) the possibility of aiding the Afghan rebels militarily so as to raise the cost of the intervention for the Soviets and divert their attention from the Persian Gulf.
(3) the use of Pakistani facilities in connection with the planned Rapid Deployment Force.
(4) the demonstration of American reliability, especially with respect to the People's Republic of China.

The obvious drawbacks were not insurmountable: "(1) Adverse effects on U.S.-Indian relations; (2) a weakening of the credibility of the U.S. nonproliferation policy; (3) high economic costs and (4) commitment to a regime of questionable staying power."

Shrewdly, Fukuyama noted that the Sino-Pakistani relationship offered a model equilibrium:

> The Chinese have supported civilian and military regimes indifferently and have not attempted to influence Pakistan's internal character. As a consequence, they have never been called to account for the failures of a particular regime. . . . Unless the United States can emulate this behavior in some fashion, the liabilities may well exceed the benefits.*

This advice was more or less accepted and reinforced by Brzezinski's "realism." General Zia-ul-Haq, the worst of Pakistan's dictators, was about to be whitewashed and transformed into a plucky freedom fighter against the Evil Empire. The newspapers and television networks did their duty.

From 1980 to 1989, Afghanistan became the focal point of the Cold War. Millions crossed the Durand Line and settled in camps and cities in the NWFP, the largest influx—3.5 million refugees—a direct result of the Soviet occupation. The result was to be catastrophic for both countries. Nobody benefited from the Afghan war except for a tiny layer of heroin smugglers, civilian middlemen, the top brass of the Pakistan army, and politicians allied to all three. Weapons, heroin, drug dollars, NGOs assigned to "help" the refugees, and would-be jihadi warriors from Saudi Arabia, Egypt, and Algeria flooded the region. Pakistan's largest city and port became the center of the heroin trade. The poppy was cultivated in the north, transformed into powder, and packaged to Karachi, from where it was smuggled out to Europe and America. The modern city and its elite were graphically depicted in Kamila Shamsie's novel *Kartography*.

All the main Western intelligence agencies (including the Israelis) were present in Peshawar, near the Afghan frontier. It began to resemble a gold-rush town. The region would never again be the same. For the first time in Pakistan's history, the market and black-market rates

---

*Francis Fukuyama, "The Security of Pakistan: A Trip Report," September 1980, Rand, Santa Monica.

for the dollar were exactly the same. Weapons, including Stinger missiles, were sold to the mujahideen and illegal-arms dealers by Pakistani officers wanting to get rich quick. At a dinner in a London restaurant in 1986, Benazir Bhutto whispered in my ear that our generous host, a certain Sindhi gentleman, waxing eloquent on matters cultural, had a day job selling Stingers and Kalashnikovs. I asked him whether I could buy a missile and how much it would set me back. He was not in the least bit curious as to why I might need such a weapon.

"No problem at all," he said with a smile. "Fly to Karachi. I'll meet you at the airport. We'll drive out of the city and you can try one. Then we'll discuss a price." Unlike me, he was quite serious.

The heroin trade funded Pakistan's thriving black economy. General Fazle Haq, Zia's governor in the Frontier Province, publicly declared his indifference, arguing that since the heroin went abroad, Pakistanis weren't that bothered. The number of registered addicts in Pakistan grew from a few hundred in 1977 to over 2 million in 1987.* The growth of gang warfare in Karachi is directly linked to its becoming a center of the heroin trade.

As for Pakistan and its people, they languished. Zia wanted a total break with the past and reached out for religion, usually the first resort of a scoundrel. On December 2, 1978, the "soldier of Islam," as he often referred to himself, had denounced politicians "who did what they pleased in the name of Islam," then proclaimed that he was preparing to enforce true Islamic laws in the country. He announced the creation of Sharia courts, whose powers were limited but which could nonetheless pronounce whether a law was "Islamic or un-Islamic." Disputes between theologians began immediately, and a number of courts had to be rapidly reconstituted. Two months later Zia promulgated a number of new ordinances and presidential orders. According to these, all legal punishments related to alcohol consumption, adultery, theft, and burglary were to be replaced by the religious punishments prescribed by the Koran and early Islamic jurisprudence. Any Muslim caught drinking would be subjected to eighty lashes; an

---

*One of the banks through which the heroin mafia laundered money was the BCCI (Bank of Credit and Commerce International), now defunct.

unmarried couple caught fornicating would get one hundred lashes, but adultery involving married partners would lead to both being stoned to death; an offense against property would require amputation of the right hand from the wrist, and robbery would be punished by chopping off both hand and foot. These were Sunni prescriptions. The Shia theologians opposed amputating at the wrist, but were happy with removing all fingers and the thumb of the right hand. And as for the absurd demand so beloved of the Peoples Party, for food, clothes, and shelter, all this, according to General Zia, could not be provided by the state or private businesses, but only by God: "Any increase or decrease in your sustenance comes from Him. Trust in God and He will bestow upon you an abundance of good things in life."

All government employees were instructed to say their prayers regularly, and the relevant authorities were instructed to make all necessary arrangements for performing prayers in government buildings, airports, railway stations, and bus stops. A special ordinance was passed insisting on total reverence for Ramadan, and cinemas were to be closed during this period for three hours after the evening prayers. Pakistan had never known anything like it, and the results were mixed. Officially encouraged religiosity now became the norm, but with a massive increase in alcohol consumption and every drunkard claiming that he was resisting the dictatorship. The figures on adultery and the observance of fasts can never be established. The Taliban did not as yet exist, but the stage was being prepared. To the credit of the medical profession, doctors refused to preside over or perform "Islamic" amputations, and these particular punishments could never be implemented. Public and prison floggings, however, occurred regularly and further brutalized the country's fragile political culture.

Unsurprisingly, under Zia, the Jamaat-e-Islami, which had never won more than 5 percent of the vote anywhere in the country, was patronized by the government. Its cadres were sent to fight in Afghanistan, its armed student wing was encouraged to terrorize campuses in the name of Islam, its ideologues were ever present on TV and in the print media. The Inter-Services Intelligence were now instructed by the military leadership to assist the formation of other, more extreme jihadi groups, which carried out terrorist acts at home and abroad. Religious schools began to be established in the countryside, especially in the frontier provinces. Soon Zia too needed his own political party, and the bureaucracy set one up, the Pakistan Muslim League, with Zia's favorite protégés: the Sharif brothers and the Chaudhrys of Gujrat. Currently at each other's throats, they at that time combined their great strengths, one of which was the use of political power to assist the primitive but rapid accumulation of capital.

The Sharif family had become favorites of Zia's mainly because they had suffered under Bhutto and their hatred for him was unrestrained. Blacksmiths by trade, they had left India and sought refuge in the new Muslim homeland, settling down in Lahore. Muhammad Sharif, a hardworking, semipious disciplinarian, made sure his sons, Nawaz and Shahbaz, were provided with a proper education. The family had done well, their small steel foundries prospered, and if anything they were disinterested in politics. Their refusal to pay protection money to some of the more thuggish Bhutto supporters in Lahore led to their business being targeted and nationalized in 1972. The decision was economically stupid and politically counterproductive. A family of neutral small businessmen were transformed into lifelong enemies of the Bhutto family. The day Zia ordered Bhutto's execution, Muhammad Sharif and his sons gave thanks to Allah for responding so rapidly to their prayers. The oldest son, Nawaz, became a protégé of the general's and was made the leader of the *khaki* Muslim League. Transmogrified into politicians by the military, the Sharif family were ever grateful to General Zia. Their primary loyalty, however, was to their own business interests. The foundries had been returned to them but they were no longer enough. Political power was now harnessed to make huge profits largely through securing massive bank loans that were not repaid. This process started early and acquired new momentum after General Zia's unexpected death.

The second family to benefit from military regimes was the Chaudhry clan based in Gujrat. This is an old Punjabi town, located near the Chenab River, built by the Mogul emperor Akbar and garrisoned by Gujjars, traditionally belonging to a seminomadic caste of cowherds and goatherds (hence the city's name). The initial function of the town was to supply the Mogul armies with food and other necessities as they tramped through the region. The Jats, descended from migrant tribes, were farmers who acquired a taste for war and supplied soldiers to the Moguls and later, in much greater numbers, to the British and their successor armies. Some of them settled in the town as well, with constant rivalry between them and the Gujjars.

Gujrat acquired a reputation for craftsmanship—especially pottery— of a high quality during the Mogul period. Few signs of this are left except in the craft of forging currency and especially passports. Before electronic safeguards were introduced, a particular Gujrati craftsman reputedly produced passports and U.S. visas of such high quality that his clients were rarely detected. Such were his skills that government ministers sometimes used him to help their poorer clansmen escape to friendlier climes, an interesting example of self-indictment.

The Chaudhry clan were Jats, and especially during British rule when living standards declined, most of them were badly off and constantly in search of employment. The founding father was Chaudhry Zahoor Elahi. Most of his friends regarded him as a warmhearted and generous rogue. He belonged to Nat, a tiny village near Gujrat, dominated by criminal fraternities whose sense of solidarity left a deep mark on him. His father was much respected locally as an effective river bandit who earned his living by recycling stolen goods. Zahoor Elahi began his adult life as a police constable in British India, a background that could not have been more remote from that of the generals he would later serve.

In 1943, Zahoor Elahi was posted to the Sikh holy city of Amritsar. His brother Manzoor Elahi accompanied him in the hope of finding employment. Zahoor was respectful and worked hard, but also had an ear on permanent alert wherever he was, just in case fate decided to help out. One day he was in the police station when he heard that a local Hindu tradesman, who had infringed some law, was about to be raided.

Sensing an opportunity here, Zahoor Elahi visited the trader that same day and warned him. When the raid took place, the police found nothing. An investigation was launched, the treachery was discovered, and poor Zahoor was sacked from the force.

The businessman was sufficiently grateful to give money to both brothers. Manzoor Elahi was helped to set up a tiny handloom workshop. Then came partition. The brothers returned to their village. One day Zahoor Elahi went to the Rehabilitation and Compensations office and demanded that they be recompensed for what they had lost (in reality very little). Like many others in those turbulent times, he exaggerated the claim. In those days it was thought that illegal gains should be converted into the most easily transportable commodity, which was either gold or jewelry. Zahoor Elahi displayed an unbridled passion for land and real estate, the genetic traces of which can still be seen in his progeny. He first obtained a large house in downtown Gujrat, in lieu of what was claimed to have been lost in Amritsar. He never looked back, skillfully deploying his natural gifts to gradually build up a large fortune. Once this had been achieved, to his credit he never forgot his past and maintained friendly relations with the local police and criminals, often bringing them together to explain that, despite a difference in profession, they had interests in common.

He was not the only booty politician in the country, but he was one of the most astute. He understood that in politics as well as everyday life, any person with an ounce of sense could reach a goal that gave the lie to his beginnings. Ethics were unnecessary. As befitted a small-town notable, he joined the Muslim League and began to rise in its ranks. With the impressive growth of his property portfolio, his regular pilgrimages to Mecca were combined with duty-free shopping. He always returned with trunkloads of presents for his friends, high and low.

He joined Field Marshal Ayub's Muslim League, the first of the *khaki* (the appellation derives from the color of their military uniforms) leagues that would become a tiny but important pillar of military rule in the country. He became a party stalwart, providing funds and busing in audiences to make the general feel popular at public meetings. For a self-made man to rise so high in Pakistan was unusual at that time. Others like him found poverty vexatious, but lacked initiative and networking skills. The process would become much more commonplace during the heroin bonanza some decades later, when the entrepreneurial spirit of the Chaudhrys and the Sharifs permeated the big cities and left a permanent mark on the political life of the country. It costs a great deal to become a prime minister.

As long as Bhutto was a cabinet minister in the military regime, Elahi played the sycophant, a role in which he had trained himself since his days as a young police constable. After Bhutto was sacked by Ayub and was still sulking in his tent thinking seriously about whether to organize a new political party, Elahi turned his back on the fallen minister. He did more. He became a key defender of Ayub inside the Muslim League and cajoled and bribed those who were tempted to leave with Bhutto and managed to keep most of them in the party. Bhutto was never one to forgive a slight, real or imagined. Once in power in 1972, he made it clear that he regarded the Chaudhrys of Gujrat as thieves and pimps who should be treated as such. Attempts by the Chaudhrys to broker a deal with the new leader via intermediaries close to him came to naught. Bhutto's hatred, once ablaze, always tended toward the indiscriminate. He had an elephant's memory, as many a civil servant who had avoided him during his years of disgrace was to discover. Zahoor Elahi bided his time. It came sooner than expected. He welcomed Zia's coup in 1977, developing close relations with the dictator and backing Bhutto's execution. He ostentatiously asked General Zia to make him a present of the "sacred pen" with which he had signed Bhutto's death warrant. The chief justice of the West Pakistan High Court, Maulvi Mushtaq Hussain, who had behaved abominably in court during Bhutto's trial for murder, had become a close friend of Zahoor Elahi's. In 1978, he was in Lahore lavishing his hospitality on the judge. Both men were in the car that was taking the judge back to his home in Lahore's Model Town district. A group of al-Zulfiqar gunmen opened fire. The judge, who was the target, ducked and avoided the bullet meant for him. Chaudhry was felled. Zahoor Elahi had not been the target, but al-Zulfiqar, embarrassed at missing the judge, claimed he was also on their list, which may have been true.

Whatever the truth, Zahoor Elahi became an instant martyr. The anniversary of his death is marked in Gujrat each year with great pomp and ceremony by his family (usually government ministers), and streets have been named after him. After his death, his oldest son, Chaudhry Shujaat Hussain, inherited the mantle and became a crucial power broker in General Zia's *khaki* Muslim League. Total power, however, continued to elude the Zahoor Elahi clan. The Sharif family had the Muslim League contract, but the Chaudhrys maintained family tradition by masking their resentment. They waited patiently. Their chance would come a decade later when another general, Pervez Musharraf, seized power.

But the Chaudhrys, along with the Sharifs, prospered well enough during the Zia years. So did the Pakistan army, to which the war in Afghanistan had given an enormous boost. It was a frontline ally of the United States against the godless Communists. And Zia and his generals knew only too well that without the financial and military support of the United States and also of China, Saudi Arabia, Israel, and Egypt, it would not have been so easy to win. The ISI and CIA watched and applauded as Russian technicians and their families were killed, disemboweled, and their heads displayed on posts. This was sweet revenge for Vietnam. Meanwhile Prince Turki bin Faisal, the Saudi chieftain promoting the war, dispatched Sheikh Osama bin Laden to Afghanistan to further advance the struggle by demonstrating to the Believers that the Saudis were behind them and not to worry too much about America. The story has been well documented, but what is not stressed often enough is how this war wrecked the northwestern regions of Pakistan. The consequences are still sharply felt.

The crude but effective ISI manuals used to fight Moscow are once again proving helpful, this time to the forces fighting the United States in Afghanistan today. One of the anti-Soviet commanders, Abdul Haq, told admiring Western journalists that the mujahideen did not actually target civilians, "but if I hit them, I don't care. . . . If my family lived near the Soviet embassy, I would hit it. I wouldn't care about them. If I am prepared to die, my son has to die for it, and my wife has to die for it." These "qualities" were then praised in the Western media as exhibitions of an indomitable warrior race. Robert Fisk, who reported on the conflict for the London *Times,* has written of the strict instructions to refer to the mujahideen as "freedom fighters," regardless of any of their activities.

Brigadier Mohammed Yousaf of the ISI, who was centrally involved in training the mujahideen and selecting Pakistani commandos to cross the border and fight alongside them, defended these tactics in 2003:

Next was sabotage and assassination from within . . . this included placing a bomb under the dining-room table of Kabul University in late 1983. The explosion, in the middle of the meal, killed nine Soviets, including a woman Professor. Educational institutions were considered fair game as the staff were all communists indoctrinating their students with Marxist dogma . . . this was corrupting the youth, turning them away from Islam.*

The same tactics and the same justifications, directed now against the United States and NATO, are said to represent the "sickness" of Islam and are traced back directly to the Koran or other Islamic teachings. In which case, one might ask, how is it that jihadi manuals circulating in the refugee camps and among the mujahideen were produced at the University of Nebraska–Omaha?

The primers, which were filled with talk of jihad and featured drawings of guns, bullets, soldiers and mines, have served since as the Afghan school-system's core curriculum. Even the Taliban used the American-produced books, though the radical movement scratched out human faces in keeping with its strict fundamentalist creed.†

Meanwhile changes were taking place in the Soviet Union. With the elevation of Mikhail Gorbachev to general secretary of the politburo in March 1985, it soon became obvious that the Soviet Union would accept defeat in Afghanistan and withdraw its troops. I had a surprising personal experience in this regard. At a UN-sponsored conference in Tashkent that spring, I was astonished when, after my speech, which was extremely critical of the Soviet intervention in Afghanistan and its aftermath, the younger members of the Soviet delegation, led by Yevgeni Primakov (subsequently head of the KGB and briefly prime minister under Yeltsin), came up and hugged me, saying

---

*Mohammed Yousaf and Mark Adkin, *The Bear Trap: Afghanistan's Untold Story* (Lahore: 2003). Should be a recommended read for all NATO personnel in Afghanistan. Exactly the same tactics are being used against them.

†Joe Stephens and David B. Ottaway, "The ABCs of Jihad in Afghanistan," *Washington Post,* March 23, 2002.

they agreed with me and so did their new general secretary. When I reported this to various Pakistani friends, they became despondent. Some refused to believe this was possible. Today, many of them are equally committed to the U.S. occupation of Afghanistan and plead with the West to send more troops.*

The Soviet Union had accepted defeat and decided on a unilateral withdrawal from Afghanistan. Nonetheless, General Gromov wanted some guarantees for their Afghan supporters who were being left behind. The United States—its mission successful—was prepared to play ball. General Zia, however, was not. The Afghan war had gone to his head (as it had to that of Osama bin Laden and his colleagues), and he wanted his own people in power there. Zia dreamed of hoisting the crescent and star in Central Asian capitals. As the Soviet withdrawal got closer, Zia and the ISI made plans for the postwar settlement. During his rule Pakistan had built a nuclear bomb, and this, coupled with the Soviet defeat, had given Zia and the generals closest to him a new confidence and the feeling that they were invulnerable.

AND THEN ZIA went up in smoke. On August 17, 1988, he took five generals to the trial of a new U.S. Abrams M1/A1 tank at a military test range near Bahawalpur. Also present were a U.S. general and the U.S. ambassador, Arnold Raphael. The demonstration did not go well and everybody was grumpy. Zia offered the Americans a lift in his specially built C-130 aircraft, which had a sealed cabin to protect him from assassins. A few minutes after the plane took off, the pilots lost control and it crashed into the desert. All the passengers were killed. All that was left of Zia was his jawbone, which was duly buried in Islamabad (the nearby roundabout became known to cabbies as Jawbone Chowk). The cause of the crash remains a mystery. The U.S. National Archives contain 250 pages of documents relating to

---

*Ahmad Rashid, "Accept Defeat by Taliban, Pakistan Tells NATO," *Daily Telegraph,* November 30, 2006. Rashid writes, "To progress in Riga, Nato will have to enlist US support to call Pakistan's bluff, put pressure on Islamabad to hand over the Taliban leadership and put more troops in to fight the insurgency while persuading Mr Karzai to become more pro-active."

the incident, but they are still classified. Pakistani intelligence experts have informally told me that it was the Russians taking their revenge for Afghanistan or, in another variant, acting on behalf of Indian leader Rajiv Gandhi, whose mother, Indira, was assassinated by her Sikh bodyguards, who had apparently visited the Sikh training camps in Pakistan. A remarkable version was supplied by John Gunther Dean, a senior diplomat serving as U.S. ambassador to India. According to Barbara Crossette, the *New York Times* South Asia bureau chief at the time:

> In New Delhi in August 1988, a lot of history came together in Dean's mind. He had an immediate suspicion about who killed Zia, but his putative perpetrator was not on the list of possible conspirators then in circulation. Dean thought the plot to rid the world of General Zia bore the hallmarks of Israel, or specifically the Israeli intelligence agency, Mossad.
>
> Dean believed in "dissent through channels," not leaks. And, knowing what a controversy such a public accusation would unleash, and the effect it would have not only in the United States and South Asia but also in the wider Islamic world, he decided to go back to Washington to explain his theory in person to his superiors at the State Department. That act cost him his diplomatic career.*

Was Dean hinting that Mossad had blown up Zia to punish him for getting a bomb? Dean never spoke again so we don't know, but it seems unlikely. The Israelis had appreciated Zia's role in defeating the Palestinians in Jordan. Zia had allowed a Mossad presence in Peshawar during the Afghan war. Furthermore, he often thought of Pakistan as a Muslim equivalent of Israel:

> Pakistan is like Israel, an ideological state. Take out Judaism from Israel and it will collapse like a house of cards. Take Islam out of Pak-

---

*Barbara Crossette, "Who Killed Zia?" *World Policy Journal,* Fall 2005.

istan and make it a secular state: it would collapse. For the past four years we have been trying to bring Islamic values to the country.*

Most Pakistanis, as is their wont, blamed the CIA. Zia's son was convinced it was Murtaza Bhutto's group, "al-Zulfiqar." Zia's widow would whisper it was "our own people," meaning the army. Benazir Bhutto described it as "an act of God." The only fact they could all agree on was that he was dead. The mystery remains unsolved to this day. When foreign leaders were pleading with him to spare Zulfiqar Ali Bhutto's life, Zia had replied that nobody was indispensable, and "I am of the opinion that the higher you go, the harder you fall." The "soldier of Islam" had left behind his own epitaph.

---

*Quoted in the *Economist,* December 12, 1981. When in 1970 I first made this comparison in the very first sentence of *Pakistan: Military Rule or People's Power?* there was outrage, especially among right-wing Pakistanis. A decade later the analogy had become halal, or kosher.

6

THE WASHINGTON QUARTET

The General
as Chief Executive

WITH ZIA'S ASSASSINATION, THE SECOND PERIOD OF MILITARY rule in Pakistan came to an end. What followed was a longish civilian prologue to Musharraf's reign, unprecedented in the country's short history. For ten years members of two political dynasties—the Bhutto and Sharif families—ran the country in turn. This ten-year spell was an important phase in Pakistan's history. Tragically, neither Bhutto's daughter, Benazir, nor Zia's protégé, Nawaz Sharif, showed any ability to govern the country in interests other than their own. Clientilism, patronage, and corruption on a gigantic scale were the hallmarks of their weak regimes.

In November 1988, a thirty-five-year-old Benazir Bhutto had, much to the annoyance of the army, won the elections held a short time after Zia's demise. Despite strong Islamist opposition, she became the country's only woman prime minister. This had been the first real opportunity people had to show their anger at her father's execution. Her program pledged a few reforms to help the poor, but was far removed from the world of "food, clothes, and shelter for all." Her options were severely limited. Her enemies were embedded in the state apparatuses and she was politically weak. When I met her a few months after her triumph, she was refreshingly honest: "I can't do anything. The army on one side and the president [Ghulam Ishaq Khan, a former bureaucrat who had supported Zia against Bhutto] on the other." It was undoubtedly a difficult situation. My advice was to go on television and tell the people, explaining why she was virtually powerless. It was the only way to educate citizens. My other suggestion was to implement certain reforms that did not require billions. She should, at the least, attempt to set up girls' schools all over the country and repeal the disgraceful Hudood Ordinances, pushed through by Zia, that treated women as second-class citizens and equated rape with adultery. She nodded approvingly, but nothing was done. As prime minister, Benazir could not even avenge herself on Zia's ghost, let alone introduce a single legislative measure that mattered. The system Zia had put in place was never challenged. Most of her party hierarchy were so happy to be back in power that all they could think about was themselves. After an inconclusive twenty months in office, President Ishaq, using the enormous powers vested in him via Zia's Eighth Amendment to the 1973 constitution, dismissed Benazir's government in August 1990, accusing her of tolerating corruption and failing to control ethnic violence in her home province of Sind. There was little public response. In the elections that followed, Nawaz Sharif won a majority and became the new prime minister. He too fell out with the president and was dismissed from office in 1993. A former World Bank employee, Moin Qureshi, was appointed caretaker prime minister pending new elections in October 1993, which returned Benazir to power.

Meanwhile the crisis in Afghanistan continued even after the unilateral Soviet withdrawal in February 1989. The two countries had become intertwined. A leading member of the Soviet politburo, Yevgeni Primakov, had proposed a deal to stabilize Afghanistan whereby Moscow would gradually take the old Afghan leaders and cadres out of the country, leaving an intact structure for the government that followed. Pakistan rejected this sensible offer. Its foreign minister, Sahibzada Yaqub Khan, an old friend of Washington, wanted no compromise. Nor did his masters. The scent of blood was in their nostrils, and so the mujahideen factions were told to continue the war. A demoralized and defeated pro-Soviet Afghan army disintegrated rapidly, and most of the Afghan leadership ultimately fled abroad. The prime minister, Mohammad Najibullah, took refuge in the UN office. Large parts of Kabul were destroyed, after which the mujahideen groups, much to the dismay of their foreign friends, began to fight each other. Political disputes were settled with artillery. Different combinations of president and ministers were not able to restore order. There was no effective central government. Gunmen became "tax collectors" and trade came to a virtual standstill. The poppy alone remained sacrosanct.

During Benazir Bhutto's second term in office (1993–96) her minister of the interior, General Naseerullah Babar, together with the ISI, devised a plan to set up the Taliban as a politico-military force that could take over Afghanistan, a move only halfheartedly approved by the U.S. embassy. The truth was, once the Soviet Union had withdrawn its troops, Washington had lost interest in the country.

Benazir Bhutto's denials that her government was the main force supporting the Taliban were never convincing. In 1994, the last time I met her, she told me that all her government was doing was sending the Afghan refugees back to Afghanistan. What this gloss concealed was the heavy involvement of the ISI in the return journey. The Taliban (the word literally means "students") were children of Afghan refugees and poor Pathan families "educated" in the madrassas in the 1980s. They provided the shock troops, but were led by a handful of experienced mujahideen including Mullah Omar. Without Pakistan's support they could never have taken Kabul, although Mullah Omar, another fantasist, sometimes preferred to forget this reality, just as Sheikh Osama and Al Qaeda had convinced themselves that the defeat of the Russians was a jihadi victory, forgetting the key role of the infidels, without whose support the jihadis could never have won at all. Omar's faction was dominant, but the ISI never completely lost control of the organization. Islamabad kept its cool even when Omar's zealots asserted their independence by attacking the Pakistan embassy in Kabul in 1999 and, in the same year, his religious police interrupted a friendly soccer match between the two countries because the Pakistani players had arrived sporting long hair and shorts. Before a stunned crowd, the police caned the players, shaved their heads, and sent them back home. A return match in Islamabad was canceled.

General Hamid Gul, a staunchly pro-jihadi director general of the ISI during Benazir's first term, whom she had unsuccessfully attempted to remove, paid her a warm tribute after her assassination in 2007:

It is not the jihadis who have killed her. She was rather protective of the jihadis in the past. Benazir was never soft on the Kashmir issue, let me tell you that. I served as the ISI director-general under her. The Taliban emerged during her second tenure in office and captured Kabul when she was still the prime minister. Her interior minister used to patronise them openly.*

Benazir Bhutto's second government ran into serious trouble when her carefully handpicked president, Farooq Leghari, a loyal and staunch PPP stalwart, became discontented. It was an old problem: corruption in high places. Visiting Islamabad in early 1996, I found the surface calm deceptive. As I was lunching with my mother in her favorite Islamabad restaurant, a jovial, mustachioed figure came over to greet us from an adjacent table. His wife, Benazir, was abroad on a state visit. Senator Asif Zardari, state minister for investment, responsible for entertaining the children in her absence, had brought them out for a special treat. An exchange of pleasantries ensued. I asked how things were proceeding in the country. "Fine," he replied with a charming grin. "All is well." He should have known better.

Behind closed doors in Islamabad, a palace coup was in motion. Benazir Bhutto was about to be luxuriously betrayed. Leghari was preparing to dismiss her government after secret consultations with the army and opposition leaders. During dinner that same week, a senior civil servant, extremely fond of Benazir, was in despair. The president, he said, had sought to defuse the crisis by asking for a special meeting with the prime minister. Benazir, characteristically, turned up with her husband. This annoyed Leghari: one of the subjects he wanted to discuss with her was her husband's legendary greed. Despite this, Leghari remained calm while attempting to convince the first couple that not

*"Get America Out of the Way and We'll Be OK," interview with Harinder Baweja, *Tehelka Magazine,* February 2, 2008.

only their political enemies were demanding action. The scale of the corruption and the corresponding decay of the administration had become a national scandal. Leghari was under pressure from the army and others to move against the government. To resist them he needed her help. He pleaded with her to discipline Zardari and a number of other ministers who were out of control. Zardari, stubborn as always in defense of his material interests, taunted the president: nobody in Pakistan, he said, including Leghari, was entirely clean. The threat was obvious: you touch us and we'll expose you.

Leghari felt the dignity of his office had been insulted. He went pale and began to tremble with anger. He suggested that the minister for investment leave the room. Benazir nodded and Zardari walked out. Leghari again entreated her to restrain her husband. She smiled and gave her president a lecture on loyalty and how much she valued it. The people who were complaining, she told him, were jealous of her husband's business acumen. They were professional whingers, has-beens, rogues resentful at being passed over. She made no concessions. She was not convinced that the army was planning a coup.

It's true that not every general is bursting to seize state power. General Asif Nawaz (chief of staff from 1991 to 1993) resisted the temptation despite advice to the contrary, and his sudden and unexpected death fueled the rumor mills in Islamabad. His widow and many others suspected murder.* His successor, General Wahid Kakar (1993–96) was to tell friends that the U.S. ambassador had made it clear that given the crisis, Washington would understand if firm action was taken. Kakar too remained outside politics, though the scale of corruption angered him, and on a famous occasion he is reported to have confronted Benazir Bhutto and complained about her husband's greed.

"Why don't you divorce him or have him bumped off?" asked the general.

"If you have any proof, General, sahib," Benazir purred in response, "please send it to me."

---

*A fascinating account of this episode and numerous others in Pakistan's military history is contained in Shuja Nawaz, *Crossed Swords: Pakistan, Its Army, and the Wars Within* (Karachi: 2008).

Kakar retired peacefully and was replaced by General Jehangir Kara-mat, another professional officer who refused to contemplate a coup.

Several months after dismissing Benazir, Leghari told me that this meeting, the last of many, had been decisive. He could no longer tol-erate her excesses: if she continued in office, the army would intervene against democracy for the fourth time in the country's history. Reluc-tantly, he said, he decided to invoke the Eighth Amendment—Zia's gift to the nation—which gives the president powers to dismiss an elected government. New elections have to be held within ninety days.

Corruption was the main charge leveled against Benazir and Zardari. The couple were alleged to have used public office to amass a large private fortune—reckoned to be in the region of $1.5 billion—and transferred their assets abroad. Zardari was arrested, but his busi-ness associates remained loyal. One of them, the chairman of Pakistan Steel, committed suicide rather than give evidence against his former patron. Benazir's closest supporters insist that her political prestige was squandered by her husband, that he was a fraud, a poseur, a wastrel, a philanderer, and much worse. In March 1999, addressing a friendly gathering at an Islamabad seminar, Benazir defended her spouse. He was much misunderstood, she said, but before she could continue, the audience began to shake their heads in disapproval. "No! No! No!" they shouted. She paused and then said with a sigh, "I wonder why I always get the same reaction whenever I mention him."

Zardari was not the only reason for her unpopularity. The Peoples Party had done little for the poor, who were its natural constituency. Most of her ministers, at the national and provincial levels, were too busy lining their own pockets. Permanently surrounded by sycophants and cronies, she had become isolated from her electorate and oblivious to reality. The country was continuing to rot. A state that has never provided free education or health care and could no longer guarantee subsidized wheat, rice, or sugar rations to the poor or protect innocent lives from random killings in its largest city had created mass despair. In January 1999, a transport worker in Hyderabad who had not been paid for two years went to the Press Club, soaked himself in petrol, and set himself alight. He left behind a letter that read like an extract from an Upton Sinclair novel:

I have lost patience. Me and my fellow workers have been protesting the nonpayment of our salaries for a long time. But nobody
takes any notice. My wife and mother are seriously ill and I have no
money for their treatment. My family is starving and I am fed up
with quarrels. I don't have the right to live. I am sure the flames of
my body will reach the houses of the rich one day.

In the general election that followed Benazir's removal from power,
the Peoples Party suffered a humiliating defeat. The Pakistani electorate
may be largely semiliterate, but its political sophistication has never
been in doubt. Disillusioned, apathetic, and weary, Benazir's supporters refused to vote for her, but they could not at that point bring themselves to vote for her enemy. Nawaz Sharif's Muslim League won a
giant majority, winning two-thirds of the seats in the National Assembly, but 70 percent of the electorate stayed indoors.

The Sharif brothers were returned to power. Once again, Shahbaz,
the younger but shrewder sibling, accepted family discipline and Nawaz
became the prime minister. In 1998, Sharif made Pervez Musharraf
army chief of staff in preference to the more senior general, Ali Kuli
Khan. Sharif's reasoning may have been that Musharraf, from a middle-
class, refugee background like himself, would be easier to manipulate
than Ali Kuli, who came from a landed Pathan family in the NWFP
and was a schoolfellow of President Farooq Leghari, whom Sharif didn't
trust either because of the latter's PPP origins. Whatever the reasoning,
it turned out to be a mistake of similar magnitude to Zulfiqar Ali
Bhutto's when he leapfrogged General Zia over the head of five senior
generals. Ali Kuli Khan, highly regarded by most of his colleagues, did
not harbor political ambitions and, like his immediate predecessors,
would probably have stayed out of politics.

On Bill Clinton's urging, Sharif pushed for a rapprochement with
India. This accorded with his own business instincts. Travel and trade
agreements were negotiated, land borders were opened, flights resumed,
but before the next stage—loosening of travel restrictions and regular
cross-border train services—could be reached, the Pakistan army began
to assemble in the Himalayan foothills.

To put it mildly, the terrain in Kargil and the neighboring region is inhospitable and for at least half the year also inaccessible. The jagged peaks reach nineteen thousand feet, and winter temperatures average -60 degrees Celsius. When the snows melt, the fierce rocks make all movement extremely difficult. Officers and soldiers serving in the region regard it as a Siberian exile. An unwritten agreement between India and Pakistan from 1977 onward was that neither side would man posts from September 15 to April 15 each year. In 1999, the Pakistan army, hoping to isolate the Indians in Kashmir, decided to bin the agreement and launched a limited war that raised the specter of a nuclear exchange.

THE INDIANS, CLEARLY taken by surprise on discovering Pakistani troops and irregulars occupying heights on the Indian side, suffered serious reverses during the first few weeks of the conflict, but subsequently moved in crack regiments and artillery together with heavy air cover and began to inflict casualties, compelling Pakistan to withdraw from some areas. After three months of fighting from May to July 1999, neither side could claim total victory, but casualties were high (several thousand on both sides). In his memoirs, Musharraf grotesquely exaggerates Pakistan's "triumph," claiming his side won. In reality, another stupid idea had backfired on the Pakistani high command. A cease-fire was agreed to and each army returned to its side of the Line of Control that separates Pakistan-occupied Kashmir from that run by India.

There were, however, a few unpleasant reminders of the ideological fanaticism introduced into the Pakistan army during the Zia period. Compulsory prayers and preachers attached to units had begun to affect the soldiery. In December 2000, I was told by a former army officer in Lahore about a disturbing incident after the Kargil cease-fire. The Indians had informed their Pakistani counterparts that one of the peaks in Kargil-Drass was still occupied by Pakistani soldiers, contrary to the cease-fire agreement. A senior officer investigated and ordered the captain in charge of the peak to return to the Pakistani side of the Line of Control. The captain accused his senior officer and the military high command of betraying the Islamist cause and shot the officer dead. The Islamist officer was finally disarmed, tried by a secret court-martial, and executed.

WHY DID THE war take place at all? In private, the Sharif brothers told associates that the army was opposed to their policy of friendship with India and was determined to sabotage the process: the army had acted without clearance from the government. In his memoir, Musharraf insists that the army had kept the prime minister informed in briefings in January and February 1999. This ties in with what my informant (a former senior civil servant) who was present at the briefing told me. The slick video presentation by the GHQ had impressed Sharif. Naturally in the video the good guys won hands down. All Sharif asked at the end was "Can you do it quickly?"

The real reason for the war went back to the defeat in Dhaka. If the Americans could avenge Vietnam in Afghanistan, why not Pakistan in Kashmir? Ever since the 1990 victory in Kabul, the ISI had been infiltrating jihadis across the Line of Control into Indian-held Kashmir, trying to mimic the Afghan operation, but this time working on their own. They succeeded in destabilizing the province, but the Indian government responded with more troops, and ordinary Kashmiris were caught in the ugly crossfire. The Indian troops were undoubtedly brutal, but the jihadis, with their Wahhabi rhetoric, also antagonized important layers of the population. Islam in Kashmir had always been of the soft Sufi variety.

The Kargil war was designed to recapture the initiative. Looking back, it is truly staggering that Pakistan's military philosophers actually thought they could defeat India. Once the latter realized that this was a full-fledged assault, it recovered and sent in heavy artillery with air and helicopter cover. A naval offensive, prelude to a blockade, was also set in motion. With only six days of fuel left, the Napoléons in Pakistan's GHQ had no alternative but to accept a cease-fire. Sharif told Washington that he had been bounced into a war he didn't want, but did not oppose. Soon afterward, the Sharif family decided to get rid of Musharraf. Constitutionally, of course, the prime minister had the power to dismiss the chief of staff and appoint a new one, as Zulfiqar

Ali Bhutto had done in the 1970s when he appointed Zia. But the army then was weak, divided, and had been defeated in a major war; this was certainly not the case in 1999. Here it was only a stupid, if costly, adventure that had gone wrong.

SHARIF'S CANDIDATE TO succeed Musharraf was General Ziauddin Butt, head of the ISI, who was widely regarded as weak and incompetent. He was bundled off to Washington for vetting and while there is said to have pledged bin Laden's head on a platter. If Sharif had simply dismissed Musharraf, he might have had a better chance of success, but what he lacked in good sense his overclever brother tried to make up for in guile. Were the Sharif brothers really so foolish as to believe that the army was unaware of their intrigues, or were they misled by their belief in U.S. omnipotence? Clinton duly warned the Pakistan army that Washington would not tolerate a military coup in Pakistan. I remember chuckling at the time that this was a first in U.S.-Pakistan relations. Sharif relied too heavily on Clinton's warning. He should have checked with the Pentagon's Defense Intelligence Agency.

The tragicomic episode that followed is described accurately enough in Musharraf's memoir, *In the Line of Fire,* a book intended largely for Western eyes.* Musharraf describes how on October 11, 1999, he and his wife were flying back from Sri Lanka on a normal passenger flight when the pilot received instructions not to land. While the plane was still circling over Karachi, Nawaz Sharif summoned General Ziauddin Butt and in front of a TV crew swore him in as the new chief of staff. Meanwhile there was panic on Musharraf's plane, by now low on fuel. He contacted the commander of the Karachi garrison, the army took control of the airport, and the plane landed safely.

---

*Pervez Musharraf's *In the Line of Fire* (New York and London: 2005) gives the official version of what has been happening in Pakistan over the last six years. Whereas Altaf Gauhar injected nonsense of every sort into Ayub's memoirs, his son Humayun Gauhar, who worked with Musharraf on this book, has avoided the more obvious pitfalls. The general's raffish lifestyle is underplayed, but enough is in the book to suggest that he is not too easily swayed by religious or social obligations.

Simultaneously, military units surrounded the prime minister's house in Islamabad and arrested Nawaz Sharif. General Zia had been assassinated on a military flight; Musharraf took power on board a passenger plane.

So began the third extended period of military rule in Pakistan, initially welcomed by all Nawaz Sharif's political opponents (including Benazir Bhutto, long before her consecration as the Mother of Democracy) and some of his former colleagues. Musharraf was initially popular in Pakistan, and if he had pushed through reforms to provide an education for all children, with English as a compulsory second language (as in Malaysia) to break the elite's monopoly on higher education abroad, instituted land reforms to end the stranglehold of the gentry on large swathes of the countryside, tackled corruption in the armed forces and everywhere else, and ended the jihadi escapades in Kashmir and Pakistan as a prelude to a long-term deal with India, he might have left behind a positive legacy. Sadly and predictably, none of this was even attempted. Musharraf did, however, implement one important shift by permitting the emergence of independent TV stations and thus breaking the deadly stranglehold of state TV. This undoubtedly enhanced media freedom in the country. A number of the networks were challenging, critical, and not at all worried about offending those in authority. Musharraf lived to regret this concession.

In the political realm, he mimicked his military predecessors. Like them, he took off his uniform, went to a landlord-organized gathering in Sind, and entered politics. His party? The ever-*khaki*, ever-available courtesan known to the country as the Muslim League. His supporters? Chips off the old corrupt block he had denounced so vigorously on taking office and whose leaders he was prosecuting for large-scale corruption. The inevitable had happened. The Chaudhrys of Gujrat had split from the Sharif family and done a deal with the general. Chaudhry Shujaat Hussain, the minister of the interior and narcotic control in Nawaz Sharif's government, had decided that becoming a broker for the military was a far more rewarding occupation than a spell in opposition. The only surprise was that anyone was surprised.

• • •

THE FIRST MAJOR crisis to hit the Musharraf regime occurred on September 11, 2001. By pure chance, that very week the long-bearded General Mahmud Ahmad, director general of the ISI, was in Washington as a guest of the Pentagon. While the 9/11 attacks were occuring, General Ahmad was enjoying a relaxed breakfast at the Capitol with the chairmen of the Senate and House Intelligence committees, Senator Bob Graham (D) and Representative Porter Goss (R). The latter had worked for the CIA black-ops (clandestine operations) section for over ten years. In a discussion of terrorism, reference was made to Osama bin Laden's base in Afghanistan. In the interval between the two attacks on the World Trade Center, General Ahmad tried to convince his hosts that Mullah Omar was totally trustworthy and could be persuaded to disgorge Osama bin Laden. The meeting carried on in this vein until the second plane hit the WTC and everyone left. It is not known if Graham questioned his guest regarding information that, it was later revealed, his staff had received from an ISI operative in August that year, warning that the Twin Towers would soon be attacked.

The next day, General Ahmad, accompanied by Maleeha Lodhi, Pakistan's ambassador in Washington, was summoned to the State Department to receive the notorious ultimatum from Richard Armitage revealed by Musharraf in Washington to promote his memoir: either you're with us or you're against us, and "we'll bomb you into the Stone Age" if you resist. Musharraf was insistent that the threat had been made. Bush was sure that those words would not have been used. Ahmad and Armitage denied it had been said at their meeting. Musharraf then claimed he had other sources of information. Clearly something had been said, but had Musharraf exaggerated to impress his corps commanders that there was no option but to do Washington's bidding, or was it a simple ploy to increase sales of his book? Maleeha Lodhi's account of the meeting was altogether more diplomatic, as befitted her status:

> "The two of them were very tense," Ms. Lodhi said of Mr. Armitage and General Ahmad. "Armitage started out by saying: 'This is a grave moment. History begins today for the United States. We're

asking all our friends—you're not the only country we're speaking to—we're asking people whether they're with us or against us.'"*

The next day, the couple were sent for again, and Armitage handed the ISI boss a seven-point list of U.S. requirements from Pakistan for waging the coming war in Afghanistan. Without even looking closely at the printed sheet, Mahmud Ahmad put it in his pocket and said that he accepted everything. As some of the demands affected Pakistan's sovereignty, even Richard Armitage was taken aback and asked the ISI boss whether he needed to consult with General Musharraf before making any commitments. "Not necessary," replied General Ahmad. "He will agree with me." Ahmad's strong antipathy to the United States was hardly a secret. He was evidently in a hurry to get back home and convince his colleagues not to accept any of the demands. These were later published in *The 9/11 Commission Report*:

1. Stop Al Qaeda operatives at its border and end all logistical support for bin Laden.
2. Give the United States blanket overflight and landing rights for all necessary military and intelligence operations.
3. Provide territorial access to U.S. and allied military intelligence and other personnel to conduct operations against Al Qaeda.
4. Provide the United States with intelligence information.
5. Continue to publicly condemn the terrorist attacks.
6. Cut off all shipments of fuel to the Taliban and stop recruits from going to Afghanistan.
7. If the evidence implicated bin Laden and Al Qaeda, and the Taliban continued to harbor them, to break relations with the Taliban government.

This was a direct challenge to Pakistan's sovereignty, reducing it to the status of Britain. Musharraf later denied that he had agreed to the second and third points, but that was certainly not the view in Wash-

---

New York Times, August 4, 2007.

ington. Colin Powell informed the National Security Council that the Pakistanis had agreed to everything. What was not in the seven points but had been demanded in secret discussions was U.S. access to the nuclear facility. This Musharraf could not and did not accept, hence the endless campaign in the U.S. and European media on the jihadi "threat" to the weapons.

The Pakistani generals were faced with a difficult choice after September 11. If they did not agree to U.S. demands, Washington might follow the Israeli example and make an anti-Muslim pact with the religious extremists ruling India at the time. But if they kowtowed, the results could be catastrophic, given that Pakistani intelligence (ISI) had been funding fundamentalist groups in Pakistan since the Zia years (1977–88). Musharraf, backed by most of his generals, decided that it was necessary to withdraw from Kabul, to persuade his supporters in the Taliban not to resist U.S. occupation, and to open up Pakistan's military and air force bases to the United States. From these bases, the U.S.-led assault on Afghanistan was mounted in October 2001.

In truth, Musharraf did not always cooperate or accept every demand. He also had a sense of humor. Why otherwise would he have decided to attend the Non-Aligned Conference in Havana timed to open on September 11, 2006? At a meeting with Hugo Chávez, the Venezuelan president, Musharraf offered this advice: "You are far too aggressive with the Americans. Do as I do. Accept what they say and then do as you want."

MEANWHILE, THE embittered ISI chief and a colleague were dispatched to Kabul to inform the Taliban that war was coming unless they handed the Al Qaeda leadership over to Pakistan. Whatever happened, the Taliban were not to resist the occupation, but pack their bags, make themselves scarce, and disappear. All Pakistan military and air force personnel in Afghanistan were recalled. The impulsive Mahmud Ahmad did transmit this message, but added his own footnote. He told Mullah Omar that he disagreed with the command and thought the Taliban should fight back. Immediately on his return to Islamabad, Ahmad was fired, and more pliant officers were sent to talk the Taliban out of any crazed attempt to resist U.S. military power. Most of the leadership did as asked and agreed to bide their time. Mullah Omar chose to tie his fate to that of his honored Al Qaeda guest, and when last seen, this veteran of the anti-Soviet war, half lame and half blind, was on a motorbike heading for the mountains to make his great escape. Unlike Steve McQueen in the movie, the mullah is still at large. All the high-tech surveillance devices have so far not succeeded in tracking him down.

Musharraf's unstinting support for the U.S. after 9/11 prompted local wags to dub him Busharraf, and in March 2005 Condoleezza Rice described the U.S.-Pakistan relationship since 9/11 as "broad and deep." Had Musharraf not, after all, unraveled Pakistan's one military victory to please Washington? He would always insist that he only agreed to become Washington's surrogate because of State Department honcho Richard Armitage's Stone Age threat. What really worried Islamabad, however, was a threat Musharraf doesn't mention: if Pakistan had refused, the United States would have used the Indian bases that were on offer.

This decision almost cost Musharraf his life. The victory in Afghanistan had struck a deep chord among the more conservative sections of the army. Ever since the war against East Bengal, soldiers had been heavily indoctrinated with anti-Hindu propaganda. The Hindus were the enemy. They would destroy Pakistan at the first opportunity. Coupled to this was the Islamization within the army pushed through by Zia especially during the jihad against the Soviet army next door. To accept a U.S. occupation of a Muslim state that they had helped set up was too much for some of the officers. For some soldiers too it was a shameful defeat. At an open GHQ seminar headed "Fall of the Taliban," the now retired ISI brigadier Mohammed Yousaf, who had been invited as a participant, walked in and added the word *Government* after *Taliban*. He would not accept that it was all over. Nor was he wrong. Jihadi militants, helped by information from within the army, had decided to kill Musharraf. They felt betrayed. Their logic was simple: if it had been right to wage jihad against the Soviet infidels, why did the same not apply to the American infidels? The textbooks from the University of Nebraska had left a mark.

When Musharraf seized power in 1999, he had refused to move from his homely, colonial bungalow in Rawalpindi to the kitsch comfort of the President's House in Islamabad, which with its gilt furniture and tasteless decor owes more to Gulf State opulence than local tradition. The cities are close to each other, but far from identical. Islamabad, laid out in a grid pattern and overlooked by the Himalayan foothills, was built in the 1960s by General Ayub. He wanted a new capital remote from threatening crowds, but close to GHQ in Rawalpindi, which had been constructed by the British as a garrison town. After partition, it became the obvious place to situate the military headquarters of the new Pakistan.

One of the nineteenth-century British colonial expeditions to conquer Afghanistan (they all ended in disaster) was planned in Rawalpindi. From here, a century and a half later, the Washington-blessed jihad was launched against the hopeless Afghan Communists. From here, the U.S. demand to use Pakistan as a base for its operations in Afghanistan was discussed and agreed upon in September 2001.

For a short while after the U.S. occupation of Kabul, a misleading calm prevailed in Pakistan. I had predicted a rapid defeat of the Taliban, since that is what GHQ had decided, and suggested that the jihadi groups would regroup in Pakistan and, sooner or later, start punishing General Musharraf's regime. This began in 2002. An unreported attempt to kill Musharraf was followed by three big hits: the kidnapping and brutal murder of *Wall Street Journal* reporter Daniel Pearl; the assassination of the interior minister's brother; and the bombing of a church in the heart of Islamabad's tightly protected diplomatic enclave. In addition, targeted assassinations of middle-class professionals took place in Karachi. Over a dozen doctors belonging to the Shia minority were killed. These acts were a warning to Pakistan's military ruler: if you go too far in accommodating Washington, your head will also roll.

Were all these acts of terrorism actually carried out by hard-line groups such as Jaish-e-Mohammed and Harkatul Ansar, who often claim them? Probably, but this is not an entirely coherent assertion. These organizations were, after all, funded and armed by the state as late as the Kargil war. Turn them upside down and the rational kernel is revealed. It is the ISI whose blatant manipulation of these groups has been obvious to everyone in the country for a long time. Those sections of the ISI who patronized and funded these organizations were livid at "the betrayal of the Taliban."

Unless this is appreciated, the random and selective terrorism that shook the country after the fall of the Taliban becomes inexplicable. Musharraf, like Bhutto and Nawaz Sharif, inherited Zia's ISI, whose size and budget had massively expanded during the first Afghan war. Secretary of State Colin Powell's statement of March 3, 2002, exonerating the ISI from any responsibility for Pearl's disappearance and murder shocked many Pakistanis. Virtually everyone I spoke to in Pakistan at the time stated the exact opposite. Musharraf was obviously not involved, but he must have been informed of what was taking place. He had referred to Pearl as an "overintrusive journalist" caught up in "intelligence games," an indication that Musharraf did know something. Had he informed his bosses in Washington? And if so, why did Powell absolve the ISI? Pearl was lured to a fashionable restaurant in Karachi, kidnapped, then executed by his captors. A video showing Pearl's throat being slit was distributed to the Western media, and a gruesome clip was shown on CBS News.

The Pearl tragedy had shed some light on the darker recesses of the intelligence networks. He was a tough-minded, investigative (as opposed to embedded) journalist with a deep regard for the truth. While he showed little interest in political or social theories or ideologies, he was sensitive to the moral and human costs of their implementation. This applied as much to the "humanitarian intervention" in Kosovo as to clerical misrule in Iran, though his reports from Iran never followed the official Washington line. Some of his best pieces in the *Wall Street Journal* were reasoned and eloquent rejections of state propaganda, including U.S. propaganda about Kosovo used to justify the bombing of Yugoslavia. He proved that the Sudanese pharmaceutical factory—bombed on Bill Clinton's orders to distract attention from the Lewinsky affair—was exactly that and not a shady installation producing biological and chemical weapons as alleged by the White House.

When Pearl's death was announced, I remember thinking that the official U.S. response was rather subdued. What if the victim had been Thomas Friedman of the *New York Times*? Would Pervez Musharraf have been able to describe Friedman at a Washington press conference as "too intrusive," which is what he said about Pearl? It was as if Pearl had connived in his own murder. The brother of Pakistan's interior minister had been killed by an Islamist group a few weeks before Pearl. When, during a private meeting, the minister muttered something about Pearl bringing it on himself, a friend Pearl's widow had brought with her asked, "With all due respect, Mr. Minister, would you blame your brother for having been murdered just because he was driving the streets of Karachi?"

Pearl's journalism was sorely missed in the run-up to the Iraq war when propaganda flooded the television networks and the "paper of record" had become almost as uncritical and unquestioning as the Pakistani media had once been under General Zia's dictatorship. There was no mystery as to why Pearl had come to Pakistan in the first place; obviously to track the big story, to see if he could uncover the links between the intelligence services and indigenous terrorism. His newspaper—and indeed the State Department—were remarkably coy on this subject, refusing to disclose the leads that Pearl was pursuing. Contrary to stories that were circulated later, Daniel Pearl was a cautious journalist. His wife, Mariane, detailed the memos he sent to his paper, arguing that they should train and protect journalists reporting from danger zones.* They were ignored. Pearl refused to go to Afghanistan—the situation was too insecure—but he also knew that the real story was in Pakistan. He decided to investigate the links between Richard Reid, the shoe bomber, and Islamist groups in Pakistan. This was presumably what Musharraf thought "too intrusive." Pakistani officials more than once told Mariane that if Pearl had behaved like other foreign journalists, the tragedy might have been averted. Neither she nor the FBI experts who flew to Pakistan were able to decipher Pearl's notes, written in code and describing, one assumes, what he found out.

Any Western journalist, however friendly, who visits Pakistan is routinely watched and followed. This is an old intelligence habit, an article of faith, dating back to the country's founding (and before), and

*Mariane Pearl, *A Mighty Heart: The Brave Life and Death of My Husband* (New York and London: 2004), subsequently a Hollywood movie.

it goes on even when elected governments are in power. In the wake of the Afghan war the intelligence agencies became overstocked with cheap labor. The notion that Danny Pearl, beavering away on his own, setting up contacts with members of extremist groups, was not at the same time being carefully monitored by the secret services is incredible. In fact, it is unbelievable. And nobody in Pakistan believed it at the time or does now.

Circumstantial evidence suggested the involvement of the intelligence agencies in Pearl's death. There was no direct proof, but it was no secret in Pakistan that Omar Saeed Sheikh, the psychopath who set up the kidnapping, had intelligence connections. In 1994, ISI-spawned Islamist groups had infiltrated him into Kashmir. A specialist in kidnapping foreigners and keeping them as hostages, he masterminded an action of this kind in Delhi to secure the release from Tihar jail of Masood Azhar, leader of an Islamist group. The kidnapping succeeded, but so did Indian intelligence: after a shoot-out, Sheikh was captured. He slapped the senior police officer who arrested him and was beaten up in return. Five years later, in December 1999, his colleagues hijacked an Indian airliner on its way to Kandahar and threatened to kill everyone on board unless Sheikh and other "liberation fighters" were freed. They were.

What drove a Sylvester Stallone fan, born in East London in 1973, to become a religious fanatic? His parents had emigrated to Britain in 1968 with enough capital to establish a small garment business. Perfect Fashions did well enough for Omar to be sent to prep school. But his fondness for drink and thuggery worried his parents, who sent him back to the Land of the Pure. He didn't last long at Aitchison College, a top private school in Lahore: after a couple of years, he was expelled for "bullying." A contemporary described him to me as having had "strong psychopathic tendencies . . . even then," and said he was always threatening to kill other boys. He returned to London and was sent to school at Snaresbrook, where he was a contemporary of Nasser Hussain, the future England cricket captain. Omar was a keen chess player and arm wrestler, ever eager to demonstrate the latter skill in local pubs.

He did well at Snaresbrook and went to study statistics at the London School of Economics. A number of active Islamist groups were on campus, and Bosnia became their cause. The involvement of Western intellectuals in Bosnia has been well publicized, usually by themselves. Less well documented is that remnants of the Afghan mujahideen, including some of Osama's men, had been taken in U.S. transport planes to fight the holy war in the Balkans. In 1993, Sheikh went to Bosnia as part of a group of Muslim students from the LSE taking medicines and supplies to victims of the civil war. Here, he first established contact with the armed-struggle Islamist groups who converted him to their version of jihad. General Musharraf later claimed that Sheikh was a double agent who had been recruited by MI6 and sent to Bosnia. By January 2002 he was in Islamabad promising Daniel Pearl a much-sought-after interview with the clerical godfather of the shoe bomber.

Many questions about Pearl's death remain unanswered. The group that kidnapped and killed Pearl supposedly called itself the National Movement for the Restoration of Pakistani Sovereignty. One of its demands—the release of the Guantánamo prisoners—was obvious, but the second was extraordinary: the delivery of F-16s, which the United States had been paid for but had not delivered, to Pakistan. A jihadi group that supposedly regards the Musharraf regime as traitorous for selling out the Taliban endorsing a twenty-year-old demand of the military and state bureaucracy? Impossible.

Sheikh surrendered to the provincial home secretary (a former ISI officer) in Lahore on February 5, 2002. Officially he was arrested in Lahore a week later. None of these matters was raised at his trial in a closed court in Hyderabad in July 2002. He was sentenced to death, his fellow conspirators to life imprisonment. Both sides appealed, Sheikh against the death sentence, the state against the sentence of life imprisonment—rather than hanging—for the other three. Sheikh wrote a statement that was read out by his lawyer: "We'll see who will die first, me or the authorities who have arranged the death sentence for me. Musharraf should know that Almighty Allah is there and can get his revenge." The three attempts on Musharraf's life, two of which took place within a fortnight and one of which came close to success, indicated that Sheikh wasn't making an empty boast.

Heavy traffic often makes the ten-mile journey from Islamabad to Rawalpindi tortuous, unless you're the president and the highway has been cleared by a security detail. Even then, carefully orchestrated assassination attempts can play havoc with the schedule. The first happened on December 14, 2003. Moments after the general's motorcade passed over a bridge, a powerful bomb exploded and badly damaged the bridge, although no one was hurt. The armored limo, fitted with radar and an antibomb device, courtesy of the Pentagon, saved Musharraf's life. His demeanor at the time surprised observers. He was said to have been calm and cheerful, making jocular allusions to living in perilous times. Unsurprisingly, security had been high—decoys, last-minute route changes, etc.—but this didn't prevent another attempt a week later, on Christmas Day. This time two men driving cars loaded with explosives came close to success. The president's car was damaged, guards in cars escorting him were killed, but Musharraf was unhurt. Since his exact route and the time of his departure from Islamabad were heavily guarded secrets, the terrorists must have had inside information. If your security staff includes angry Islamists who see you as a traitor and want to blow you up, then, as the general states in his memoir, Allah alone can protect you. He has certainly been kind to Musharraf.

The culprits were discovered and tortured till they revealed details of the plot. Some junior military officers were also implicated. The key plotters were tried in secret and hanged. Amjad Farooqi, the supposed mastermind and a jihadi extremist, was shot dead by security forces. Two questions haunt both Washington and Musharraf's colleagues: How many of those involved remained undetected, and would the command structure of the army survive if a terrorist succeeded next time around? Musharraf didn't seem worried and adopted a jaunty, even boastful tone. Before 9/11 he was treated like a pariah abroad and beset by problems at home. How to fortify the will of a high command weakened by piety and corruption? How to deal with the corruption and embezzlement that had been a dominant feature of both the Sharif and Bhutto governments? Benazir Bhutto was already in self-exile in Dubai; the Sharif brothers had been arrested and Nawaz was charged with high treason. Washington rapidly organized an offer of asylum from Saudi Arabia, a state whose ruling family has institutionalized the theft of public funds. These questions soon disappeared from the agenda as the Chief Executive of Pakistan, a title more in keeping with the spirit of the age and preferable to the old-fashioned Chief Martial Law Administrator, began to settle down, adjust to the realities of elite existence, and prepare to make himself president.

As for Omar Saeed Sheikh, who could certainly reveal a great deal, he continues to live in a death cell in a Pakistani prison, chatting amiably to his guards and e-mailing newspaper editors in Pakistan to tell them that if he is executed, papers he has left behind will be published exposing the complicity of others. Perhaps this is a bluff, or perhaps he was a triple agent and was working for the ISI as well.

What the Pearl killing revealed was that Musharraf had not yet succeeded in establishing total control over the intelligence agencies. He would only do so after the attempts on his own life. General Ashfaq Kayani, another senior officer trained in the United States, was appointed director general of the ISI. He supervised the gathering of information that led to the capture of those in the army who had helped Musharraf's would-be assassins. Kayani was promoted to chief of army staff, replacing Musharraf in November 2007. In a dispatch from Carlotta Gall on January 7, 2008, the *New York Times* reflected the tremor of excitement felt in Washington:

> "He's loyal to Musharraf to the point where Musharraf is a liability and no longer an asset to the corporate body of the Pakistani military," said Bruce Riedel, a former C.I.A. and White House official who is an expert on Pakistan. "They will say: 'Thank you very much for your interest in security affairs. Here is your ticket out of the country.'"
>
> As he has risen through the military, General Kayani has impressed American military and intelligence officials as a professional, pro-Western moderate with few political ambitions.

Musharraf had been described in similar language ten years previously, but now his allies were not pleased. The foreign policy half of the apple was beginning to shrivel, but what of the other half? The Chaudhrys were permanently reaping the harvest of power. Musharraf's favorite prime minister, Shaukat "Shortcut" Aziz, formerly a senior executive of Citibank with close ties to the eighth-richest man in the world, the Saudi prince Al-Walid bin Talal, was spouting a great deal of nonsense. The model preferred by some Western commentators on permanent military rule with technocrats running the Finance Ministry has proved a total failure. Watching Aziz flattering the Chaudhrys with wild assertions of their genius in what passes for a parliament in Islamabad reminded one of a paid piper rather than an "impartial technocrat." One wondered what had recommended him in the first place. Whose choice was he? As it became clear that nothing much was going to change, a wave of cynicism engulfed the country.

The score-settling with perceived enemies at home was crude, and for that reason Musharraf's book, *In the Line of Fire,* caused a commotion in Pakistan, demonstrating that the title, at least, was accurate. A spirited controversy erupted in the media, something that could never have happened during previous periods of military rule. Scathing criticism came from ex-generals (Ali Kuli Khan's detailed rejoinder was published in most newspapers), opposition politicians, and pundits of every sort. In fact there was more state interference in the media during Nawaz Sharif's tenure than under Musharraf prior to the desperate state of emergency imposed in the fall of 2007. The level of debate in the Pakistani media is much higher than that in neighboring India, once greatly admired for its vigorous and critical press, but now taken over by a middle-class obsession with shopping and celebrity that has led to widespread trivialization of TV and most of the print media.

Musharraf was better than Zia and Ayub in many ways, but the more unpopular he became, the more he began to resort to the time-honored style of dictators. Human rights groups noticed a sharp rise in the number of political activists who were being "disappeared": four hundred in 2007 alone, including Sindhi nationalists and a total of twelve hundred in the province of Baluchistan, where the army has become trigger-happy once again. The war on terror has provided many leaders with the chance to sort out their domestic opponents, but that doesn't make it any better.

And then there is Operation Enduring Freedom in Afghanistan, where the only thing that endures is violence and the heroin trade. Despite the fake optimism sometimes evinced in the Western media, it is hardly a secret that it is a total mess. A revived Taliban is winning popularity by resisting the occupation. NATO helicopters and soldiers are killing hundreds of civilians and describing them as "Taliban fighters." Hamid Karzai, the man with the nice shawls, is seen as a hopeless puppet, totally dependent on NATO troops. He has antagonized both the Pashtuns, who are turning to the Taliban once again in large numbers, and the warlords of the Northern Alliance, who openly denounce him and suggest it's time he was sent back to the States. In western Afghanistan, only Iranian influence has preserved a degree of stability. If Ahmadinejad is provoked into withdrawing his support, Karzai will not last more than a week. Islamabad waits and watches. Military strategists are convinced that the United States has lost interest and NATO will soon leave. If that happens, Pakistan is unlikely to permit the Northern Alliance to take Kabul. Its army will move in again. A Pakistan veteran of the Afghan wars joked with me, "Last time we sent in the beards, but times have changed. This time, inshallah, we'll dress them all in Armani suits so it looks good on U.S. television."

The region remains fogbound. Pakistan's first military leader was seen off by a popular insurrection. The second was assassinated. What will happen to Musharraf? Once he took off his uniform and handed over the army to General Ashfaq Kayani, he left himself totally dependent on the goodwill of his successor and Washington. General Kayani's decision some weeks before the elections to withdraw all military personnel from civilian duties (army officers were running public utilities and numerous other nonmilitary institutions) may or may not have been a broad hint to his predecessor to follow suit, but its result was to stop the "election cell" of the ISI from "intervening" in the elections. The "mother of all election victories" that Musharraf had predicted could only have been achieved with the connivance of military intelligence. In previous years it was never a surprise when captains and majors accosted local or national politicians and civil servants to inform them what was required. Their absence meant that the Chaudhrys of Gujrat received a heavy blow, and senior ministers in Musharraf's cabinet were defeated in the Punjab. I received a euphoric e-mail from an old friend: "The people know that the mouths of military dictators are the home of lies."

The February 2008 elections were viewed as a referendum on Musharraf's rule. Despite the low turnout, he lost badly. The PPP emerged as the largest party with eighty-seven seats, with the Sharif brothers' Muslim League winning sixty-six. The two old rivals between them had an overall majority. The Chaudhrys of Gujrat slumped to thirty-eight seats in the National Assembly, with serious allegations that at least ten of these were won through large-scale manipulation. The Islamists lost control of the Frontier Province to the secular PPP and ANP. Musharraf should have offered to resign as soon as the new parliament was in session, giving the newly elected national and provincial assemblies the opportunity to elect a new president.

His supporters insist that the Bush administration wanted him to continue in office, and U.S. ambassador Anne Patterson summoned the widower Bhutto to the embassy in Islamabad to remind him of the deal that had been agreed to by his late wife, that she was to become Musharraf's junior partner and not bargain with the Sharif brothers, whose Islamist sympathies made them suspect. The scale of the general's defeat, however, made such a prospect suicidal. Except for the most slavish pro-Bush Pakams (Pakistani-Americans), whose dross regularly pollutes the blogosphere, the serious advice Zardari received was that the days of the Republicans were numbered. Far better, in these conditions, to help Musharraf become a private citizen voluntarily before the Democrats got rid of him.

7

THE HOUSE OF BHUTTO
Daughter of the West

ARRANGED MARRIAGES CAN BE A MESSY BUSINESS. DESIGNED principally as a means of accumulating wealth, circumventing undesirable flirtations, or transcending clandestine love affairs, they often don't work. Where both parties are known to loathe each other, only a rash parent, desensitized by the thought of short-term gain, will continue with the marriage knowing full well that it will end in misery and possibly violence. Occasionally the husband's side will agree to a wedding, pocket the dowry, and burn the bride. That this is equally true in political life became clear in the ill-fated attempt by Washington to tie Benazir Bhutto to Pervez Musharraf.

The single, strong parent in this case was a desperate State Department—with John Negroponte as the ghoulish go-between and British prime minister Gordon Brown as the blushing bridesmaid—fearful that if it did not push this through, both parties might soon be too old for recycling. The bride was certainly in a hurry, the groom less so. Brokers from both sides engaged in lengthy negotiations on the size of the dowry. Her broker was Rehman Malik, a former boss of Pakistan's FBI-equivalent FIA (Federal Investigation Agency), who was himself investigated for corruption by the National Accountability Bureau and served nearly a year in prison after Benazir's fall in 1996, then became one of her business partners and is currently under investigation (with her) by a Spanish court looking into a company called Petroline FZC, which made questionable payments to Iraq under Saddam Hussein. Documents, if genuine, show that she chaired the company. She may have been in a hurry, but she did not wish to be seen taking the arm of a uniformed president. He was not prepared to forgive her past. The couple's distaste for each other yielded to a mutual dependence on the United States. Neither party could say no, though Musharraf hoped the union could be effected inconspicuously. Fat chance.

Both parties made concessions. A popular opposition demand had been that Musharraf relinquish his military post before he stood for the presidency. Bhutto now agreed that he could take off his uniform after his "reelection" by the existing parliament, but it had to be before the next general election. (He did so, leaving himself dependent on the goodwill of his successor as army chief of staff.) He pushed through a legal ruling—yet another sordid first in the country's history—known as the National Reconciliation Ordinance, which withdrew all cases pending against politicians (these included Nawaz Sharif) accused of looting the national treasury. The ruling was crucial for Bhutto since she hoped that the money-laundering and corruption cases pending against her, her husband, and her fixer Iftikhar Malik in three European courts—Barcelona, Geneva, and London—would now be dismissed. The Spanish obliged, but the Swiss remain adamant and London bowed to the wishes of the Pakistani government.

Many Pakistanis—not just the mutinous and mischievous types who have to be locked up at regular intervals—were repelled, and coverage of "the deal" in the Pakistani media was universally hostile, except on state television. The "breakthrough" was loudly trumpeted in the West, however, and a whitewashed Benazir Bhutto was presented on U.S. networks and BBC TV news as the champion of Pakistani democracy—reporters loyally referred to her as "the former prime minister" rather than the fugitive politician facing corruption charges in several countries.

She had returned the favor in advance by expressing sympathy for the U.S. wars in Iraq and Afghanistan, lunching with the Israeli ambassador to the UN (a litmus test), and pledging to "wipe out terrorism" in her own country. In 1979, a previous military dictator had bumped off her father with Washington's approval, and perhaps she thought it would be safer to seek permanent shelter underneath the imperial umbrella. HarperCollins had paid her half a million dollars to write a new book. The working title she chose was *Reconciliation*. It was published posthumously and contained little that had not already been said by commentators on Islam, the types who appear on the approved list of Daniel Pipes and the Campus Watch folk. The real struggle was not between the world of Islam and the United States, but within Islam itself. Moderate Islam, as represented no doubt by herself, Hamid Karzai, Hosni Mubarak, and other modernists, did not pose a threat to any Western values. Nor does the Koran. Nor do most Muslims. Evil extremism had to be destroyed.* Like Musharraf's predecessors, he promised he would stay in power for a limited period, pledging in 2003 to resign as army chief of staff in 2004. Like his predecessors, he ignored his pledge. Martial law always begins with the promise of a new order that will sweep away the filth and corruption that marked the old one. In this case it toppled the civilian administrations of Benazir Bhutto and Nawaz Sharif. But "new orders" are not forward movements, more military detours that further weaken the shaky foundations of a country and its institutions. Within a decade the uniformed ruler will be overtaken by a new upheaval.

Dreaming of her glory days in the last century, Benazir wanted a large reception on her return. The general was unhappy. The intelligence agencies (as well as her own security advisers) warned her of the dangers. She had declared war on the terrorists, and they had threatened to kill her. But she was adamant. She wanted to demonstrate her popularity to the world and to her political rivals, including those inside her own fiefdom, the Pakistan Peoples Party (PPP). She had been living in self-exile in Dubai since 1996, occasionally

---

*To her credit, Bhutto generously acknowledged the help she had received from Husain Haqqani, a former Jamaat-e-Islami militant and Zia sympathizer who later became attached to the PPP and was Pakistan's ambassador to Sri Lanka, a post from which he was removed following a security breach. He subsequently obtained an academic post in the United States, acting simultaneously as an adviser to first Benazir and more recently Zardari. Haqqani's interests and those of the United States have always coincided, which is why, one assumes, he has been appointed the new Pakistani ambassador to the United States.

visiting London to shop and Washington to meet her contacts in the State Department. For a whole month before she boarded the Dubai-Karachi flight, the PPP busily recruited and paid volunteers from all over the country to welcome her. Up to two hundred thousand people lined the streets, but it was a far cry from the million who turned up in Lahore in 1986 when a very different Benazir had returned to challenge General Zia-ul-Haq. The plan had been to move slowly in the Bhuttomobile from Karachi airport to the tomb of the country's founder, Muhammed Ali Jinnah, where she would make a speech. It was not to be. As darkness fell, the bombers struck. Who they were and who sent them remains a mystery. She was unhurt, but 130 people died, including some of the policemen guarding her. The wedding reception had led to mayhem. Fingers were immediately pointed at jihadi groups in Pakistan, but the leader of the most prominent of these, Baitullah Masood, denied involvement. She herself singled out rogue elements from "within the government" and ex-military officers linked to the Taliban.

The general, while promising to collaborate with Benazir, was coolly making arrangements to prolong his stay at President's House. Even before her arrival, he had considered taking drastic action by imposing a state of emergency to dodge the obstacles that stood in his way, but his generals (and the U.S. embassy) seemed unconvinced by the timing. The bombing of Benazir's cavalcade reopened the debate. Pakistan, if not exactly the erupting volcano portrayed in the Western media, was being shaken by all sorts of explosions. The legal profession, up in arms at Musharraf's recent dismissal of the chief justice, had won a temporary victory, resulting in a fiercely independent Supreme Court. The independent TV networks continued to broadcast reports that challenged official propaganda. Investigative journalism is never popular with governments, and the general often contrasted the deference with which he was treated by the U.S. networks and BBC television with the "unruly" questioning inflicted on him by local journalists: it "misled the people." He had loved the coverage his book received in the United States and, in particular, his appearance with Jon Stewart on *The Daily Show*.

At home it was very different. He had become obsessed with the media coverage of the lawyers' revolt. A decline in his popularity had increased the paranoia. His advisers were people he had promoted. Generals who had expressed divergent opinions in what he referred to as "frank and informal get-togethers" had been retired. His political allies were worried that their opportunities to enrich themselves even further would be curtailed if they had to share power with Benazir.

What if the Supreme Court now declared his reelection by a dying and unrepresentative assembly illegal? To ward off disaster, the ISI had been preparing blackmail flicks: agents secretly filmed some of the Supreme Court judges in flagrante. But so unpopular had Musharraf become that even the sight of judicial venerables in bed might not have done the trick. It might even have increased their support.* Musharraf decided that blackmail wasn't worth the risk. Only firm action could "restore order"—i.e., save his skin. The usual treatment in these cases is a declaration of martial law. But what if the country is already being governed by the army chief of staff? The solution is simple. Treble the dose. Organize a coup within a coup. That is what Musharraf decided to do. Washington was informed a few weeks in advance, Downing Street somewhat later. Benazir's patrons in the West told her what was about to happen, and she, foolishly for a political leader who has just returned to her country, evacuated to Dubai.

On November 3, 2007, Musharraf, as chief of the army, suspended the 1973 constitution and imposed a state of emergency: all non-government TV channels were taken off the air, the mobile phone networks were jammed, paramilitary units surrounded the Supreme Court. The chief justice convened an emergency bench of judges, who—heroically—declared the new dispensation "illegal and unconstitutional." They were unceremoniously removed and put under house arrest. Pakistan's judges have usually been acquiescent. Those who in the past resisted military leaders were soon bullied out of it, so

---

*In 1968, when a right-wing, pro-military rag in Lahore published an attack on me, it revealed that I "had attended sex orgies in a French country house organised by [my] friend, the Jew Cohn-Bendit. All the fifty women in the swimming-pool were Jewish." Alas, this was totally false, but my parents were amazed at the number of people who congratulated them on my virility.

the decision of this chief justice took the country by surprise and won him great admiration. Global media coverage of Pakistan suggests a country of generals, corrupt politicians, and bearded lunatics; the struggle to reinstate the chief justice had presented a different picture.

Aitzaz Ahsan, a prominent member of the PPP, minister of the interior in Benazir's first government, and currently president of the Bar Association, was arrested and placed in solitary confinement. Several thousand political and civil rights activists were picked up. The former cricket hero, Imran Khan, a fierce and incorruptible opponent of the regime, was arrested, charged with "state terrorism"—for which the penalty is death or life imprisonment—and taken in handcuffs to a remote high-security prison. Musharraf, Khan argued, had begun yet another shabby chapter in Pakistan's history.

Lawyers were arrested all over the country; many were physically attacked by policemen. The order was to humiliate them, and the police obliged. A lawyer, "Omar," circulated an account of what happened:

> While I was standing talking to my colleagues, we saw the police go wild on the orders of a superior officer. In riot gear . . . brandishing weapons and sticks, about a hundred policemen attacked us . . . and seemed intensely happy at doing so. We all ran. Some of us who were not as nimble on their feet as others were caught by the police and beaten mercilessly. We were then locked in police vans used to transport convicted prisoners. Everyone was stunned at this show of brute force but it did not end. The police went on mayhem inside the court premises and court buildings. . . . Those of us who were arrested were taken to various police stations and put in lockups. At midnight, we were told that we were being shifted to jail. We could not get bail as our fundamental rights were suspended. Sixty lawyers were put into a police van ten feet by four feet wide and five feet in height. We were squashed like sardines. When the van reached the jail, we were told that we could not get [out] until orders of our detention were received by the jail authorities. Our older colleagues started to suffocate, some fainted, others started to panic because of claustrophobia. The police ignored our screams and refused to open the van doors. Finally, after three hours . . . we were let out and

taken to mosquito-infected barracks where the food given to us smelled like sewage water.

Geo, the largest Pakistani TV network, had long since located its broadcasting facilities in Dubai. It was a strange sensation watching the network in London when the screens were blank in Pakistan. On the first day of the emergency I saw Hamid Mir, a journalist loathed by the general, reporting from Islamabad and asserting that the U.S. embassy had given the green light to the coup because it regarded the chief justice as a nuisance and wrongly believed him to be "a Taliban sympathizer." Certainly no U.S. spokesperson or State Department adjunct in the Foreign Office criticized the dismissal of the eight Supreme Court judges or their arrest: that was the quid pro quo for Washington's insistence that Musharraf take off his uniform. If he was going to turn civilian, he wanted all the other rules twisted in his favor. A newly appointed stooge Supreme Court would soon help him with the rule-bending. As would the authorities in Dubai, who helpfully suspended Geo's facilities. Benazir Bhutto too, in the first few days after the state of emergency was declared, maintained an opportunist silence on the judiciary.

In the evening of that first day, and after several delays, a flustered General Musharraf, his hair badly dyed, appeared on TV, trying to look like the sort of leader who wants it understood that the political crisis is to be discussed with gravity and sangfroid. Instead, he came across as an inarticulate dictator fearful for his own political future. His performance as he broadcast to the nation, first in Urdu and then in English, was incoherent. The gist was simple: he had to act because the Supreme Court had "so demoralized our state agencies that we can't fight the war on terror" and the TV networks had become "totally irresponsible." "I have imposed emergency," he said halfway through his diatribe, adding, with a contemptuous gesture, "You must have seen it on TV." Was he being sarcastic, given that most channels had been shut down? Who knows? Mohammed Hanif, the sharp-witted head of the BBC's Urdu Service, which monitored the broadcast, confessed himself flummoxed when he wrote up what he heard. He had no doubt that the Urdu version of the speech was the general's own work. Hanif's deconstruction—

he quoted the general in Urdu and in English—deserved a broadcast all of its own:

> Here are some random things he said. And trust me, these things were said quite randomly. Yes, he did say, "Extremism *bahut* extreme *ho gaya hai* [extremism has become too extreme]. . . . Nobody is scared of us anymore. . . . Islamabad is full of extremists. . . . There is a government within government. . . . Officials are being asked to the courts. . . . Officials are being insulted by the judiciary."
>
> At one point he appeared wistful when reminiscing about his first three years in power: "I had total control." You were almost tempted to ask: "What happened then, uncle?" But obviously, uncle didn't need any prompting. He launched into his routine about three stages of democracy. He claimed he was about to launch the third and final phase of democracy (the way he said it, he managed to make it sound like the Final Solution). And just when you thought he was about to make his point, he took an abrupt turn and plunged into a deep pool of self-pity. This involved a long-winded anecdote about how the Supreme Court judges would rather attend a colleague's daughter's wedding than just get it over with and decide that he is a constitutional president. . . . I have heard some dictators' speeches in my life, but nobody has gone so far as to mention someone's daughter's wedding as a reason for imposing martial law on the country.
>
> When for the last few minutes of his speech he addressed his audience in the West in English, I suddenly felt a deep sense of humiliation. This part of his speech was scripted. Sentences began and ended. I felt humiliated that my president not only thinks that we are not evolved enough for things like democracy and human rights, but that we can't even handle proper syntax and grammar.

The English-language version put the emphasis on the "war on terror": Napoléon and Abraham Lincoln, he said, would have done what he did to preserve the "integrity of their country"—the mention of Lincoln was obviously intended for the U.S. market. In Pakistan's military academies the usual soldier heroes are Napoléon, de Gaulle, and Atatürk.

What did Benazir, now outmaneuvered, make of the speech as she watched it on TV in her Dubai sanctuary? She first said she was shocked, which was slightly disingenuous. Even if she had not explicitly been told in advance that an emergency would be declared, it was hardly a surprise. U.S. secretary of state Condoleezza Rice had already made a token public appeal to Musharraf not to take this course, indicating clearly what lay ahead. Yet for more than twenty-four hours Benazir Bhutto was unable to give a clear response. At one point she even criticized the chief justice for being too provocative.

Agitated phone calls from Pakistan persuaded her to return immediately to Karachi. To put her in her place, the authorities kept her plane waiting on the tarmac. When she finally reached the VIP lounge, her PPP colleagues told her that unless she denounced the emergency, the party would split. Outsmarted and abandoned by Musharraf, she couldn't take the risk of losing key figures in her own organization. And so she criticized the emergency and its perpetrator, established contact with the beleaguered opposition, and, as if putting on a new lipstick, declared that she would now lead the struggle to get rid of the dictator. She also tried to call on the chief justice to express her sympathy, but wasn't allowed near his residence.

She could have followed the example of her imprisoned colleague Aitzaz Ahsan, a senior minister in both her governments, but she was envious of him: he had become far too popular in Pakistan. He'd even had the nerve to go to Washington without her patronage, where he was politely received by society and inspected as a possible substitute should things go badly wrong. Not a single message had flowed from her BlackBerry to congratulate him on his victories in the struggle to reinstate the chief justice. Ahsan had advised her against any deal with Musharraf. When generals are against the wall, he is reported to have told her, they resort to desperate and irrational measures. Others who offered similar advice in gentler language were also batted away. She was the PPP's "chairperson for life" and brooked no dissent. That Ahsan had been proved right irritated her even more. Any notion of political morality had long ago been dumped. The very idea of a party with a consistent set of beliefs was regarded as ridiculous and outdated. Ahsan was now safe in prison, far from the madding hordes of Western journalists whom she received in style during the few days she spent under house arrest and afterward. She made a few polite noises about his imprisonment, but nothing more.

Sensing trouble, Washington dispatched a go-between at short notice to sort out the mess. Negroponte spent time with Musharraf and spoke to Benazir, still insisting that they make up and go through with the deal. She immediately toned down her criticisms, but the general was scathing and said in public that she would never win the elections scheduled for January 2008. Perhaps he thought the ISI would rig them in style as they had done so often in the past. Opinion polls revealed that her old rival Nawaz Sharif was well ahead of her. Musharraf's hasty pilgrimage to Mecca was no doubt an attempt to secure Saudi mediation in case he had to cut a deal with the Sharif brothers—who had been living in exile in Saudi Arabia—and sideline her completely. The Saudi king insisted that Nawaz Sharif should now be permitted to return to his country. Both sides denied that a deal was done, but Sharif returned to Pakistan soon afterward with Saudi blessings and an armor-plated Cadillac as a special gift from the king. There seemed little doubt that Riyadh would rather have him than Benazir.

With Pakistan still under a state of emergency and the largest media network refusing to sign the oath of allegiance that would allow them back on air, the vote scheduled for January could only have been a general's election. It was hardly a secret that the ISI and the civilian bureaucracy would decide who won and where, and because of this some of the opposition parties were considering not contesting the election. Nawaz Sharif told the press that he had in a long telephone call failed to persuade Benazir to join a boycott and thereby render the process null and void from the start. But once he was back in the country, he became less certain. His supporters insisted that their popularity in the Punjab had risen because of their refusal to deal with Musharraf, and a boycott would be counterproductive. Sharif accepted this view.

What would Benazir do now? Washington's leverage in Islamabad was limited, which is why they wanted her to be involved in the first place. "It's always better," the U.S. ambassador half joked at a reception, "to have two phone numbers in a capital." That may be so, but they could not guarantee her the prime ministership or even a fair election.

In his death cell, three decades previously, her father had mulled over similar problems and come to slightly different conclusions. *If I Am Assassinated,* Zulfiqar Ali Bhutto's last will and testament, contained some tart assessments whose meaning wasn't lost on his colleagues:

> I entirely agree that the people of Pakistan will not tolerate foreign hegemony. On the basis of the self-same logic, the people of Pakistan would never agree to an internal hegemony. The two hegemonies complement each other. If our people meekly submit to internal hegemony, a priori, they will have to submit to external hegemony. This is so because the strength and power of external hegemony is far greater than that of internal hegemony. If the people are too terrified to resist the weaker force, it is not possible for them to resist the stronger force. The acceptance of or acquiescence in internal hegemony means submission to external hegemony.

After Bhutto was hanged in April 1979, the text became semisacred among his supporters. But, when in power, Bhutto père had failed to develop any counterhegemonic strategy or institutions, other than the 1973 constitution, drafted by the veteran civil rights lawyer Mahmud Ali Kasuri (whose son Khurshid was until recently Musharraf's foreign minister). A personality-driven, autocratic style of governance had neutered the spirit of Bhutto's party, encouraged careerists, and finally paved the way for his enemies. He was the victim of a grave injustice; his death removed all the warts and transformed him into a martyr. More than half the country, mainly the poor, mourned his passing.

The tragedy led to the PPP's being treated as a family heirloom, which was unhealthy for both party and country. It provided the Bhuttos with a vote bank and large reserves. But the experience of her father's trial and death had radicalized and politicized his daughter. She would have preferred, she told me at the time, to be a diplomat. Her two brothers, Murtaza and Shahnawaz, were in London, having been forbidden to return home by their imprisoned father. The burden of trying to save her father's life fell on Benazir and her mother, Nusrat, and the courage they exhibited won them the silent respect of a frightened majority. They refused to cave in to General Zia's military dictatorship, which apart from anything else was invoking Islam to claw back rights won by women in previous decades. Benazir and Nusrat Bhutto were arrested and released several times. Their health began to suffer. Nusrat was allowed to leave the country to seek medical advice in 1982. Benazir was released a little more than a year later, thanks, in part, to U.S. pressure orchestrated by her old Harvard friend Peter Galbraith, who had useful contacts in the State Department. She later described the period in her memoir, *Daughter of the East* (1988); it included photo captions such as "Shortly after President Reagan praised the regime for making 'great strides towards democracy,' Zia's henchmen gunned down peaceful demonstrators marking Pakistan Independence Day. The police were just as brutal to those protesting at the attack on my jeep in January 1987."

Benazir moved to London, where her tiny Barbican flat in the heart of the old city became a center of opposition to the dictatorship, and here we often discussed a campaign to take on the generals. Benazir had built up her position by steadfastly and peacefully resisting the military and replying to every slander with a cutting retort. Her brothers had been operating on a different level. They set up an armed group, al-Zulfiqar, whose declared aim was to harass and weaken the regime by targeting "traitors who had collaborated with Zia." The principal volunteers were recruited inside Pakistan, and in 1980 they were provided with a base in Afghanistan, where the pro-Moscow Communists had taken power three years before. It is a sad story with a fair share of factionalism, show trials, petty rivalries, fantasies of every sort, and death for the group's less-fortunate members.

In March 1981, Murtaza and Shahnawaz Bhutto were placed on the FIA's most wanted list. They had hijacked a Pakistan International airliner soon after it left Karachi (a power cut had paralyzed the X-ray machines, enabling the hijackers to take their weapons on board); it was diverted to Kabul. Here Murtaza took over and demanded the release of political prisoners. A young military officer on board the flight was murdered. The plane refueled and went on to Damascus, where the legendary Syrian spymaster General Kholi took charge and ensured there were no more deaths. That American passengers were on the plane was a major consideration for the generals, and for that reason alone the prisoners in Pakistan were released and flown to Tripoli.

This was seen as a victory and welcomed as such by the PPP in Pakistan. For the first time the group began to be taken seriously. A key target inside the country was Maulvi Mushtaq Hussain, the chief justice of the High Court in Lahore, who had in 1978 sentenced Zulfiqar Ali Bhutto to death, and whose behavior in court (among other charges, he had accused Bhutto of "pretending to be a Muslim"—his mother was a Hindu convert) had enraged the entire Bhutto family. Mushtaq was in a friend's car being driven to his home in Lahore's Model Town area when al-Zulfiqar gunmen opened fire. The judge survived, but his friend and the driver died.

The friend was the founding father of the Chaudhrys of Gujrat: Chaudhry Zahoor Elahi, whom we have met earlier in this narrative. It is the next generation of Chaudhrys that currently provides Musharraf with civilian ballast: Zahoor Elahi's son Shujaat organized the split with Nawaz Sharif and created the splinter PML-Q to ease the growing pains of the new regime. He still fixes political deals and wanted an emergency imposed much earlier to circumvent the deal with Benazir. He was to be the mastermind of the general's election campaign. His cousin Pervez Elahi was chief minister of the Punjab; the latter's son, in turn, is busy continuing the family tradition by evicting tenants and buying up all the available land on the edge of Lahore.

The hijacking meanwhile had annoyed Moscow, and the regime in Afghanistan asked the Bhutto brothers to find another refuge. While in Kabul, they had married two Afghan sisters, Fauzia and Rehana Fasihudin, daughters of a senior official at the Afghan Ministry of Foreign Affairs. Together with their wives they now left the country and after a sojourn in Syria and possibly Libya ended up in Europe. The reunion with their sister took place on the French Riviera in 1985, a setting well suited to the lifestyles of all three siblings.

The young men feared General Zia's agents. Each had a young daughter. Shahnawaz lived in an apartment in Cannes. He had been in charge of the "military apparatus" of al-Zulfiqar, responsible for the purchase of weapons, and life in Kabul had exacted a heavier toll on him. He was edgy and nervous. Relations with his wife were stormy, and he told his sister that he was preparing for a divorce. "There's never been a divorce in the family. Your marriage wasn't even an arranged one. . . . You chose to marry Rehana. You must live with it" was Benazir's revealing reply, according to her memoir. This was to be her own attitude when her husband's philandering was brought to her notice. Then on July 18, 1985, Shahnawaz was found dead in his apartment. His wife claimed he had taken poison, but according to Benazir, nobody in the family believed her story; there had been violence in the room and his papers had been searched. Rehana looked immaculate, which disturbed the family. She was imprisoned for three months under the Good Samaritan law for not having gone to the assistance of a dying person. After her release she settled in the United States. "Had the CIA killed him as a friendly gesture towards their favourite dictator?" Benazir speculated. She raised another question too: had the sisters become ISI agents? The truth remains hidden. Not long afterward Murtaza divorced Fauzia, but kept custody of their three-year-old daughter, Fatima, and moved to Damascus. Here he had plenty of time for reflection and told friends that too many mistakes had been made in the struggle against the dictatorship. In 1986 he met Ghinwa Itaoui, a young teacher who had fled Lebanon after the Israeli invasion of 1982. She calmed him down and took charge of Fatima's education. They were married in 1989, and a son, Zulfiqar, was born the following year.

Benazir returned to Pakistan in 1986 and was greeted by large crowds, nearly a million people in Lahore, who came out to show their affection for her and to demonstrate their anger with the regime. She campaigned all over the country, but felt increasingly that for some of the more religious-minded a young, unmarried woman was not acceptable as a leader. How, for instance, could she visit Saudi Arabia without a husband? An offer of marriage from the Zardari family was accepted, and she married Asif in 1987. The Zardaris were small landowners. The father, Hakim Zardari, had been a supporter of the National Awami Party and owned some cinemas in Karachi. They were not wealthy but had enough to indulge Asif Zardari's passion for polo. He loved horses and women and was not interested in politics. Benazir told me that she was slightly nervous that it was an arranged marriage, but was hoping for the best. She had been worried that any husband would find it difficult to deal with the periods of separation her nomadic political life would entail, but this never bothered Zardari, who was perfectly capable of occupying himself.

A year later General Zia's plane blew up in midair. In the elections that followed the PPP won the largest number of seats. Benazir became prime minister, but was hemmed in by the army on one side and the president, the army's favorite bureaucrat, Ghulam Ishaq Khan, on the other. She told me at the time that she felt powerless. Being in power, it seemed, was satisfaction enough. She went on state visits: met and liked Mrs. Thatcher and later, with her new husband in tow, was received politely by the Saudi king. In the meantime, plots were afoot—the opposition was literally buying off some of her MPs—and in August 1990 her government was removed by presidential decree and Zia's protégés the Sharif brothers were back in power.

By the time she was reelected in 1993, she had abandoned all idea of reform, but that she was in a hurry to do something became clear when she appointed her husband minister for investment, making him responsible for all investment offers from home and abroad. The Pakistani press widely alleged that the couple accumulated $1.5 billion. The high command of the Pakistan Peoples Party now became a machine for making money, but without any trickle-down mechanism. This period marked the complete degeneration of the party. The single tradition that had been passed down since the foundation of the party was autocratic centralism. The leader's word was final. Like her father in this respect, Benazir never understood that debate is not only the best medium of confutation, of turning the ideological tables. It is also the most effective form of persuasion. The debate urgently needed to be shifted out of the paddock of religion and into a more neutral space. This never happened.

All that shamefaced party members could say on corruption, when I asked them during several visits to Pakistan, was "Everybody does it all over the world," thus accepting that the cash nexus was now all that mattered. Money was now the sacred center of all politics. In foreign policy Benazir's legacy was mixed. She refused to sanction an anti-Indian military adventure in Kargil on the Himalayan slopes, but to make up for it, as I wrote at the time,* her government pushed through the Taliban takeover in Kabul—which makes it doubly ironic that Washington and London were promoting her as a champion of democracy before her tragic demise.

Murtaza Bhutto had contested the elections from abroad and won a seat in the Sind provincial legislature. He returned home and expressed his unhappiness with his sister's agenda. Family gatherings became tense. Murtaza had his weaknesses, but he wasn't corrupt, and he argued in favor of the old party's radical manifesto. He made it clear that he regarded Zardari as an interloper whose only interest was money. Nusrat Bhutto suggested that Murtaza be made the chief minister of Sind; Benazir's response was to remove her mother as chairperson of the PPP. Any sympathy Murtaza may have felt for his sister turned to loathing. He no longer felt obliged to control his tongue and at every possible opportunity lambasted Zardari and the corrupt regime over which his sister presided. It was difficult to fault him on the facts. The incumbent chief minister of Sind was Abdullah Shah, one of Zardari's creatures. He began to harass Murtaza's supporters. Murtaza decided to confront the organ-grinder himself. According to some, he rang Zardari and invited him round for an informal chat to try to settle the problems within the family. Zardari agreed. As the two men were pacing the garden, Murtaza's retainers appeared and grabbed Zardari. Someone brought out a cutthroat razor and some warm water and Murtaza shaved off half of Zardari's mustache to the delight of the retainers, then told him to get lost. A fuming Zardari, who had probably feared much worse, was compelled to shave off the other half at home. The media, bemused, were informed that the new clean-shaven consort had accepted intelligence advice that the mustache made him too recognizable a target. Benazir's private version for friends was somewhat different. She said the kids disliked it because it prickled when he kissed them and so he dispensed with it for their sake. Both explanations were negated by Zardari's allowing it to grow again immediately afterward.

Some months later, in September 1996, as Murtaza and his

---

*London Review of Books, April 15, 1999.

entourage were returning home from a political meeting, they were ambushed, just outside their house, by some seventy armed policemen accompanied by four senior officers. A number of snipers were positioned in surrounding trees. The streetlights had been switched off. Murtaza clearly understood what was happening and got out of his car with his hands raised; his bodyguards were instructed not to use their weapons. Instead, the police opened fire. Seven men were killed, Murtaza among them. The fatal bullet had been fired at close range. The trap had carefully been laid, but as is the way in Pakistan, the crudeness of the operation—false entries in police logbooks, lost evidence, witnesses arrested and intimidated, the provincial PPP governor (regarded as untrustworthy) dispatched to a nonevent in Egypt, a policeman killed who was feared might talk—made it obvious that the decision to execute the prime minister's brother had been made at a high level. Shoaib Suddle, deputy inspector general of Sind when Murtaza was murdered, was charged with involvement in the killing, but the case was dismissed before it went to trial. He was subsequently promoted to inspector general by Zardari in April 2008. Two months later, he was appointed director general of the Intelligence Bureau in Islamabad.

While the ambush was being prepared, the police had sealed off Murtaza's house (from which his father had been lifted by Zia's commandos in 1977). The family inside felt something was wrong, and a remarkably composed Fatima Bhutto, age fourteen, rang her aunt at Prime Minister's House. The conversation that followed remains imprinted on her memory, and a few years ago she gave me an account of it. Zardari took her call.

> FATIMA: I wish to speak to my aunt, please.
> ZARDARI: It's not possible.
> FATIMA: Why? [At this point, Fatima says she heard loud wails and
>   what sounded like fake crying.]
> ZARDARI: She's hysterical, can't you hear?
> FATIMA: Why?
> ZARDARI: Don't you know? Your father's been shot.

Fatima and Ghinwa found out where Murtaza had been taken and rushed out of the house. The street outside showed no sign that anything had happened: the scene of the killing had been wiped clean of all evidence, with no traces of blood or signs of disturbance. They drove straight to the hospital, but it was too late: Murtaza was already dead.

When Benazir arrived to attend her brother's funeral in Larkana, angry crowds stoned her limo. She had to retreat. In another unusual display of emotion, local people encouraged Murtaza's widow to attend the actual burial ceremony in defiance of Islamic tradition. According to Fatima, one of Benazir's hangers-on instigated legal proceedings against Ghinwa in a religious court for breaching Islamic law. Nothing was sacred.

Anyone who'd witnessed Murtaza's murder was arrested; one witness died in prison. When Fatima rang Benazir to ask why witnesses were being arrested and not the killers, she was told, "Look, you're very young. You don't understand things." Perhaps for this reason the kind aunt decided to encourage Fatima's blood mother, Fauzia, whom she had previously denounced as a murderer in the pay of General Zia, to come to Pakistan and claim custody of Fatima. No mystery as to who paid her fare from California. Fatima and Ghinwa Bhutto resisted and the attempt failed. Benazir then tried a softer approach and insisted that Fatima accompany her to New York, where she was going to address the UN Assembly. Ghinwa Bhutto approached friends in Damascus and had her two children flown out of the country. Fatima later discovered that Fauzia had been seen hobnobbing with Benazir in New York.

In November 1996 Benazir was once again removed from power, this time by her own president, Farooq Leghari, a PPP stalwart. He cited corruption, but what had also angered him was the ISI's crude attempt at blackmail—the intelligence agencies had photographed Leghari's daughter meeting a boyfriend and threatened to go public. The week Benazir fell, the chief minister of Sind, Abdullah Shah, who had helped organize Murtaza's murder, hopped on a motorboat and fled Karachi for the Gulf and then to the United States.

A judicial tribunal had been appointed by Benazir's government to inquire into the circumstances leading to Murtaza's death. Headed by a Supreme Court judge, it took detailed evidence from all parties. Murtaza's lawyers accused Zardari, Abdullah Shah, and two senior police officials of conspiracy to murder. Benazir (now out of power) accepted that there had been a conspiracy, but suggested that "the hidden hand responsible for this was President Farooq Ahmad Leghari." The intention, she said, was to "kill a Bhutto to get rid of a Bhutto." Nobody took this seriously. Given all that had happened, it was an incredible suggestion.

The tribunal said no legally acceptable evidence linked Zardari to the incident, but asserted, "This was a case of extra-judicial killings by the police," and concluded that such an incident could not have taken place without approval from the highest quarters. Nothing happened. Eleven years later, Fatima Bhutto publicly accused Zardari; she also claimed that many of those involved that day appear to have been rewarded for their actions. In an interview on an independent TV station just before the emergency was imposed, Benazir was asked to explain how her brother had bled to death outside his home while she was prime minister. She walked out of the studio.

A sharp op-ed piece by Fatima Bhutto appeared in the *Los Angeles Times* on November 14, 2007. She did not mince words:

> Ms. Bhutto's political posturing is sheer pantomime. Her negotiations with the military and her unseemly willingness until just a few days ago to take part in Musharraf's regime have signaled once and for all to the growing legions of fundamentalists across South Asia that democracy is just a guise for dictatorship. . . .
>
> My father was Benazir's younger brother. To this day, her role in his assassination has never been adequately answered, although the tribunal convened after his death under the leadership of three respected judges concluded that it could not have taken place without approval from a "much higher" political authority. . . .
>
> I have personal reasons to fear the danger that Ms. Bhutto's presence in Pakistan brings, but I am not alone. The Islamists are waiting at the gate. They have been waiting for confirmation that the reforms for which the Pakistani people have been struggling have been a farce, propped up by the White House. Since Musharraf seized power in 1999, there has been an earnest grass-roots movement for democratic reform. The last thing we need is to be tied to a neocon agenda through a puppet "democrat" like Ms. Bhutto.

This elicited the following response from its target: "My niece is angry with me." Well, yes.

Musharraf may have withdrawn the corruption charges against Benazir, but three other cases were proceeding in Switzerland, Spain, and Britain. The latter two appear to have been dropped, but the Swiss court is refusing to close the case.

In July 2003, after an investigation lasting several years, Daniel Devaud, a Geneva magistrate, convicted Mr. and Mrs. Asif Ali Zardari, in absentia, of money laundering. They had accepted $15 million in bribes from two Swiss companies, SGS and Cotecna. The couple were sentenced to six months in prison and ordered to return $11.9 million to the government of Pakistan. "I certainly don't have any doubts about the judgments I handed down," Devaud told the BBC. Benazir appealed, thus forcing a new investigation. On September 19, 2005, she appeared in a Geneva court and tried to detach herself from the rest of the family. She hadn't been involved, she said: it was a matter for her husband and her mother, who was afflicted with Alzheimer's. She knew nothing of the accounts. And what of the agreement her agent Jens Schlegelmilch had signed according to which, in case of her and Zardari's death, the assets of Bomer Finance Company would be divvied out equally between the Zardari and Bhutto families? She knew nothing of that either. And the £120,000 diamond necklace in the bank vault paid for by Zardari? It was intended for her, but she had rejected the gift as "inappropriate." The case is still pending. In November 2007, Musharraf told Owen Bennett-Jones of the BBC World Service that his government would not interfere with the proceedings: "That's up to the Swiss government. Depends on them. It's a case in their courts."

In Britain the legal shenanigans concerned the $3.4 million Rockwood estate in Surrey, bought by offshore companies on behalf of Zardari in 1995 and refurbished to his exacting tastes. Zardari denied owning the estate. Then, when the court was about to instruct the liquidators to sell it and return the proceeds to the Pakistani government, Zardari came forward and accepted ownership. In 2006, Lord Justice Collins had ruled that, while he was not making any "findings of fact," there was a "reasonable prospect" that the Pakistani government might be able to establish that Rockwood had been bought and furnished with "the fruits of corruption." A close friend of Benazir Bhutto's informed me that she was genuinely not involved in this one, since Zardari wasn't thinking of spending much time there with her.

Even these fragments of the past emerged only fleetingly and rarely on television. What was interesting was the short memory of the U.S. press. In 1998, the *New York Times* had published a sharp and lengthy indictment of Bhutto-Zardari corruption. John F. Burns described how "Asif Ali Zardari turned his marriage to Ms. Bhutto into a source of virtually unchallengeable power" and went on to cite several cases of corruption. The first involved a gold bullion dealer in Dubai who had paid $10 million into one of Zardari's accounts in return for being awarded the monopoly on gold imports that were vital to Pakistan's jewelry industry. Two other cases involved France and, again, Switzerland:

> In 1995, a leading French military contractor, Dassault Aviation, agreed to pay Mr. Zardari and a Pakistani partner $200 million for a $4 billion jet fighter deal that fell apart only when Ms. Bhutto's Government was dismissed. In another deal, a leading Swiss company hired to curb customs fraud in Pakistan paid millions of dollars between 1994 and 1996 to offshore companies controlled by Mr. Zardari and Ms. Bhutto's widowed mother, Nusrat. . . .
>
> In 1994 and 1995, [Zardari] used a Swiss bank account and an American Express card to buy jewelry worth $660,000—including $246,000 at Cartier and Bulgari Corp. in Beverly Hills, Calif., in barely a month.*

Given the scale of the corruption, why was Washington so desperate? Daniel Markey, formerly of the State Department and currently senior fellow for India, Pakistan, and South Asia at the Council on Foreign Relations, explained why the United States had pushed the marriage of convenience: "A progressive, reform-minded, more cosmopolitan party in government would help the U.S." As their finances revealed, the Zardaris were certainly cosmopolitan.

---

*John F. Burns, "House of Graft: Tracing the Bhutto Millions . . . A Special Report," *New York Times,* January 9, 1998.

What then is at stake in Pakistan as far as Washington is concerned? "The concern I have," Robert Gates, the U.S. secretary for defense, told the world, "is that the longer the internal problems continue, the more distracted the Pakistani army and security services will be in terms of the internal situation rather than focusing on the terrorist threat in the frontier area." But one reason for the internal crisis has been Washington's overreliance on Musharraf and the Pakistani military. Washington's support and funding have given him the confidence to operate as he pleases. But the thoughtless Western military occupation of Afghanistan is obviously crucial, since the instability in Kabul seeps into Peshawar and the tribal areas between the two countries. The state of emergency targeted the judiciary, opposition politicians, and the independent media. All three groups were, in different ways, challenging the official line on Afghanistan and the "war on terror," the disappearance of political prisoners, and the widespread use of torture in Pakistani prisons. The issues were being debated on television in a much more open fashion than happens anywhere in the West, where a blanket consensus on Afghanistan drowns all dissent. Musharraf argued that civil society was hampering the war on terror. Hence the emergency. It's nonsense, of course. It's the war in the frontier regions that is creating dissent inside the army. Many do not want to fight. Hence the surrender of dozens of soldiers to Taliban guerrillas. This is the reason many junior officers are taking early retirement.

Western pundits blather on about the jihadi finger on the nuclear trigger. This is pure fantasy, reminiscent of a similar campaign almost three decades ago, when the threat wasn't the jihadis who were fighting alongside the West in Afghanistan, but nationalist military radicals. The cover story of *Time* magazine for June 15, 1979, dealt with Pakistan; a senior Western diplomat was quoted as saying that the big danger was "that there is another Gadhafi down there, some radical major or colonel in the Pakistani army. We could wake up and find him in Zia's place one morning and, believe me, Pakistan wouldn't be the only place that would be destabilized."

The Pakistan army is half a million strong. Its tentacles are everywhere: land, industry, public utilities, and so on. It would require a cataclysmic upheaval (a U.S. invasion and occupation, for example) for this army to feel threatened by a jihadi uprising. Two considerations unite senior officers: the unity of the organization and keeping politicians at bay. One reason is the fear that they might lose the comforts and privileges they have acquired after decades of rule; but they also have the deep aversion to democracy that is the hallmark of most armies. Unused to accountability within their own ranks, it's difficult for them to accept it in society at large.

As southern Afghanistan collapses into chaos, and as corruption and massive inflation take hold, the Taliban are gaining more and more recruits. The generals who once convinced Benazir that control of Kabul via the Taliban would give them "strategic depth" may have retired, but their successors know that the Afghans will not tolerate a long-term Western occupation. They hope for the return of a whitewashed Taliban. Instead of encouraging a regional solution that includes India, Iran, and Russia, the United States would prefer to see the Pakistan army as its permanent cop in Kabul. It won't work. In Pakistan itself the long night continues as the cycle restarts: military leadership promising reforms degenerates into tyranny, politicians promising social support to the people degenerate into oligarchs. Given that a better functioning neighbor is unlikely to intervene, Pakistan will oscillate between these two forms of rule for the foreseeable future. The people, who feel they have tried everything and failed, will return to a state of semisleep, unless something unpredictable rouses them again. This is always possible.

Before the story could move further, another tragedy struck Pakistan and the House of Bhutto. Determined to fulfill her part of the Faustian deal brokered in Washington, Benazir Bhutto, despite some hesitation, agreed to participate in an election regarded at the time as deeply flawed by virtually every independent commentator in Pakistan and by many in her own party.

She decided to begin her campaign in the country's military capital, Rawalpindi, where she arrived on December 27, 2007. She came to address a public meeting at Liaquat Bagh (formerly Municipal Park), a popular public space named after the country's first prime minister, Liaquat Ali Khan, who was killed there by an assassin in October 1951. The killer, Said Akbar, was immediately shot dead on the orders of a police officer involved in the plot. Not far from here, a colonial structure where nationalists were imprisoned once stood. This was Rawalpindi jail. Here, Benazir's father, Zulfiqar Ali Bhutto, was hanged in April 1979. The military tyrant responsible for his judicial murder made sure the site of the tragedy was destroyed as well.

The rally was not disrupted on this occasion, but the killers were waiting in the vicinity of her car. As she was about to leave, she decided on a last wave to her supporters and the television cameras. A bomb blew up and she appeared to have been felled by bullets fired at her car. The assassins, mindful of their failure in Karachi a month previously, had taken out double insurance this time. They wanted her dead at any cost. Government pathologists claimed that Bhutto caught her head on the sunroof of the car she was speaking from as she ducked inside, fracturing her skull, and that was the cause of her death. Her party disagreed. Scotland Yard was asked for help. After a brief investigation it concurred with the government report. Exhuming the body and a new postmortem would have been definitive, but Zardari refused to permit it.

Her death was greeted with anger throughout the country. The people of her home province, Sind, responded with violent demonstrations, targeting government buildings and cars of non-Sindhis. While the global media networks assumed, without any investigation, that she was killed by local jihadi terrorists or Al Qaeda, the crowds in Pakistan had different ideas and pointed accusing fingers at the president, while the streets resounded to chants of Peoples Party supporters: *"Amreeka ne kutta paala, vardi wallah, vardi wallah"* ("America trained a dog / the one in uniform, the one in uniform").

Even those sharply critical of Benazir Bhutto's behavior and policies—both while she was in office and more recently—were stunned and angered by her death. Indignation and fear stalked the country once again. This event made a crude rigging of the February 2008 elections virtually impossible. An odd coexistence of military despotism and anarchy created the conditions leading to her assassination. In the past, military rule was designed to preserve order—and did so for a few years. No longer. Today it creates disorder and promotes lawlessness. How else can one explain the sacking of the chief justice and other judges of the country's Supreme Court for attempting to hold the government's intelligence agencies and the police accountable to courts of law? Their replacements lack the backbone to do anything, let alone conduct a proper inquest into the misdeeds of the agencies to uncover the truth behind the carefully organized killing of a major political leader. Pakistan today is a conflagration of despair. It is assumed that the killers were jihadi fanatics. This may well be true, but were they acting on their own? Conspiracy theories mushroomed after her death. General Hamid Gul, a former director general of the ISI during Benazir's first prime ministership, told the media that despite promising the United States that she would hand over A. Q. Khan, the self-styled "father of the Pakistani bomb," for questioning and permit the entry of U.S. troops and planes to deal with Al Qaeda in Pakistan, she had "drifted from her agenda" after her arrival and the first attempt on her life. Hamid Gul insisted that "the Israeli lobby will never rest in peace until they have snatched our nuclear weapons. In the war against terror, Pakistan is the target." For this, according to General Gul, she was eliminated. This is a popular view among retired segments of the military and civilian bureaucracy, but is it credible?

It is certainly the case that Musharraf refused to send A. Q. Khan to Washington. Government officials told me that the United States was desperate to question Khan about his dealings with Iran, and what he said under questioning in the United States might be used as a pretext to bomb Iran's nuclear reactors. If Benazir Bhutto had agreed to this, which is possible, nothing suggests that she had undergone any political conversion after her return. She had hitched her future to the United States for a number of reasons. They would help whitewash her past and get her back into power, after which she would still need Washington's support to deal with the army. The United States as the sole imperial power was too powerful to oppose anyway, and those, like her late father, who did not do its bidding had ended up dead. For these reasons she had decided on a historic compromise and promised a rapid recognition of Israel as well, to appease Washington. This explains the unusual Israeli media coverage of her death as a "massive loss" and several full-page advertisements in the *New York Times* and other newspapers by a Los Angeles–based pro-Israeli organization, the Simon

Wiesenthal Center. A large picture of Bhutto was beneath the words "SUICIDE TERROR: What more will it take for the world to act?" and the ad called on the United Nations for a special session devoted to the issue. "Unless we put suicide bombing on the top of the international community's agenda, this virulent cancer could engulf us all," it reads. "The looming threat of WMDs in the hands of suicide bombers will dwarf the casualties already suffered in 30 countries." The ad demanded that the UN declare suicide bombings a "crime against humanity."

Benazir, according to some close to her, had been tempted to boycott the Pakistani elections, but had lacked the political courage to defy Washington, which was insisting that the elections go ahead as scheduled. She certainly had plenty of physical courage and had refused to be cowed by threats from local opponents. She chose to address an election rally in Liaquat Bagh. Her death further poisoned relations between the Pakistan Peoples Party and the army. That had started in 1977 when her father was removed by a military dictator and killed. Party activists, particularly in the province of Sind, were brutally tortured, humiliated, and, sometimes, disappeared or killed.

Pakistan's turbulent history, a result of continuous military rule and unpopular global alliances, confronts the ruling elite now with serious choices. They appear to have no positive aims. The overwhelming majority of the country disapproves of the government's foreign policy. They are angered by its lack of a serious domestic policy except for further enriching a callous and greedy elite that includes a swollen, parasitic military. Now they watch helplessly as politicians are shot dead in front of them.

I FIRST MET Benazir at her father's house in Clifton, Karachi, in 1969, when she was a fun-loving teenager, and eight years later at Oxford, when she invited me to speak at the Oxford Union when she was its president. At that time she was not particularly interested in politics and told me she had always wanted to be a diplomat. History and personal tragedy pushed her in another direction. Her father's death transformed her. She became a new person, determined to take on the military dictator of that time. We would endlessly discuss the future of the country in her tiny flat in London. She agreed that land reforms, mass education programs, a health service, and an independent foreign policy were constructive aims and crucial if the country was to be saved from the vultures in and out of uniform. Her constituency was the poor, and she was proud of that.

I was in regular communication with political activists and intellectuals in Lahore. Their virtually unanimous view was that since her return would be the first occasion for people to publicly mourn the execution of her father, at least half a million would come out to greet her. Having experienced firsthand the terrors of the Zia dictatorship, she was less sure about the turnout, and who can blame her. The country had been silenced by repression, but my instincts were the same as those of friends in Lahore. She asked me to write her speech. One day she rang. "Last night I dreamt I'd arrived in Lahore, the crowds were there, I went to the podium, opened my handbag, but the speech was missing. Can't you hurry up?" I did, and then we rehearsed it once a week before she left. Her Urdu was rudimentary, but when I suggested that she ask the assembled masses a question in Punjabi, she balked at the thought. The question was simple: *"Zia rehvay ya jahvay?"* (Should Zia stay or go?). Her pronunciation was abysmal. She would laugh and try again till it became as good as it was ever going to be. There was another moment of panic. "What should I do if they reply he should stay." This time I laughed. "They wouldn't be there if they felt that." Film footage shows her asking the question in Punjabi, and the affecting response of the crowd, which turned out to be closer to a million people strong. That campaign was the high point of her life, when a combination of political and physical courage created a wave of hope in the benighted country.

She changed again after becoming prime minister. In the early days, when I met her on a number of occasions in Islamabad, we would gently argue. In response to my numerous complaints, all she would say was that the world had changed. She couldn't be on the "wrong side" of history. And so, like many others, she made her peace with Washington. This finally led to the deal with Musharraf and her return home after more than a decade in exile. On a number of occasions she told me that she did not fear death. It was one of the dangers of playing politics in Pakistan. The last time we met was in the prime minister's residence in 1995, a year before she was dismissed from office for corruption. I asked whether she was worried by the threat of assassination. There had been an attempt already, she informed me, but the assassin, Aimal Kansi, almost blew himself up, but escaped. She smiled. I was astonished by the revelation.

Kansi was a former CIA agent recruited during the first Afghan war. He felt betrayed by the agency when they cut off his salary after the Russians left Afghanistan. His subsequent behavior resembled the script of *The Bourne Identity.* In 1993, Kansi returned to the United States, made his way to Langley, Virginia, waited with a sniper's rifle, and unleashed a deadly rampage, killing two CIA employees, including his former boss, and wounding several others. He returned to Pakistan and was on the most wanted list of the CIA and the FBI. In 1997, he was finally captured by FBI agents in a seedy hotel in Islamabad. He had been betrayed by his own bodyguards, the CIA having spent more than $3.5 million to pay informants and others to entrap him. He was extradited to the United States, where he was tried and killed by lethal injection. Till she told me, I had no idea that he had tried to kill her as well.

It is difficult to imagine any good coming out of the tragedy of her death, but there is one possibility. Pakistan desperately needs a political party that can give voice to the social needs of the bulk of the people. The Peoples Party, founded by Zulfiqar Ali Bhutto, was built by the activists of the only popular mass movement the country has known: students, peasants, and workers who fought for three months in 1968–69 to topple the country's first military dictator. They saw it as their party, and that feeling persists in some parts of the country to this day, despite everything.

Benazir's horrific death should have given her colleagues pause for reflection. To be dependent on a person or a family may be necessary at certain times, but it is a structural weakness, not a strength for a political organization. The Peoples Party needed to be refounded as a modern and democratic organization, open to serious debate and discussion, defending social and human rights, uniting the many disparate groups and individuals in Pakistan desperate for any halfway decent alternative, and coming forward with concrete proposals to stabilize occupied and war-torn Afghanistan. The Bhutto family should not have been asked for any more sacrifices. But it was not to be. When emotions run high, reason goes underground, and in Pakistan it can lie buried for a long time.

Six hours before she was executed, Mary, Queen of Scots, wrote to her brother-in-law, Henry III of France: "As for my son, I commend him to you in so far as he deserves, for I cannot answer for him." The year was 1587. On December 30, 2007, a conclave of feudal potentates gathered in the home of the slain Benazir Bhutto to hear her last will and testament being read out, its contents subsequently announced to the world media. Where Mary was tentative, her modern equivalent left no room for doubt. She could certainly answer for her son.

Her will specified that her nineteen-year-old boy, Bilawal Zardari, a student at Oxford University, should succeed her as chairperson of the party. Her husband, Asif Zardari (one of the most venal and discredited politicians in the country and still facing corruption charges in two European courts), would lead the party till Bilawal came of age. He would then become chairperson for life, as was the custom. That this is now official does not make it any less grotesque. The Peoples Party had now formally become a family heirloom, a property to be disposed of at the will of its proprietor.

Pakistan and the supporters of the party deserved something better than this distasteful, medieval charade. Benazir's last decision, alas, was in the same autocratic mode as its predecessors, an approach that would tragically cost her . . . her own life. Had she heeded the advice of some party leaders and not agreed to the Washington-brokered deal with Pervez Musharraf or, even later, decided to boycott his parliamentary election without cast-iron guarantees regarding her safety, she might still have been alive.

That most of the PPP inner circle consists of spineless timeservers leading frustrated and melancholy lives is no excuse for the farcical succession. All this could be transformed if inner-party democracy was implemented. A tiny layer of incorruptible and principled politicians are inside the party, but they have been sidelined. Dynastic politics is a sign of weakness, not strength. Benazir was fond of comparing her clan to the Kennedys, but chose to ignore the fact that the Democratic Party is not the instrument of any one family.

The issue of democracy is enormously important in a country that has been governed by the military for over half of its life. Pakistan is not a "failed state" in the sense of the Congo or Rwanda. It is a dysfunctional state and has been for almost four decades.

At the heart of this dysfunction is the domination by the army, and each period of military rule has made things worse. This has prevented the emergence of stable political institutions. Here the United States bears direct responsibility, since it has always regarded the military as the only institution it can do business with and, unfortunately, still does so. This rock has forced choppy waters into a headlong torrent.

The military's weaknesses are well-known and amply documented. But the politicians are not in a position to cast stones. After all, it was not Musharraf who pioneered the assault on the judiciary so conveniently overlooked by the U.S. deputy secretary of state, John Negroponte, and the British foreign secretary, David Miliband. The first attack on the Supreme Court was mounted by Nawaz Sharif's goons, who physically assaulted judges because they were angered by a decision that ran counter to their master's interests when he was prime minister.

Those who had hoped that, with Benazir's death, the Peoples Party might start a new chapter are likely to be disappointed. Zardari's ascendancy will almost certainly split the party over the next few years. He was loathed by many activists, who held him responsible for his wife's downfall. Now he is their leader.

The global consensus that jihadis or Al Qaeda killed Benazir Bhutto fell apart within a fortnight of her murder. It emerged that when Benazir asked the United States for a Karzai-style phalanx of privately contracted former U.S. marine bodyguards, the Pakistan government saw it as a breach of sovereignty and contemptuously rejected the suggestion. Hillary Clinton and Senator Joseph Biden, chairman of the Senate Foreign Relations Committee, publicly hinted that the convict's badge should be pinned on General Musharraf and not Al Qaeda for the murder, a sure sign that sections of the U.S. establishment were thinking it was time to dump the Pakistani president. He, of course, angrily denied any association with the Bhutto murder and asserted that even if she had survived, she would not have been able to handle the crisis in Pakistan:

The United States thought Benazir was the right person to fight terrorists. Who is the best person to fight? You need three qualities
today if you want to fight the extremists and the terrorists. Number
one, you must have the military with you. Well, she was very
unpopular with the military. Very unpopular. Number two, you
shouldn't be seen by the entire religious lobby to be alien—a nonreligious person. The third element: don't be seen as an extension of
the United States. Now I am branded as an extension, but not to the
extent she was. Pakistanis know that I can be tough. I can speak out
against Hillary Clinton. I can speak out against anyone. These are
the elements. You be the judge.*

Washington's problem is that, with Benazir dead, the only phone
number in Islamabad they can call is that of General Ashfaq Kayani, the
Fort Leavenworth–trained head of the army. Nawaz Sharif is regarded
in Washington as a lightweight and a Saudi poodle (his close business
and religious affinities with the kingdom are well-known) and hence
not 100 percent reliable, though, given the U.S.-Saudi alliance, poor
Sharif is puzzled as to why this should exclude him from consideration.
He and his brother are both ready to do Washington's bidding but
would prefer the Saudi king to Musharraf as the imperial messenger.

A temporary solution to the crisis was available. This would have
required General Musharraf's replacement as president by a less contentious figure, an all-party government of unity to prepare the basis
for genuine elections within six months, and the reinstatement of the
sacked Supreme Court judges to investigate Benazir's murder without
fear or favor. Musharraf has finally discarded his uniform and handed
over the military to Kayani. He should simultaneously have retired
from political life since it was the uniform that had led him to the presidency. It would have been a new start, but Pakistan's history is replete
with leaders who had no desire to besmirch themselves with new ideas.
Politics of the short term is always in command. This turbulent year
virtually telescoped the entire history of the country, barring a province

---

*Interview with *Newsweek*, January 12, 2008.

on the verge of defection. One of the more depressing features of the Pakistani military-bureaucratic elite—which has governed the country almost continuously since it was founded in 1947—is its startling lack of originality. It regularly repeats old mistakes. Never is this more obvious than during extended periods of direct or indirect military rule (1958–71, 1977–89, 1999–2008).

Social and political rank in much of today's world is determined by wealth. Power and money cohabit the same space. The result is a mutant democracy whose function is to seal off all possibilities of redistributing wealth and power or enhancing its own standing with the citizenry. Some exceptions remain. In China, for instance, the party hierarchy remains dominant, a partial reflection, perhaps, of the ancient mandarin tradition that insisted on educational qualifications as the principal criteria for social advancement. In Pakistan, the brightest kids dream of becoming stockbrokers in New York; the most ambitious imagine themselves in uniform. The immeasurable importance of the army determines the entire political culture of the country. The chief of staff is the single person on whom the gaze of the political community in Pakistan rests semipermanently. Next in line of importance is the U.S. ambassador. A failure to grasp this basic reality makes it genuinely difficult to understand the past or present of the country.

Throughout its sixty-year history, political life in Pakistan has been dominated by a series of clashes between general and politician, with civilian bureaucrats pretending to be impartial seconds, while mostly favoring the military. The final arbiter is usually Washington. The statistics reveal the winner. Bureaucrats and unelected politicians ran Pakistan for eleven years, the army has ruled the country for thirty-four years, and elected representatives have been in power for fifteen years. It is a dismal record, but it had Washington's strong approval as revealed by an inspection of each of the dictatorships in turn.

8

On the Flight Path of
American Power

The 9/11 Commission Report, published in July 2004, pronounced, among other things, that the Musharraf government was the
best if not the only hope for long-term stability in Pakistan and
Afghanistan. The turbulence required a strongman, and as long as Pakistan was on board in the "war against terror" and prepared to fight the
forces of extremism, the United States owed long-term and comprehensive support to a regime committed to "enlightened moderation."

The word association forces me to digress briefly and recall the late
conservative senator Barry Goldwater's dictum in his speech accepting
the Republican presidential nomination in 1964: "I would remind you
that extremism in the defense of liberty is no vice! And let me remind
you also that moderation in the pursuit of justice is no virtue." Mal-
colm X defended this view eloquently in one of his last public appear-
ances, at which I was present. Leaving aside important differences of
how to interpret "liberty," this is also the view today of many who resist
the United States in Iraq and Afghanistan, though unfortunately most
of them would not agree with a 1981 assessment by the same senator
during a Senate speech in which he offered sage advice to his own party
that applied equally to the Washington-backed Afghan insurgents bat-
tling the godless Russians at the time:

On religious issues there can be little or no compromise. There is no position on which people are so immovable as their religious beliefs. There is no more powerful ally one can claim in a debate than Jesus Christ, or God, or Allah, or whatever one calls this supreme being. But like any powerful weapon, the use of God's name on one's behalf should be used sparingly. The religious factions that are growing throughout our land are not using their religious clout with wisdom. They are trying to force government leaders into following their position one hundred percent. If you disagree with these religious groups on a particular moral issue, they complain, they threaten you with a loss of money or votes or both.

I'm frankly sick and tired of the political preachers across this country telling me as a citizen that if I want to be a moral person, I must believe in A, B, C, and D. Just who do they think they are? And from where do they presume to claim the right to dictate their moral beliefs to me? And I am even more angry as a legislator who must endure the threats of every religious group who thinks it has some God-granted right to control my vote on every roll call in the Senate. I am warning them today: I will fight them every step of the way if they try to dictate their moral convictions to all Americans in the name of "conservatism."

These strictures had little real impact. Religious fundamentalism soon occupied the White House, and its equally fundamentalist enemy targeted Wall Street and the Pentagon. The advice of *The 9/11 Commission Report* was subsequently accepted by Congress and the Intelligence Reform and Terrorism Prevention Act of 2004 (Public Law 108–458). The recommendations in relation to Pakistan were put into effect by calling for a program of sustained U.S. aid to Pakistan and instructing the president to report to Congress what a long-term U.S. strategy to engage with and support would entail. This was followed in November 2005 by a subsidiary appraisal from the commissioners that offered only a C grade to U.S. efforts in encouraging Pakistan's anti-extremism policies and contained a warning that the country "remains a sanctuary and training ground for terrorists." This view, widespread in the United States and Europe, is regularly reflected in the media and appears to have infected the political culture of both regions.

Stanley Kurtz, a fellow of the Hudson Institute and Hoover Institution, recently wrote, "In a sense global Islam is now Waziristan writ large. . . . Waziristan now seeks to awaken the tribal jihadist side of the global Muslim soul." It is not uncommon to read gibberish of this variety from a number of neocon pundits. As suggested earlier in this book, their equivalents were expressing equally nonsensical views in the eighties when the tribal areas were regarded as freedom writ large and most Western journalists meekly followed "advice" and referred to the mujahideen as "freedom fighters." The same people continue to inhabit the same region. Once a necessary steamroller to defeat the Russians, now it appears that they themselves have to be steamrollered into oblivion. What has changed is the global priorities of the United States. This explains the new language. It is relatively easy for state intellectuals (those employed by instrumentalist think tanks and swathes of the academy) in the United States to somersault themselves into new positions and fall into line with imperial needs as required. It's much more difficult for client states to behave in exactly the same way. This explains the crisis that has erupted on Pakistan's western frontiers.

The British Empire was once embroiled in the same region. For them too Waziristan was evil writ large. Their ideologues (and later their Pakistani mimics) produced a great deal of literature on this rugged region, a crude anthropology to justify war and imperial domination. What is today ascribed to Islam alone was in those earlier times seen as a genetic characteristic of the Pashtun race and some of its more recalcitrant tribal components. Here is Mr. Temple, a senior British civil servant in 1855, sharing his opinions with his colleagues in terms and language that would have been appreciated by General Custer:

> Now these tribes are savages—noble savages perhaps—and not without some virtue and generosity, but still absolutely barbarians nevertheless. . . . In their eyes their one great commandment is blood for blood, and fire and sword for all infidels. . . . They are a sensual race . . . very avaricious . . . thievish and predatory to the last

degree. . . . The Pathan mother offers prayers that her son may be a successful robber. . . . It would never even occur to their minds that an oath on the Koran was binding. . . . They are fierce and blood-thirsty.*

Here is another cultivated imperial officer, Mr. Ibbetson, writing in 1881:

The true Pathan is perhaps the most barbaric of all the races with which we are brought into contact. . . . He is bloodthirsty, cruel and vindictive in the highest degree. . . . He does not know what truth or faith is. . . . It is easy to convict him out of his own mouth; here are some of his proverbs: "a Pathan's enmity smoulders like a dung fire"; "speak good words to an enemy very softly; gradually destroy him root and branch."

To demonstrate that the Scots were not going to be left behind, here is Mr. MacGregor a few years later:

. . . There is no doubt, like other Pathans, they would not shrink from any falsehood, however atrocious, to gain an end. Money could buy their services for the foulest deed.

The author who cites these dozens of similar references also reveals:

The Wazirs are Muhammadans of the Sunni sect, but, like any other Pathan tribe, they are not particularly strict in the performance of their religious duties. The mullahs have influence only as far as the observances of religion go, and are powerless in political matters, but the Wazirs are an especially democratic and independent peo-ple, and even their own Maliks [tribal leaders] have little real con-trol over them.†

---

*Colonel H. C. Wylly, *From the Black Mountain to Waziristan* (London: 1912).
†Ibid.

The Afghan wars of the twentieth century changed all that and the mullahs became much more powerful, but what remains true is that the use of force, as the British discovered, can never be a permanent solution. Britain's successor state in the region carried on in similar fashion, first using mercenary tribesmen to invade Kashmir in 1948 and subsequently using them during the first Afghan war from 1979 to 1989. This raises interesting questions regarding the place occupied by Pakistan in relation to the United States.

For instance, whose interests are really being served by Pakistan's foreign policy from 1947 till today, give or take Zulfiqar Ali Bhutto's last few years in office? Is it the case that some senior cabinet ministers, generals, diplomats, and selected civil servants have often reported directly to Washington, circumventing their own respective chains of command? And, if so, why has this been the case for sixty years? It is not a pretty tale.

The Great Leader had tried to rent his house to the new world power and failed. His colleagues were altogether more ambitious. With Jinnah's encouragement the new rulers of Pakistan developed an early communal awareness that to survive they had to rent their country. An open auction was considered unrealistic. There was only one possible buyer. They were quite frank on this level and told Washington that after an initial fee of $2 billion to meet their "administrative expenses" for the first few years, they would still need "a regular source of finance" to keep going. This demand has been a constant of Pakistani politics. As their lobbyist in the United States in 1947, the shrewd, if foul-tongued, bureaucrat Ghulam Mohammed, doubling then as the country's first minister of finance, chose the Chase National Bank of New York. Jinnah sent a trusted aide, Laiq Ali, with a memorandum spelling out the country's needs to the bank chairman, Winthrop W. Aldrich. He read it carefully, improved its language, and suggested some changes, and then it was officially forwarded to Foggy Bottom.

When Laiq met State Department officials, he stressed that the new country "presently faced a Soviet threat on its Western frontier." This was a foolish fabrication as the State Department was well aware. The Soviet Union, wrecked by the war, was concentrating its energies on rebuilding the country and shoring up Eastern Europe. The United

States was busy securing Western Europe and Japan, as well as keeping an eye on China, where the Eighth Route Army was beginning to threaten a Communist victory. The offer to buy Pakistan and its armed forces in perpetuity had no real appeal at the time. An internal memorandum circulated by the Office for Near Eastern Affairs was blunt: "It was obvious from this approach that Pakistan was thinking in terms of the U.S. as a primary source of military strength, and since this would involve virtual U.S. military responsibility for the new Dominion, our reply to the Pakistan request was negative."

This was made clear to Laiq Ali, though a sweetener was offered in the shape of an emergency loan to help alleviate social needs. A dejected Laiq then asked if money could be made available for certain specialist development projects. When his American interlocutors queried if these had been worked out in detail, he responded that he had knowledge only of a projected paper mill, in which he himself was interested. Unfortunately the official documents do not minute the informal reactions of officials. Washington did not even bother responding to the generous Pakistani offer to sell its army.

Confronted with this unexpected rejection, the Great Leader's special envoy asked if some money could be provided to buy some blankets and medicines for the refugees from India. This request was also turned down, but with the possibility that the United States might sell army surplus to Pakistan at a rate considerably lower than the market price. All the while Laiq was cabling Jinnah that the talks were going well. The Great Leader must have had his doubts. He instructed a veteran pro-British Muslim League leader and later prime minister, Sir Feroze Khan Noon, then on his way to Turkey, to call on the U.S. ambassador in Ankara and exert a bit more pressure. "Darkness at Noon" (a sobriquet subsequently awarded him by the *Pakistan Times*) sprang to his task with alacrity and penned the following "confidential memorandum," so crude that it must have both appalled and entertained what was at the time a sophisticated State Department under George C. Marshall's leadership:

> The Mussalmans in Pakistan are against Communism. The Hindus
> have an Ambassador in Moscow, Mrs Pandit, who is the sister of the
> Hindu Prime Minister in Delhi, Mr Nehru, and the Russians have

got an Ambassador in Delhi, the Hindu capital. We the Mussul-
mans of Pakistan have no Ambassador in Moscow nor is there any
Ambassador in Karachi—our capital. . . . If USA help Pakistan to
become a strong and independent country . . . then the people of
Pakistan will fight to last man against Communism to keep their
freedom and preserve their way of life.

There was no response. A desperate Noon then appealed to the
Turkish government for military equipment, but they turned him
down and immediately informed Washington of their decision. The
reason for the indifference was not a mystery. The United States,
Britain, and the Soviet Union agreed that the single most important
country in the region was India. In 1948, Pakistan had attempted to
solve the dispute with India over Kashmir by force. Kashmir was a
Muslim-majority province in India, but its Hindu maharaja had signed
the papers of accession and joined the Indian federation without consulting the people. This created real anger, and to keep Kashmiri
nationalists on his side, the Indian prime minister, Jawaharlal Nehru,
had promised a referendum that would allow Kashmiris to determine
their own future. It never happened. An enormous literature exists on
this subject, and I have written about it elsewhere at some length.*
Here it is only necessary to recall that the irregulars dispatched by Pakistan to take Kashmir were the same "terror tribes" that occupy the
news headlines today. They were much less disciplined at the time.
They were led by Pakistan army officers but were often out of control.
Their untamed tribal egoism—looting and raping nuns en route—led
to military disaster, holding back the assault on Srinagar. Indian troops
secured the airport in that capital city, landed more troops, and the
fighting was soon over. The British generals commanding both armies
had had enough and refused to tolerate any escalation of the conflict.
A Line of Control was established and Kashmir was unfairly divided.
India obtained what its prime minister described as the "snowy bosom"
of this stunningly beautiful region, leaving Pakistan with what can only

---

* *Clash of Fundamentalisms: Crusades, Jihads and Modernity* (London and New York: 2002),
chapter 18, "The Story of Kashmir."

be referred to as its bony posterior. Since then the dispute has led to semipermanent tension between the two countries. Even at the height of the Cold War, by which time, as is outlined below, Pakistan had become its closest of allies, the United States maintained an even-handed approach to Kashmir, a clear signal that it was not prepared to jeopardize its long-term interests in South Asia.

Pakistan kept trying to sell itself. Jinnah, deeply hostile to the British Labour government, told the U.S. ambassador not to be "misled by the UK," which was pro-India, but to understand that Pakistan alone could be a crucial ally against Soviet expansionism. Jinnah, who must have overdosed on Rudyard Kipling's novels, insisted that Soviet agents were present in Kalat and Gilgit in search of a base in Baluchistan. It was pure fantasy. More of the same was on offer from Pakistan's foreign minister, Zafarullah Khan, in New York. His line was marginally more sophisticated. Accepting that India was the major power, he pleaded with the United States to shore up Pakistan, whose people were genetically anticommunist, since this was the best way to protect India against the Soviet Union, which would send its armies through the Khyber Pass. This ploy did not work either, but Pakistan's persistence would ultimately pay off.

During the Korean War (1950–53) the United States finally turned to Pakistan and slowly began to incorporate its military and bureaucracy into its new security arrangements for the region. In 1953, former Pakistani ambassador to the United States Mohammad Ali Bogra was prime minister and, while opening a General Motors assembly plant in Karachi, once again suggested that "ties of goodwill and friendship can be forged on a permanent basis."

The United States responded by sending wheat as "aid." It was in fact part of the U.S. government's domestic price-support scheme to reduce a large domestic wheat surplus. Simultaneously John Foster Dulles, the secretary of state, put out a statement branding Pakistan as "a bulwark for freedom in Asia." The Pakistani prime minister responded obsequiously.

The country's largest English-language daily, the *Pakistan Times,* was not impressed and blasted the statement editorially on July 27, 1953:

They [Pakistanis] will find it somewhat difficult to understand the meaning of the Prime Minister's assertion, on the occasion of the first US food ship, that Pakistan and America speak the "same language regarding the ideals of freedom and democracy." They will indeed find it hard to work out a common factor between their ideals of freedom and such concrete expressions of American foreign policy as innumerable strategic bases round the globe, open support to the crumbling Western Empires and their indigenous puppets in the Orient, alliance with such retrograde elements as the Kuomintang and the Rhee gang, and the strengthening of Wall Street's hold on various Middle Eastern economies. They will also wonder how to reconcile their cherished dreams of a democratic political and social order with the cruel realities of American life such as racial discrimination and the lynching of Negroes, persecution of intellectuals and witchhunting.*

Military pacts and aid came together and would soon be followed by military dictatorships. In September 1954, Pakistan publicly declared it had become a willing tool by joining the Southeast Asia Treaty Organization together with Thailand and the Philippines. Other Southeast Asian countries included the United States, Britain, France, Australia, and New Zealand. Exactly one year later, in September 1955, Pakistan joined another Western outfit known as the Baghdad Pact, which included King Faisal's Iraq, Iran, Turkey, and Britain. Naturally, all this took place without the benefit of a single general election in Pakistan. Public anger could not be registered democratically. A U.S. Senate report, "Technical Assistance: Final Report of Committee on Foreign Relations," published on March 12, 1957, confirmed what

---

*These newspapers were part of the Progressive Papers Ltd chain, which included an Urdu political-cultural weekly, *Lail-o-Nahar* (Day and Night). Set up in Lahore with Jinnah's support in 1946, the newspapers were, in fact, owned and edited by left-wing intellectuals, some of them sympathetic to or members of the tiny Pakistan Communist Party. They included the poet Faiz Ahmed Faiz, literary critics Sibte Hasan and Ahmed Nadeem Qasmi. My father, Mazhar Ali Khan, was the editor of the *Pakistan Times*. I recently found a letter in his archives from the U.S. ambassador disinviting him from dinner because of a "hostile" editorial on the United States. The entire chain, a permanent irritation to every regime, was taken over by the military dictatorship of Ayub Khan in April 1959.

many Pakistanis were beginning to suspect: "From a political view-point, U.S. military aid has strengthened Pakistan's armed services, *the greatest single stabilizing force in the country* [my italics—TA], and has encouraged Pakistan to participate in collective defense arrangements."

IN JULY 1959, General Ayub, now firmly in control, agreed to the establishment of a top-secret U.S. military base in Badaber, near Peshawar. The aim was to spy on the Soviet Union. In May of the following year, the Russians downed a U-2 spy plane that had taken off from Peshawar and captured the pilot, Gary Powers. When the United States denied the spy flights, the Russians produced the poor pilot. The Soviet leader, Nikita Khrushchev, entertaining General Maxwell Taylor at a banquet in Moscow, reportedly clambered onto the table in a rage and shouted, "You Americans are like dogs. You eat and shit in the same place." Khrushchev later addressed a press conference at which he announced that he knew where the plane had taken off from and that Peshawar was now a Soviet target, marked with a red circle. I remember well the panic that gripped the Pakistani military establishment, not to mention the brave burghers of Peshawar, some of whom hurriedly left the city. It was empty rocket-rattling, but it highlighted Pakistan's dependent status. A few years previously, the acting foreign minister, Zulfiqar Ali Bhutto, had asked the U.S. embassy whether he could visit the base. He was politely told it was out of bounds, but that the base commanders would be happy to serve him coffee and cakes in the cafeteria. Decades later a general could write about how "Pakistan felt deceived because the US had kept her in the dark about such clandestine spy operations launched from Pakistan's territory," but this was pious nonsense. Ayub Khan knew perfectly well that the USAF base was not a rest and recreation stop for crews en route to the Far East.

Following the U-2 incident, policy makers in Washington (always more concerned with India) suggested to Ayub Khan that the best way to safeguard the subcontinent against Communism was to set up a "joint defense" system. The general agreed and suggested this to the Indian prime minister, Jawaharlal Nehru, who had carefully kept India nonaligned in the Cold War. Nehru's response was a clear rejection. "Joint defense against who?" he asked frostily.

Ayub had done as he was asked, and his reward was an official state visit to Camelot in 1961, where he was given the red-carpet treatment, reserved for special clients. A presidential yacht transported him to Mount Vernon with the Kennedys. Later he addressed a joint session of Congress, saying, "The only people who will stand by you in Asia are the people of Pakistan—provided you are prepared to stand by them." This was not completely accurate, and the use of the word *people* enraged many back home. He was a dictator who had denied citizens the franchise, so they felt he had no right to speak for them. There was much anger and many poems written.

The following year India suffered a heavy defeat in the mysterious Sino-Indian border war launched by China to regain disputed territory that was of little significance. The short war was actually intended as a shot across Soviet bows via its Indian friend and was, in fact, the first real indication of a serious rift between the Soviet Union and China, though few interpreted it as such at the time. For the United States it was a case of "unprovoked Communist aggression" on the part of the Chinese. The United States and Britain began to provide the Indian armed forces with the latest weaponry. Ayub was livid but impotent. Not till a decade after Beijing's public break with Moscow did Washington begin to think seriously about cultivating China. And here Pakistan would prove extremely helpful as a go-between, a role its leaders always relished.

When it became obvious even to Ayub Khan that the United States would never back Pakistan militarily in any conflict with India, he began to get slightly nervous. Public opinion had been opposed to the security pacts for some time. After the Pakistan-Indian war of 1965 the United States stopped its military aid to Pakistan. This shook the military-bureaucratic regime to its core. Zulfiqar Ali Bhutto, the foreign minister, was sacked for demanding a new turn based on bilateral relations. He would later explain his position thus:

Each of Pakistan's multilateral and bilateral military commitments became useless the moment the United States unilaterally termi-

nated military assistance to Pakistan. With the removal of reciproc-
ity, the agreements became void ipso facto. Notwithstanding this
incontestable position, the Government of Ayub Khan, committing
dereliction of its elementary duty to the people of Pakistan, refused
to renounce the agreements. It chose to endanger the security of
Pakistan without an iota of corresponding protection. It cannot be
forgotten that Pakistan assumed the liabilities of the Cold War in
return for military assistance and political support on Kashmir. The
military assistance ended three years ago and the political support
went earlier. The United States' position on Kashmir began to shift
imperceptibly since the first Sino-Indian conflict of October 1959.
This was established beyond doubt when Pakistan took the dispute
to the Security Council in 1964. The United States imposed an
embargo on the delivery of military equipment to Pakistan when
the country was struggling for its survival against an aggressor five
times its size. For three years a complete ban was placed on the sale
of weapons and spare parts to Pakistan. The government of a country in three military alliances had to run from pillar to post in search
of armaments and spare parts, from black market centers and notorious arms peddlers. Throughout this difficult period, Ayub Khan
refused to free the country from the burden of these obsolete
alliances. On the contrary, he permitted the United States' base in
Peshawar to operate until the expiry of its lease in July 1969. Not
even those countries which are the pillars of NATO would find it
possible to assume such onerous one-sided military obligations on
behalf of the United States or any other country.*

As this lengthy extract reveals, even in his most radical phase when
he was out of power, Pakistan's most intelligent and least provincial
political leader was obsessed with the idea of India as a primary enemy.
This had formed the cornerstone of the country's foreign policy since
1947. It affected how the country functioned internally and produced
a warped political culture. During a lengthy conversation with Bhutto

---

*Zulfiqar Ali Bhutto, *Pakistan and Alliances* (Lahore: 1972).

in the summer of 1969 at his Clifton residence in Karachi, I questioned him about this, pointing out that playing on national chauvinism did not advance any progressive cause. This was soon after the 1965 war with India, which he had strongly pushed for. "How else do you think we're going to get rid of this bloody army which rules the country? Defeat in this war weakened them. That's why the big movement succeeded."* Bhutto was capable of extreme forms of cynicism, but did he actually believe this? I don't know. Privately he was a great admirer of Jawaharlal Nehru's and had read all his books, one of which he referred to in his death-cell memoir. Perhaps he understood at some level that Jinnah had created a state but not a nation. Pakistani nationalism was incredibly weak, and Bengali, Pashtun, Sindhi, and Baluch identities were much stronger. Bengal would soon be detached, but the others remained. The only way of forging a Pakistani identity was by identifying an enemy. India or "the Hindu." It was crude, but largely ineffective outside the Punjab. Even there many were ready for a different message from the stale chauvinism and the constant sloganizing that "Kashmir is in danger" mouthed by most politicians to garner cheap support. And so "anti-Indianism" became a substitute for any genuine anticolonial nationalism, a problem India never had to confront. Despite the vast number of ethnicities, languages, and varied cultural traditions, with a sense of their own epic literature and place in the region, there was never any serious problem about the people considering themselves Indian, with a few temporary exceptions—Sikhs in the Punjab, tribals in Nagaland—resulting from the political stupidity of the ruling elite.

Reading speeches made by Pakistan's first batch of bureaucrats-

---

*Also present were Mustafa Khar and Mumtaz Bhutto, staunch members of the PPP. Our conversation rapidly changed course when General Yahya's son was announced. I had just written a savage "Letter from Pakistan" for the satirical magazine *Private Eye* in which I had denounced the son as well as the father. On seeing me, Yahya junior turned to Bhutto and asked, "Sir, who do you think writes these lies about my family in *Private Eye*?" Bhutto responded with a twinkle in his eye, "Ask Tariq. He lives there." Yahya junior looked at me. "I have no idea" was my response, "but I suspect it's their editor, Richard Ingrams, who knows a lot about this world." There was much merriment after Yahya junior departed. That this surreal conversation took place at all surprises me more now than it did at the time.

turned-politicians, one is struck by a permanent "inferiority complex" in relation to India. To counter the latter, they avoid mentioning that Pakistan has only a brief history. Instead they hark back to the Muslim warriors of the early medieval period and sometimes the Mogul emperors, though these were never a good role model for young Pakistan since religion mattered little to the emperors and even the pious Aurungzeb—the last of the great Moguls—preserved an imperial army led by Hindu generals and did not attempt to make the mosque the center of state power. And so Pakistani history was never written as a common history with the rest of India till 1947, but as a crude separatist account of Indian Muslims and their glorious past.

As the United States moved closer to India after the Sino-Indian border war in 1959, Pakistan made a concerted effort to develop friendly relations with China. Ayub Khan's trip to Beijing in 1964 prefigured Richard Nixon's a decade later. The "mass welcome" laid on by the Chinese went to Ayub's head, and long after he had been driven out by a genuine mass upsurge in his own country, he would watch home movies of his China triumph. Washington was not too pleased, but found the relationship useful, and Pakistanis working for the CIA were sometimes used to spy on China, including at least one pilot, known to me, who flew PIA passenger flights to China. The friendship was instrumental for both sides, and Pakistani bureaucrats and government ministers were often debriefed in Washington. The poet Habib Jalib joked in a long satirical poem entitled "Adviser" in which the eponymous hero says to the president:

> This is what I said to him:
> "China now our dearest friend
> On it does our life depend
> But the system that there prevails
> Do not go near it,
> Salute it from afar
> Salute it from afar"

In time the Chinese system too would be turned upside down, becoming a model for Asian capitalism and making a wholehearted embrace extremely desirable for Pakistan. Throughout, the cold war with India remained a constant. The official view that India rather than the structural crisis inherent in the Pakistani state since its foundation had led to the explosion in East Bengal remained embedded in official thinking, hardening into the basis for policy making. But it was impossible to ignore that in 1971 neither China nor the United States helped "save Pakistan," as had been predicted by some and hoped by others. They let it bleed. What was the dominant view in India?

Is it the case that the triumphalist Indian leadership was planning to eliminate West Pakistan as well? There are divergent views. The first is that of Indira Gandhi, the Indian prime minister at the time, as divulged to the author during a lengthy off-the-record discussion in 1984, some months before her assassination.

After a formal interview for a book on India that I was working on at the time,* Mrs. Gandhi turned to me and said, "Now my turn to ask you some questions. I've read your new book [*Can Pakistan Survive?*]. You know these generals and how they think and operate. I am being told by my people here that Pakistan is preparing a surprise attack on us in Kashmir. What do you think?" I was taken aback. The first thought that went through my mind was that a preemptive strike by India was being considered. I was blunt in my response, pointing out that with Pakistan heavily involved in running the mujahideen on behalf of the United States, it was inconceivable that they would want to open up a second front. It would be so irrational that even if some blowhards in the high command wanted to, it would immediately be vetoed by Washington. She persisted with her questioning, and I, in turn, refused to accept that any such plan existed or was possible. I had used the word *irrational* a great deal and she turned on me.

"I am amazed that someone like you thinks that generals are rational human beings."

I burst out laughing. There was a certain irony. I, with a near hydrophobic horror of military dictators, had been put in the position of "defending" the Pakistan army.

---

*The book was *The Nehrus and the Gandhis: An Indian Dynasty,* the latest edition of which was published in 2005.

"But this would be so irrational that it would be insane," I replied. "It would mean a state and its generals deciding to commit suicide. They will not do that, and I say this as someone who is completely opposed to them and am still persona non grata because of my views on what they did in Bengal."

The discussion then took an amazing turn.

"Let me tell you something," she said. "And this is about *our* generals. After Pakistan had surrendered, General Manekshaw walked into this very office and saluted me."

Mrs. Gandhi, like Zulfiqar Bhutto, was a good mimic, and her description was very diverting. What she then described surprised me a great deal. After the salute Manekshaw asked her whether the military high command had permission to "finish the job." This meant crossing the border and taking West Pakistan. Given the demoralized state of the Pakistan army, the outcome was preordained unless the Chinese and the United States entered the conflict.

"This being India," Mrs. Gandhi continued, "I thanked the general and said the cabinet would consider the suggestion."

She then summoned an urgent cabinet meeting.

"When I reported the military request, the ministers were initially very excited and many of them were prepared to go along with it. When the meeting began, I was alone. When it ended, I had a unanimous vote for an immediate cease-fire. I tell you this to show you that in India too generals can be very irrational. In Pakistan they run the country."

I repeated what I had said earlier, and discussion on this subject ended. She then told me that the Israelis had offered to carry out a lightning strike against Pakistan's nuclear reactor provided they could use an Indian air force base. "I turned down this offer. I told them we can do it ourselves if we wanted."

Our conversation concluded with her talking about Bhutto and his visit to Simla to sign the peace treaty after the war in Bangladesh and how nervous he had been. She asked after his children and asked me to convey her warm regards to Benazir.

"You know, I was in prison myself when they hanged Bhutto. It upset me a great deal. Had I been prime minister, I would not have let it happen." Mrs. Gandhi seemed very sure on this front.

The next day I was invited to an "off-the-record" discussion at the India International Centre, where I was staying with twenty or so people, mainly civil servants, intelligence officials, journalists representing the Soviet and American lobbies, etc. "We hear you had a very interesting discussion with our prime minister yesterday," said the chair. "That's what we want to discuss." For two hours they tried to convince me that I was wrong and that Pakistan was preparing a strike in Kashmir. I remained patient, explaining at great length why this was impossible given the Afghan involvement and given that General Zia was extremely unpopular in the Sind, Baluchistan, parts of the Frontier, and sections of the Punjab. Zia could not afford any crazy war that he would lose. That is why he was desperate at the moment for some form of rapprochement and kept turning up in India uninvited on the pretext of watching cricket matches. Most of the spooks present were not convinced, and finally I told them that if India wanted a preemptive strike against Pakistan, I couldn't stop them, but they should think up a better excuse since nobody in the world would believe India had been attacked first.

This story has an amusing footnote. Back in London several months later, I described this conversation to Benazir Bhutto. She listened carefully, then asked, "But why did you tell them that our generals weren't preparing an attack?" At that moment she reminded me most of her father. She too thought the best way to break the military's grip on politics was by helping them to be defeated in a war.

I recalled my Delhi conversations most vividly when I heard that Mrs. Gandhi was assassinated by her two Sikh bodyguards in October 1984. It later emerged that one of them had visited Sikh training camps in Pakistan. For though no frontal assault was being prepared, the desire for revenge among sections of the military never evaporated. Mrs. Gandhi's internal problems with the Sikh community were of her own making, and Pakistan took advantage of Sikh discontent by training Sikh terrorists. Could it be that the CIA and the DIA had obtained information from their agents inside the Indian establishment suggesting that the Indians were seriously considering a "preemptive strike" against Pakistan? This would certainly have destabilized the entire Afghan operation, not to mention the military dictatorship in Pakistan.

A high-powered secret decision might have made Washington get rid of the Indian prime minister using Sikh hitmen trained in Pakistan. That certainly was the view of senior civil servants in New Delhi, who told me that the internal report submitted to the new prime minister linked Pakistan to the assassins and had not been made public for fear of creating a new war fever.

Further evidence in this vein was offered to me on a trip to Pakistan in 2006. On the flight back to London I encountered an old acquaintance. I had first spotted him in the departure lounge at the airport, surrounded by uniformed policemen as I waited to board the PIA flight. He took a seat not far from me in the business class, which was virtually empty. I was buried in a novel when he came and stood near my seat. We exchanged salaams.

"Recognize me?" he asked.

"Forgive me," I replied, "I . . ."

"I never forgave you when you were young. Why should I now? Look at me closely and try again."

I did as he asked. Slowly a picture formed of a pimply teenager who many decades ago used to hang out with my gang of friends during the delightful summer months we spent in the Himalayan foothills in Nathiagali. I remembered his mother first as cooking the best semolina *halwa* in the country, and that helped recall his name. He roared with delight.

"What do you do these days?" I asked him.

"You're going to kill me."

"Try me."

"I was a senior security officer for Bhutto and later Zia."

"You served both."

"It was my job."

I sighed in despair. "And after that?"

He was now an even more senior intelligence officer, on his way to a European conference to discuss better ways of combatting terrorism.

"Is OBL still alive?"

He didn't reply.

"When you don't reply, I'll assume the answer is yes."

I asked the question again. He didn't reply.

"Do you know where he is?"

He burst out laughing. "I don't, and even if I did, do you think I'd tell you?"

"No, but I thought I'd ask anyway. Does anyone know where he is?"

He shrugged his shoulders.

I insisted, "Nothing in our wonderful country is ever a secret. Someone must know."

"Three people know. Possibly four. You can guess who they are."

I could. "And Washington?"

"They don't want him alive?"

"And your boys can't kill him."

"Listen, friend, why should we kill the goose that lays the golden eggs?"

As long as Osama was alive, the official seemed to be saying, the flow of dollars would never stop. It sounded credible, but was it true? I shifted the conversation to another subject. Why had General Zia's assassination never been properly investigated? He shrugged his shoulders, saying Washington wasn't keen to dig any deeper. His own view was that the Russians were responsible. This is not an uncommon view among sections of Pakistani intelligence. For most of them the explanation is linked to Afghanistan: it was revenge by Moscow. I think this is pure fantasy. What my informant suggested was more original and contained a sting in the tail. According to him, the Russians owed the Indians a favor (he didn't explain why), and Indian prime minister Rajiv Gandhi (Indira's son) had asked for Zia's head.

"Why?" I inquired in as innocent a tone as I could muster.

"In return for his mother's death."

This was the only semiofficial confirmation I ever received from the Pakistani side regarding Mrs. Gandhi's assassination.

All this is in the past. The current obsession is with the nuclear status of both countries, which could, it is feared, lead to a wipeout of large parts of the subcontinent. The assessment of a "jihadi threat" to Pakistan's nuclear facilities is particularly virulent and not simply on the blogosphere. Otherwise intelligent people are making regular statements that border on hysteria. The following three samples are representative of this overreaction, and numerous others are even less restrained. Matthew Bunn of the Managing the Atom Project at Harvard has said:

> If you can have over forty heavily armed terrorists show up in the middle of Moscow and seize a theatre. How many might show up at some remote Pakistani nuclear weapon storage facility? This is a country that has you know substantial armed remnants of Al Qaeda still operating in the country, that are able to hold off big chunks of the Pakistani regular army and the frontier provinces for weeks at a time. If a huge Al Qaeda force arrives at one of these nuclear weapon storage facilities, what do the guards do? Do they fight, do they help? This strikes me as a very open question.

Art Brown, former CIA operations director, Asia, regards Musharraf as a vital asset without whom there might be serious trouble:

> I think that if Musharraf is removed from office, particularly if he is assassinated and there is a power grab, I think the control over the Pakistani nuclear program would obviously be a concern. We would be concerned over any government that had that kind of a program and lost its leader in a bloody coup. The laboratories themselves are probably less of a concern just because it would take longer to do something with those materials in the laboratories, take them out and sell them. We might be able to intercept that at some point, but the ready-made nuclear weapons that are sitting there in the Pakistani arsenal, those indeed could go out somebody's door and appear in our opponents' box overnight.

Robert Joseph, from the Arms Control section of the U.S. State Department, is equally worried:

> What concerns me the most is that a terrorist has to be successful only one time in terms of acquiring the material and acquiring the nuclear device and detonating that device on an American city or a city anywhere in the world. So what we need to do is have a comprehensive approach for dealing with that threat. We are emphasiz-

ing two key elements. One of course is prevention. So that we deny the terrorist access to fissile material or other weapons of mass destruction of related materials. We also need to put in place, and we are working hard, the protection capabilities, the ability to detect the transfer of this type of material for example. As well as to interdict this material.

Add to this the views of the nuclear historian Scott Sagan in his book and a new dimension emerges:

Pakistan is clearly the most serious concern in the short run. Pakistani weapons lack the advanced Permissive Actions Link (PALS) locks that make it difficult for a terrorist or other unauthorized individual to use a stolen nuclear weapon. In June 2001, Pakistani officials also acknowledged that there were no specialized Pakistani teams trained on how to seize or dismantle a nuclear weapon if one was stolen. No dedicated personnel reliability program (PRP) was in place to ensure the psychological stability and reliability of the officers and guards of Pakistan's nuclear forces. Instead, Pakistani soldiers and scientists with nuclear responsibilities were reviewed and approved for duty if they were not suspected of being Indian agents by the Inter Services Intelligence (ISI) agency.

This is what partially explains U.S. support for Pakistan's military leadership at the expense of democracy and democratic institutions. If we take each argument in turn, what is being said is either risible or applies to Israel and India as well. What if forty heavily armed ultra-right Jewish settlers tried to seize Israeli weapons of mass destruction? Or a small group of hard-core Hindu fundamentalists attempted the same in India? As in Pakistan, they would be apprehended and dealt with. None of these countries has a security force known for its softness to dissidents of any variety. As for "substantial armed remnants" of Al Qaeda, cited by Matthew Bunn, most intelligence reports put their number at well below five hundred. The Pakistan army is currently half a million strong.

And if Musharraf resigns or is removed from the presidency, the military high command would not be affected in the slightest. They would continue to control the security of the nuclear facilities. As for the acquisition of nuclear weapons by "a terrorist," this was much more likely in Russia under Yeltsin than in Pakistan today. After all, much of the fissile material obtained by Pakistan came from Western Europe. Sagan's points are far more relevant, but since he wrote his book in 2003, all the measures whose absence he noted, according to Pakistan's military security experts, are now in place, and the United States is aware of this. The loopholes that existed in terms of selling nuclear technology to friendly states have long since been sealed.

As I have suggested elsewhere in this book, the only way any jihadi groups could penetrate the nuclear facilities would be if the army wanted them to. This is virtually excluded as long as the military does not split, though the possibility of a rupture in the armed forces would be real if the United States insisted on expanding the Afghan war by occupying parts of Pakistan or systematically bombing Pashtun villages suspected of harboring "terrorists." Continuous U.S. pressure on Pakistan's stance toward Israel is also linked to the country's nuclear status. Pakistani officials are told that were they to recognize Israel, some of the pressure on the nuclear issue would dissipate.

Early in March 2008, Shireen Mazari, director general of the Institute of Strategic Studies, revealed that Washington had sent Pakistan a list of eleven demands. These included providing U.S. military and auxiliary staff the right to enter and leave the country without visa restrictions, to carry arms and wear uniforms throughout Pakistan; only U.S. jurisdiction would apply to U.S. nationals, as in Japan. They would also be free to import and export anything, as they currently can in Iraq. In addition to this they wanted free movement of all vehicles and aircraft and total immunity from all claims for damage of property or personnel. The demands were rejected. Mazari concluded her report with the following advice:

> So, for those who feel there is bonhomie and complete understanding between the Pakistan military and the US military, and the trouble only exists at the political level, it is time to do a serious rethink. The first step in dealing rationally with our indigenous terrorist

problem holistically and credibly is to create space between ourselves and the US. As the US adage goes: "There is no such thing as
a free lunch."*

Two months later, Dr. Mazari was unceremoniously sacked from
her job by the Foreign Office and given fifteen minutes to vacate her
office. She was even more angered by a call from Husain Haqqani,
ambassador designate to Washington, who arrived with a bouquet of
flowers to bid her farewell and apologize for the manner of her dismissal. Mazari was blunt in her response. "I know my independent
views have upset the U.S. lobby in Pakistan which dominates the PPP.
That's why I have been sacked."

If this is the prelude to something bigger, such as a partial U.S.
occupation of the North-West Frontier Province, it could trigger a
severe crisis in the army, already under strain carrying out CENTCOM
instructions on the Pakistan-Afghan border. The fallout could have
unpredictable consequences.

AS FAR AS nuclear weapons are concerned, the double standards of the
West are not helpful and are viewed with contempt in most parts of the
world. Nonetheless it's a fact that neither India nor Pakistan benefits
from this weaponry, which has become a new form of sacred property.
The figures speak for themselves. Following the nuclear tests of 1998
the Indian government announced an allocation of $9.9 billion for
defense spending in 1999, an increase of 14 percent over the previous
year. Pakistan, in turn, raised its budget by 8.5 percent to $3.3 billion.
South Asia today is one of the world's most heavily militarized regions.
The Indian and Pakistani armies are two of the world's ten largest war
machines. There is a combined 6:1 ratio of soldiers to doctors. The
social costs of arms spending are horrendous.

It would be to the great advantage of both countries if the billions
spent on nuclear weapons were used to build schools, universities, and

---

*Shireen M. Mazari, "US Yearns for Pak Capitulation," *News* (Islamabad), March 8, 2008.

hospitals and to provide clean water in the villages. Rationality, alas, is the first victim when these two countries quarrel. During the military skirmishes in the snow deserts of Kargil, nuclear threats were exchanged by both states on thirteen separate occasions within three months. This was followed by new terrorist attacks in India. Pakistan denied any responsibility, but New Delhi was unconvinced.

On December 13, 2001, five suicide terrorists armed with automatic rifles, grenades, and explosives killed nine people and wounded two dozen others before being killed themselves in a forty-five-minute battle with security forces outside the Indian parliamentary building. Mercifully parliament wasn't in session that day. Had Indian politicians been killed in the attack, another war between the two states would have been a near certainty.

The Indian home minister, L. K. Advani, a leader of the Hindu-chauvinist Bharatiya Janata Party (BJP), which was then in power, pointed the finger at two well-known Islamist terror groups—Jaish-e-Mohammed and Lashkar-e-Taiba—created and backed by Pakistan's Inter-Services Intelligence. He described what had taken place as the "most alarming act of terrorism in the history of two decades of Pakistan-sponsored terrorism in India. . . . The terrorists and their mentors . . . [wanted] to wipe out the entire political leadership of India." This was clearly an invitation to a military response, and it led to an intense and sharp debate within the Indian elite as to whether they should hit back with a surgical strike on training camps in Pakistani-controlled Kashmir. In the end, thankfully, they decided not to do so.

The groups that attacked the Indian parliament were not only targeting India. Their aim was evidently to provoke a conflict between the two countries. They despised Musharraf for betraying the cause and siding with Washington after 9/11. Their hatred for "Hindu" India was nothing new and had been enhanced by BJP rule in that country. The tragedy is that they came so close to inciting a war. Senior Indian strategists argued that if the United States could bomb a country and change its government while searching for terrorists who ordered the hits on the Pentagon, why could India not do the same? The logic was impeccable, but the outcome could have been a catastrophe of massive proportions. Pakistan's rulers responded with a nuclear threat: if their country's sovereignty was threatened, they would not hesitate to use nuclear weapons. An ugly chill gripped the atmosphere.

Washington sought to reassure India. Simultaneously, it pressured Islamabad to shift rapidly into reverse gear. On January 12, 2002, Musharraf made a landmark speech. He offered India a no-war pact, denuclearization of South Asia, closure of the jihadi training camps in Pakistan, and a total transformation of Indo-Pak relations. While hardline fundamentalist newspapers attacked him, the country remained calm. Not a bird twittered, not a dog barked. So much for the view that ordinary Pakistanis are obsessed with the "Islamic bomb." Pakistan's nuclear capacity had often been used by the jihadi groups as a guarantee of their untouchability. No longer. A positive response from India was vital and could have altered the entire political landscape to the benefit of both countries. But India refused to budge. Its spokesmen continued to mouth platitudes but insisted on "minimum nuclear deterrence" and refused the offer of a no-war pact.

By rejecting Pakistan's denuclearization offer, the Indian government exposed the hollowness of its professed commitment to nuclear disarmament. The folly was compounded by the test-firing of a new Agni missile on the eve of the Republic Day celebrations on January 26, 2002. Apart from being an irresponsible and provocative gesture, the test was a reaffirmation of New Delhi's resolve to proceed with nuclear armaments.

The advocates of a short sharp war against Pakistan are largely confined to the well-off, urban middle classes in India. The poor, in the main, do not favor conflict. They know the dangers it would create inside India with its 200 million Muslims. They know that wars don't come cheap and that they would bear the brunt of the suffering. Three hundred million Indians already live below the poverty line.

Even among the gung ho middle classes the desire for a war would fade were they faced with conscription and required to fight themselves. Unlike bin Laden's followers, these are armchair fundamentalists.

Meanwhile, the Pakistani and Indian armies are on full alert and confront each other across a mine-strewn border. The mines are especially concentrated in cultivated farmlands near the international border and the Line of Control in Kashmir. The local villagers will suffer the consequences for years to come. Already there have been numerous civilian casualties.

New Delhi sees itself as a potential world power. It craves a seat on the UN Security Council. It argues that if small European countries such as Britain and France can possess nuclear weapons, then why not India? The simplest response would be to extend nuclear disarmament and for Europe to initiate the process. The West seems unlikely to oblige. The U.S. military budget remains inflated and accounts for one-half of the world's expenditure on armaments. The old enemy no longer exists, but the Cold War scenarios remain in place. U.S. military planners continue to target Russia and China. The latest wave of NATO expansion that both preceded and followed the war in Yugoslavia hardened Russian opposition to nuclear disarmament. When NATO patrols the Black Sea, what price the "Partnership for Peace"?

Herein lies the crux of the problem. Unless the West begins nuclear disarmament, it has no moral or material basis on which to demand that others do the same. Only a twisted logic accepts that London and Paris can have the bomb, but New Delhi and Islamabad cannot. India and Pakistan are only too aware that nuclear rain and radiation are no respecters of frontiers. It is unlikely that they would resort to first use of these weapons, but that is not sufficient reassurance for the citizens of either country.

While Pakistan's principal preoccupation remains India, its senior partners in Washington have been trying hard to shift Islamabad's focus to the western frontier. This has briefly been discussed in an earlier chapter, but the impact of U.S.-occupied Afghanistan on Pakistan is such that it necessitates a more detailed mapping of the new turbulence afflicting the region.

9

OPERATION ENDURING FREEDOM

Mirage of the "Good" War

THE BUSH-CHENEY ERA IS DRAWING TO A CLOSE, BUT THEIR replacements, despite the debacle in Iraq, are unlikely to settle the American giant back to a digestive sleep. The leitmotif of Cheney's foreign policy was "either you're for us or for terrorism against us." The application of this line meant isolating, intimidating, or invading individual states that did not accept shelter under the U.S. umbrella.

In 2004, as the chaos in Iraq deepened, the war in Afghanistan became the "good war" by comparison. It had been legitimized by the UN—even if the resolution was not passed until after the bombs had finished falling—and backed by NATO. If tactical differences had sharpened over Iraq, they could be resolved in Afghanistan. First Zapatero in Spain, then Prodi in Italy, and most recently Rudd in Australia compensated for pulling troops out from Iraq by dispatching them to Kabul.* France and Germany could extol their peacekeeping or civilizing roles there. For the Scandinavians it became a feel-good war.

---

*Visiting Madrid, after Zapatero's election triumph of March 2008, I was informed by a senior government official that they had considered a total withdrawal from Afghanistan a few months before the elections but had been outmaneuvered by a U.S. promise to Spain that the head of its military was being proposed for commander of the NATO forces and a withdrawal from Kabul would disrupt this possibility. Spain drew back only to discover that they had been tricked.

Meanwhile, the number of Afghani civilians killed has exceeded nearly a hundredfold the 2,746 who died in Manhattan. Unemployment is around 60 percent, and maternal, infant, and child mortality levels are now the highest in the world. Opium production has soared, and the "Neo-Taliban" is growing stronger year by year. A CIA assessment of late 2006 painted a somber picture of Karzai and his regime as hopelessly corrupt and incapable of defending Afghanistan against the Taliban.[*] Increasingly Western commentators have evoked the specter of failure—usually to spur *encore un effort.* But all those who supported the folly must share the misfortune.

TWO PRINCIPAL ARGUMENTS, often overlapping, are put forward as to "what went wrong" in Afghanistan. For liberal interventionists, the answer can be summarized in two words: "not enough."[†] The invasion organized by Bush, Cheney, and Rumsfeld was done "on the cheap." The "light footprint" demanded by the Pentagon meant that too few troops were on the ground in 2001–2. Financial commitment to "nation-building" was insufficient. Though it may now be too late, the answer is to pour in more troops, more money—"multiple billions" over "many years," according to the U.S. ambassador in Kabul.[‡] The second answer to what has gone wrong—advanced by Karzai, the White House, but also the Western media generally—can be summed up in one word: Pakistan. Neither of these arguments holds water.

As suicide bombings increased in Baghdad, Afghanistan became—for American Democrats keen to prove their "security" credentials—the "real front" of the war on terror, supported by every U.S. presidential candidate in the run-up to the 2008 elections, with Senator Barack Obama pressuring the White House to violate Pakistani sovereignty

---

[*]"C.I.A. Review Highlights Afghan Leader's Woes," *New York Times,* November 5, 2006.

[†]See inter alia "The Good War, Still to Be Won," *New York Times,* August 20, 2007; "Gates, Truth and Afghanistan," *New York Times,* February 12, 2008; Francis Fukuyama, ed., *Nation-Building: Beyond Afghanistan and Iraq* (Baltimore: 2006); and successive International Crisis Group reports.

[‡]*New York Times,* November 5, 2006.

whenever necessary. On March 15, 2007, for instance, Obama told NBC, "If you look at what's happening in Afghanistan now, you are seeing the Taliban resurgent, you are seeing Al Qaeda strengthen itself. We have not followed through on the good starts we made in Afghanistan, partly because we took so many resources out and put them in Iraq. I think it is very important for us to begin a planned redeployment from Iraq, including targeting Afghanistan." A few months later on August 1, with the Stars and Stripes providing a suitable backdrop, he addressed the Woodrow Wilson Center in Washington and made it clear that if necessary he would authorize U.S. troops to enter Pakistan on search-and-destroy missions: "Let me make this clear. There are terrorists holed up in those mountains who murdered three thousand Americans. They are plotting to strike again. It was a terrible mistake to fail to act when we had a chance to take out an Al Qaeda leadership meeting in 2005. If we have actionable intelligence about high-value terrorist targets and President Musharraf won't act, we will."

His embittered rival, Senator Hillary Clinton, was not going to let him get away with this too easily. One of her staunchest supporters, Senator Chris Dodd of Connecticut, rebuked Obama the same day (as did the White House) and said, "It is dangerous and irresponsible to leave even the impression that the United States would needlessly and publicly provoke a nuclear power." A week later, during a Democratic presidential debate, Hillary Clinton rapped her rival on the knuckles while raising the specter of a jihadi finger on Pakistan's nuclear trigger:

> Well, I do not believe people running for president should engage in hypotheticals, and it may well be that the strategy we have to pursue on the basis of actionable intelligence—but remember, we've had some real difficult experience with actionable intelligence. . . . But I think it is a very big mistake to telegraph that and to destabilize the Musharraf regime, which is fighting for its life against Islamic extremists, who are in bed with Al Qaeda and Taliban. And remember, Pakistan has nuclear weapons. The last thing we want is to have Al Qaeda–like followers in charge of Pakistan and having access to nuclear weapons. So, you can think big, but remember,

you shouldn't always say everything you think if you're running for
president because it can have consequences across the world, and we
don't need that right now.

With varying degrees of firmness, the occupation of Afghanistan is
also supported by China, Iran, and Russia, though in the case of the latter, there was always a strong element of schadenfreude. Soviet veterans of the Afghan war were amazed to see their mistakes now being
repeated by the United States, despite attempts to portray this as the
ultimate humanitarian conflict. This did not prevent Russian veterans,
especially helicopter pilots, from offering themselves as mercenaries in
Afghanistan. Over two dozen are currently engaged in action over a terrain they know well.

Soon after its launching, the NATO war on Afghanistan was referred
to—including by Cherie Blair and Laura Bush—as a "war to liberate the
women of Afghanistan." Had this been true, it would have been a path-
breaking conflict: the first imperial war in human history to liberate
women. But it wasn't true. This became obvious even before the harsh
realities of the location had dispelled the haze of spin, intended in any
case for the children-citizens at home to make them feel good about
bombing another foreign land (though this did not convince Jenna
Bush, who confided to Daniel Pearl's widow that she was opposed to the
bombing of Afghanistan). And the latest reports from Afghan women's
organizations paint a grim picture of the condition of women in NATO-
occupied Afghanistan. They fared much better during the Russian
period.

HISTORICALLY, ATTEMPTS by the more enlightened sections of the
Afghan elite to improve the condition of the country were regularly sabotaged by the British Empire. Since the nineteenth century, all political
and administrative power in Afghanistan as well as virtually all the land
was under the control of the king, his nobles, and a mosaic of tribal
chiefs. The king was seen as the symbol of Afghan unity and responsible for relations with foreign powers, but his effective authority was
limited to the Pashtun region of the country. Most of the population

were peasants and herdsmen, with artisans and traders, merchants and craftsmen concentrated in the old medieval towns that included Herat, Ghazni, Kandahar, and Kabul.

The two nineteenth-century British attempts to occupy the country ended in partial failure. After the retreat of the second expeditionary force in 1893, the British took over the country's foreign policy while agreeing to its status as a buffer state between British India and czarist Russia. This was accompanied by a further weakening of the buffer as the British divided the Pashtun tribes and their lands by drawing the Durand Line through the mountains as their semipermanent frontier with Afghanistan. The purpose of this was to weaken the Pashtun tribes and thus reduce their political potential, but also to make British India impregnable. Imposed by force, the treaty was meant to last a hundred years, after which the border would no longer exist and the lands would revert to Afghanistan, though this interpretation is, unsurprisingly, disputed by Pakistan.

During the twentieth century outside influences were indirect, as in the impact of the Russian and Kemalist revolutions after the collapse of czarism and the Ottoman Empire, respectively. In the second decade of the last century, a reforming monarch, Amanullah, proposed a constitution that included an elected parliament and the right of women to vote. The British imported T. E. Lawrence "of Arabia" to help organize a tribal revolt and topple the monarch. The propaganda campaign mounted by the British to convince tribal conservatives included doctored photographs of the Afghan queen, a proto-feminist, in a swimming costume.

Stagnation continued after the Second World War, and few considered the possibility of a republic, let alone a more radical outcome. Zahir Shah, the last king of Afghanistan, was a mild nationalist but with an intense dislike of the British Empire and had, for that reason, maintained friendly relations with Mussolini and the Third Reich till 1945.

When Zahir Shah, less of a despot than those who succeeded him, was removed in a palace coup by his cousin Daud in 1973 and exiled to the Italian Riviera, most observers agreed that the country had made surprisingly little progress over the preceding 150 years. Its rentier economy and landlocked status had made it heavily dependent on aid, with a huge gulf between the wealthy elite and the bulk of the population. The modern world barely intruded even in the cities, with the exception of Kabul. Five years later, Daud too was overthrown by his erstwhile allies in a Communist-led coup d'état, thus ending the rule of the Durranis. This regime too imploded. In 1979, to prevent its collapse, the Soviet Union sent the Red Army across the border to try to save a crumbling and isolated regime. It was obvious at the time that the entry of Soviet troops would bring a horrific counterreaction and wreck the region for decades. Few, however, foresaw the speed with which a once valued U.S. ally would be transformed into an unspeakable antagonist, creating mayhem in neighboring Pakistan, a country that was vital to the whole operation in the first place, as it is again today.

When the bombing began in October 2001, I argued the following scenario:

> . . . the Taliban are effectively encircled and isolated. Their defeat is inevitable. Both Pakistan and Iran are ranged against them on two important borders. It is unlikely they will last more than a few weeks. Obviously some of their forces will go to the mountains and wait till the west withdraws before attacking the new regime, likely to be installed in Kabul when the octogenarian King Zahir Shah is moved from his comfortable Roman villa to less salubrious surroundings in the wreckage of Kabul.

> The Northern Alliance backed by the west is marginally less religious than the Taliban, but its record on everything else is just as abysmal. Over the last year they have taken over the marketing of heroin on a large scale, making a mockery of Blair's claim that this war is also a war against drugs.

> The notion that they would represent an advance on the Taliban is laughable. Their first instinct will be revenge against their opponents. However the Alliance has been weakened in recent days by the defection of Gulbuddin Hekmatyar, once the favourite "freedom fighter" of the west, welcomed in the White House and Downing Street by Reagan and Thatcher.

> This man has now decided to back the Taliban against the infi-

del. Sustaining a new client state in Afghanistan will not be an easy affair given local and regional rivalries. General Musharraf has already told Pakistanis he will not accept a regime dominated by the Northern Alliance. This is hardly surprising since his army has been fighting the Alliance for over a decade.

Till now the Pakistan army (unlike its Arab counterparts) has avoided a coup mounted by captains and colonels. It has always been the generals who have seized power and kept the army united, largely by sharing out the pieces of silver.

It is an open question whether that will be enough on this occasion. A lot will depend on the aftermath of the current war. A major concern for the overwhelming majority of Pakistanis is that the Taliban, cornered and defeated in their own country, will turn on Pakistan and wreak havoc on its cities and social fabric. Peshawar, Quetta, Lahore and Karachi are especially vulnerable. By that time the west, having scored a "victory," will turn a blind eye to the mess left behind.

As for the supposed aim of this operation—the capture of Bin Laden—this is unlikely to be easy. He is well-protected in the remote Pamir mountains and might well disappear. But victory will still be proclaimed. The west will rely on the short memory of its citizens. But let us even suppose that Bin Laden is captured and killed. How will this help the "war against terrorism"? Other individuals will decide to mimic the events of September 11 in different ways.*

At that time the entire leadership of the Western world, with hardly an exception, was convinced that the bombing and occupation were right and necessary. That the "good war" has now turned bad is no longer disputed by the more knowledgeable analysts. There is, however, no agreed prescription for dealing with the problems, not least of which, for some, is the future of NATO, stranded far away from the Atlantic in a mountain fastness, whose people, after offering a small window of opportunity to the occupiers, realized it was a mistake and

*"Into Pakistan's Maelstrom," *Guardian,* October 10, 2001.

became stubbornly hostile to the occupation. As early as 2003, a special report commissioned by the U.S. Council on Foreign Relations painted a gloomy picture:

> Nineteen months after the defeat of the Taliban and its al-Qaeda allies, Afghanistan remains a long way from achieving the U.S. goal of a stable self-governing state that no longer serves as a haven for terrorists. Indeed, failure to stem deteriorating security conditions and to spur economic reconstruction could lead to a reversion to warlord-dominated anarchy and mark a major defeat for the U.S. war on terrorism. To prevent this from happening, the Task Force recommends that the United States strengthen the hand of President Hamid Karzai and intensify support for security, diplomatic, and economic reconstruction in Afghanistan. Although Karzai is trying to assert his authority outside Kabul, he lacks the means to compel compliance by recalcitrant warlords and regional leaders who control most of the countryside. Current policy for the 9,000 U.S. troops in Afghanistan rules out support for Karzai against the regional warlords and also active participation in the planned effort to demobilize the 100,000-strong militias. In the Afghan setting, where the United States has the primary military power, this approach is mistaken and leaves a dangerous security void outside Kabul, where the 4,800-strong International Security Assistance Force (ISAF) maintains the peace.

Five years later, on February 28, 2008, Admiral Michael McConnell, director of national intelligence, a firm supporter of Vice President Cheney, informed the Senate Armed Services Committee that U.S.-supported Hamid Karzai controlled under a third of Afghanistan and the Taliban controlled 11 percent and had a presence virtually everywhere. Asked whether the insurgency had been contained, the admiral could offer little solace: "I wouldn't say it's been contained. It's been sustained in the south; it's grown a bit in the east and the north." Given the extent of the crisis, can the United States afford to enlarge the scale and transform the style of Operation Enduring Freedom?

They certainly seem to think so at Fort Riley in Kansas, where selected U.S. troops and thirty-one Afghan soldiers were training in March 2008. The Afghans were present to help U.S. soldiers imbibe "cultural sensitivity." The Voice of America reported, "The training takes place in a mock Afghan village complete with so-called enactors, usually Afghan-Americans, who play the role of villagers and combatants. Soldiers must safely enter the village, locate the house of the insurgents and enter without harming any of the civilians who wander the streets nearby. . . . Lieutenant Colonel John Nagi, one of the authors of the U.S. military handbook on counterinsurgency, says gaining a better understanding of the Afghan people is a key factor in defeating Al Qaeda and the Taliban."*

But what if the Afghan people obstinately refuse to accept that a foreign occupation is in their interests and continue to help those resisting it? This elementary question tends to escape counterinsurgency experts, but should occupy minds in the Pentagon.

The initial war aim appeared to be limited to the capture of Osama bin Laden, dead or alive, and the destruction of Al Qaeda bases in Afghanistan. There was no deep hostility in the West to the Taliban regime prior to 9/11. Even immediately afterward it was made clear to Pakistan that if the Al Qaeda leaders were handed over, the regime could stay. Mullah Omar refused to hand over bin Laden on the grounds that he was a guest and no proof was available linking him to the attacks on the United States. Omar was, however, as *The 9/11 Commission Report* makes clear, prepared to carry on negotiations with the United States. The National Security Council had been toying with the idea of using 9/11 to invade Iraq, but Omar's refusal to capitulate immediately left the NSC with little option but to concentrate on Afghanistan. An avalanche of fear, hatred, and revenge now descended on the country. With Pakistan officially committed to the U.S. side, the Taliban regime in Kabul fell without a serious struggle. The reason so many zealots of the cause disbanded so rapidly was obvious. Pakistan forbade any frontal confrontation and, despite some ISI defections, got its way. The more recalcitrant Mullah Omar faction decided, of their own accord, to evac-

---

*Greg Flakus, "Afghan Soldiers Train at U.S. Army Base," Voice of America, March 25, 2008.

uate to the mountains and bide their time. This was why Kabul fell
without a fight, the Northern Alliance heroes entering the town soon
after the BBC's war correspondent.

Pakistan's key role in securing this "victory" was underplayed in the
Western media. The public was told that elite Special Forces units and
CIA "specialists" had liberated Afghanistan, and having triumphed
here, they could now be sent on to Iraq. It was a gross miscalculation
on every level. Once the situation began to unravel and could no longer
be concealed, former U.S. ambassadors began to speak publicly of a
lack of resources, not enough money and not enough soldiers. "We're
tough, we're determined, we're relentless," the U.S. president informed
the world in April 2002. "We will stay until the mission is done."

That same month a wave of new refugees fled from the terror of
history and most of the Taliban middle cadres crossed the border into
Pakistan to regroup and plan for what lay ahead. Zalmay Khalilzad, the
Afghan-American proconsul in Afghanistan, now began the hard task
of assembling a new government. It was impossible to transplant a
whole generation of Americans (or Afghan-Americans) to run the
country as the old colonial powers had done. Even then they had
required local allies. Khalilzad knew that the United States could not
run the country without the Northern Alliance, and he toned down
the emancipatory rhetoric that had been used to justify the occupation.

The coalition constructed by Khalilzad was intended as an octopus
with Karzai as its eye. Militias of rival groups, united only by opposition to the toppled Taliban, occupied Kabul, and their representatives
had to be accommodated on every level. In these conditions it was difficult to install a surrogate regime. Meanwhile, U.S. forces stationed
themselves in former Soviet bases and the prisons once again began to
echo with the screams of tortured victims. The "Chicago boys" had
brought the peace of the graveyard to Pinochet's Chile, the "Berkeley
mafia" had injected "macroeconomic stability" in Suharto's Indonesia.
Could the swarm of NGO locusts descending on Kabul pull off something similar in Afghanistan? Both Pinochet and Suharto had drowned
the opposition in blood, with almost a million corpses in Indonesia.
Afghanistan could not be subjugated in similar fashion, both because
of its more "primitive" social structure based on tribal dominance and

the institutionalized decentralization represented by the Northern Alliance. The chaos encountered in Afghanistan was closer to the Somalian debacle of 1993.

The Taliban regime had been a "purer" model of the Wahhabi state in Saudi Arabia. Repressive and cruel, it had nonetheless restored order in a country racked by foreign and civil wars since 1979. According to virtually every source, the rape that had been endemic in the country was ended with the public execution of rapists, though an overruled radical-feminist wing of the Taliban had suggested that castration would be sufficient punishment. Attempts were also being made to reduce the heroin output, with some success. On the economic front, Wahhabi Islam is perfectly at home with the neoliberal dispensation that rules the world. Koranic literalists can find passages in favor of free trade, and the Taliban delegation received full honors when they visited UNOCAL (now part of Chevron) headquarters in Texas. On December 17, 1997, the London *Daily Telegraph* headlined, "Oil Barons Court Taliban in Texas," and informed its readers that the bearded visitors were prepared to sign a "£2 billion contract with an American oil company to build a pipeline across the war-torn country" and, then more mysteriously noted, "The Islamic warriors appear to have been persuaded to close the deal, not through delicate negotiation but by old-fashioned Texan hospitality. . . . Dressed in traditional *salwar kameez*, Afghan waistcoats and loose, black turbans, the high-ranking delegation was given VIP treatment during the four-day stay." A deal was a deal regardless of sartorial differences, and the few images recording this event were later immortalized in Michael Moore's *Fahrenheit 9/11*. The pipeline project was delayed not so much by Taliban doubts, but by rival offers emanating from Russia and supported by Tehran. Despite this, the U.S. oil company was confident of its success, and a final deal was close to being stitched when the planes hit the Twin Towers.

What many Afghans now expected from a successor government was a similar level of order, without the repression and social restrictions, and a freeing of the country's spirit. What they were instead presented with was a melancholy spectacle that blasted all their hopes.

The problem was not a lack of funds but the Western state-building project itself. By its nature a top-down process, it aims to construct an army constituted not to defend the nation but to impose order on its own people, on behalf of outside powers; a civil administration that will have no control over planning, health, education, etc., all of which will be run by NGOs whose employees will be far better paid than the locals, and answerable not to the population but to their overseas sponsors; and a government whose foreign policy is identical to Washington's. In September 2006, a German correspondent in Kabul sent a dispatch home in which she explained the reasons for local hostility to the West and why so many Afghans were joining the resistance. The contrast between the wealth displayed by the occupiers, including corporate expense accounts that charged the cost of prostitutes to their firms, and the poverty of most Afghans created resentment and anger. Add to this the weekend partying in Kabul:

> Now hordes of Westerners are chauffeured to the ministries of a morning, and picked up in air-conditioned vehicles of an afternoon. The foreigners have brought new customs to the capital as well; jeans are now on sale, although many women still walk the streets in burkas. Every Thursday, before the Afghan weekend starts, UNHAS—the UN air service that transports embassy and aid organization employees around the country—registers a miraculous spike in passengers to Kabul from the provinces: It's party time! And the revelry behind the façades of the capital's aging mansions is as riotous as anything to be found in Berlin or New York.
>
> At a French shipping company's toga bash, men donned fake laurel wreaths, bared their torsos, wrapped themselves in sheets and pranced around like Roman emperors. At the garden party arranged by an international consulting firm, hundreds of foreigners whooped it up until the wee hours, dancing amid a decorative backdrop of camels.*

It is amazing colonial arrogance to fail to notice that an occupied country is no longer sovereign, even if the occupation has been legally

---

*Susanne Koelbl, "The Wild East," *Der Spiegel*, September 29, 2006.

sanctioned by the United Nations Security Council. How can any government in these conditions be considered legitimate?

The Bonn Conference organized two months after the occupation, from November 27 to December 5, 2001, could not discuss this central issue and instead became bogged down with power-sharing arrangements. Joschka Fischer, the German foreign minister, ignorant of the realities on the ground, pressed for a federal solution on the German model to neutralize separatist attractions, but this was not a problem. The contentious issue was who exercised power and where. To concentrate Western minds, components of the Northern Alliance organized at least three different coup attempts to topple Karzai in 2002–3. They were obstructed by NATO, providing a vivid illustration of both sovereignty and legitimacy to the population at large.

The reality on the ground was clear enough. After the fall of the Taliban government, four major armed groups reemerged as strong regional players. In the gas-rich and more industrialized north, bordering the Central Asian republics of Uzbekistan and Tajikistan, with his capital in Mazar-i-Sharif, the Uzbek warlord Rashid Dostum was in charge. Allied first to the Communists, later to the Taliban, and most recently NATO, General Dostum had reportedly demonstrated his latest loyalty by massacring hundreds of Taliban and Arab prisoners.

Not far from Dostum, in the mountainous northeast of the country, a region rich in emeralds, lapis lazuli, and opium, the late Ahmed Shah Massoud built his fighting organization of Tajiks, who regularly ambushed troops on the Salang Highway, which linked Kabul to Tashkent during the Soviet occupation. The most dynamic, if overpraised, guerrilla leader of the anti-Taliban groups, Massoud hailed from Panjshir province. During the anti-Russian war he had become a favorite pinup in Paris, usually portrayed as a rugged romantic, a Muslim, an anticommunist Che Guevara, a man of the people. His membership in the Jamaat-e-Islami, led by Burhanuddin Rabbani, and his own reactionary views on most social issues were barely mentioned. These were tiny defects at a time when Islamic groups were considered staunch allies of the West.

Had Massoud not been killed by a suicide bomber two days before 9/11, he would have been the most obvious candidate to head a post-

Taliban government. The French government issued a postage stamp with his portrait, and NATO named Kabul airport after him. But Massoud could never have been as reliable a client as the transplanted Hamid Karzai, and it is an open question whether the indigenous guerrilla leader would have accepted a lengthy foreign occupation or agreed to permanent U.S. military bases in the country. He had been the leader of the armed wing of Burhanuddin Rabbani's Islamist group, which operated in tandem with an allied Islamist leader, Abdul Rasul Sayyaf. Both men were lecturers in Sharia, or Islamic law, on the faculty at Kabul University in 1973. Their movements were incubated and, until 1993, funded by Saudi Arabia, after which the latter gradually shifted its support to the Taliban. Massoud maintained a semi-independence during the Taliban period. To his supporters in the West he had presented an image of pure, incorruptible masculinity. It was not the same at home. Rape and the heroin trade were not uncommon in areas under his control. His supporters are currently in the government, but not as reliable as Karzai, which worries NATO.

On the west, sheltered by neighboring Iran, lies the ancient city of Herat, once a center of learning and culture where poets, artists, and scholars flourished. Here, for over three centuries, important books were written and illustrated, including the fifteenth-century classic *Miraj-nameh,* an early medieval Islamic account of the Prophet's ascent to heaven from the Dome of the Rock and the punishments he observed as he passed through hell. Some European scholars maintain that a Latin translation of this work inspired Dante. The book has sixty-one paintings in all, created with great love for the Prophet of Islam. He is depicted with Central Asian features and seen flying to heaven on a magical steed, which has a woman's head. There are also illustrations of a meeting with Gabriel and Adam, a sighting of houris at the gates of paradise, and renderings of wine bibbers being punished in hell. These stunning illustrations are accompanied by the exquisite calligraphy of Malik Bakshi in the Uighur script.

The sophisticated culture required to produce such a work is a far cry from modern Herat and its outlying regions, where the Shia warlord Ismail Khan today holds sway and where the majority of Hazaras live. A former army captain inspired by the Islamic revolution in neighboring Iran, Ismail achieved instant fame by leading a garrison revolt against the pro-Moscow regime in 1979. Backed by Tehran, he built up a strong force that united all the Shia groups and was to trouble the Russians throughout their stay. Tens of thousands of refugees from this region (where a Persian dialect is the spoken language) were given work, shelter, and training in Iran. From 1989 to 1992, the province was run on authoritarian lines. The harsh regime and Ismail Khan's half-witted effrontery began to alienate supporters. His high-tax and forced-conscription policies angered peasant families. When the Taliban took power in Kabul, support had already drained away from the warlord. Herat fell without a struggle. Ismail and his supporters quietly crossed the border to Iran, where they bided their time, to return in October 2001 under NATO cover.

Iran has certainly given covert support to the occupations of Iraq and Afghanistan, which removed their enemies from power. This proved more beneficial in Iraq, where pro-Iranian parties were given a large share in the Green Zone government. In Afghanistan the situation was different. Here the Tajiks make up 27 percent of the population; the Uzbeks and Hazaras, 8 and 7 percent respectively; and 54 percent of Afghans are Pashtuns, who live in the south and east of the country along the border with Pakistan. During the first Afghan war (1979–92) three militant Sunni groups acquired dominance, and soon after they took Kabul the tiny non-Muslim minority of Hindus and Sikhs, mainly shopkeepers and traders, were displaced. Some were killed. Ten thousand refugees fled to India. Gulbuddin Hekmatyar, an ISI asset, was provisioned by Pakistan and had been groomed by the Saudis to take over, but found himself confronted by Massoud and others. The jihad was long over and now the jihadis were at each other's throats. The brutal power struggle wrecked the country and had little to do with religion. They were, after all, all Muslims. Rather than matters of faith, what was at stake was control of the drug trade.

Meanwhile, serious problems confronted the occupying forces. The brutality of U.S. and British troops alienated the population, and talk of "victory" began to sound hollow to Afghan ears. By 2003–4 existing Taliban guerrilla factions were mounting serious resistance, attacking troop carriers, occasionally bringing down helicopters, and punishing collaborators. NATO retaliation resulted in extensive civilian casualties, leading to further disenchantment with the occupation. With some exceptions this was barely reported in the West. *Time* magazine became a serial offender (though it was by no means alone) by running unfiltered NATO spin, as typified by Tim McGirk's report of March 28, 2005, which summons every conceivable cliché to bang the drum for the official case:

> "The Taliban is a force in decline," says Major General Eric Olson, who conducted the U.S. military's counterinsurgency battle until last month. . . . The Taliban's fall has been a long time coming . . . what turned the tide? In a word, nation-building. . . . Last October's Presidential elections were crucial. . . . "It was a moral and psychological defeat for the Taliban," Olson told *Time*. . . . Now the Taliban is a busted flush. . . . Says Major Mike Myers, a spokesman for the U.S. forces in Kandahar, "The Taliban class of 2004 was smaller than the class of 2003." . . . In Kabul, Karzai is hoping that the Taliban are now demoralized enough to consider an amnesty. Soon, Karzai is expected to announce a "reconciliation" with all Taliban except Omar and his top commanders.

That this was pure propaganda must soon have become obvious to the editors of *Time*. Less than a year later, on February 26, 2006, an attempted assassination of Dick Cheney by the Taliban occurred while he was visiting the "secure" U.S. air base at Bagram (once an equally secure Soviet air base). Cheney's survival provoked some controversy on U.S. television when *Real Time* host Bill Maher expressed consternation that comments posted that same week on the Huffington Post website had been removed because "they expressed regret that the attack on Dick Cheney failed." Maher went on to say, "I have zero doubt that if Dick Cheney was not in power, people wouldn't be dying needlessly tomorrow. . . . I'm just saying if he did die, other people, more people would live. That's a fact." No European TV pundit would have dared to make this sort of comment in public. They were too cowed by the "war on terror."

Two U.S. soldiers and a mercenary ("contractor") died in the attack on Cheney, as did twenty other people working at the base. This episode alone should have focused the U.S. vice president's mind on the scale of the Afghan debacle. The casualty rates rose substantially in 2006 as NATO troops lost forty-six soldiers, shot down in helicopters or caught in clashes with what was now being referred to as the neo-Taliban. In the confrontation with their Afghan antagonists, the United States was facing a number of closely interrelated problems.

The first was the failure of "nation-building." Few tears were shed in Afghanistan and elsewhere when the Taliban fell, but the hopes aroused by Western demagogy did not last long. It soon became clear that the new transplanted elite would cream off a fair portion of the foreign aid and create its own criminal networks of graft and patronage. Then there were the NGOs. Even those sympathetic to the occupation had lost patience with these organizations. The Karzai government, of course, disliked them because it felt all the aid money should be channeled through the government. But disaffection with these organizations extended throughout the populace. In a state with hardly any stability, the notion of "civil society," which the NGOs were committed to building, had little appeal. In addition, the resources available to them provoked considerable resentment. "The NGOs," according to an experienced and well-versed U.S. academic, "brought scores of overpaid young people into their communities, where they flaunted their high salaries and new motor vehicles. Worse, their well-funded activities highlighted the poverty and ineffectiveness of the civil administration and discredited its local representatives in the eyes of the local populace."* Unsurprisingly, they began to be targeted by the insurgents and had to hire mercenary protection.

There are few signs that the $19 billion in "aid and reconstruction" money devoted to Afghanistan has served to ease the suffering of the majority of its people. The electricity supply is worse now than five years ago. As one commentator noted, "While foreigners and wealthy Afghans power air conditioners, hot-water heaters, computers and satellite televisions with private generators, average Kabulis suffered a sum-

---

*S. Frederick Starr, "Sovereignty and Legitimacy in Afghan Nation-Building," in Francis Fukuyama, ed., *Nation-Building: Beyond Afghanistan and Iraq* (Baltimore: 2006).

mer without fans and face a winter without heaters."* As a result, hundreds of homeless Afghans are literally freezing to death each winter.

Overall, "nation-building" in Afghanistan has so far produced only a puppet president dependent for his survival on foreign mercenaries, a corrupt and abusive police force, a "nonfunctioning" judiciary, a burgeoning criminal layer, and a deepening social and economic crisis. Even the West's own specialists and institutions concede much of this to be the case. It beggars belief to argue that more of the same will be the answer to Afghanistan's problems.

IN SEPTEMBER 2005, a quick-fix election was organized at high cost with the help of U.S. public relations firms. The lion's share of the profits was pocketed by the Rendon Group of Washington, D.C., which has received contracts worth millions of dollars. The elections were organized, at least partly, for the benefit of Western public opinion, but the realities on the ground soon overcame the temporary feel-good impact. NATO troops guarded polling booths in some areas and the Northern Alliance in others. There were widespread reports of coercion, and residents of Baghlan, Kapisa, and Herat provinces told reporters from the Pajhwok Afghan News agency that some polling agents, staff, and police officials had forced them to cast votes for particular candidates. Karzai had to vote in a special voting booth constructed inside the presidential palace.

The results failed to bolster support for NATO inside the country. While 12 million Afghan citizens were eligible to vote, just over 4 million did so. The violence preceding the elections symbolized the absurdity of the process. Though newly elected, President Karzai symbolized his own isolation, as well as an oft-tested instinct for self-preservation, by refusing to be guarded by a security detail from his own ethnic Pashtun base. He wanted and was given tough, Terminator-look-alike U.S. marines. They were later replaced by mercenaries or privatized soldiers.

In September 2006, exactly a year after the elections had been

---

*Barnett Rubin, "Saving Afghanistan," *Foreign Affairs,* January–February 2007, 8.

trumpeted as an enormous success in the Western media, an attempted bombing of the U.S. embassy came close to hitting its target. A CIA assessment that same month painted a somber picture, describing Karzai and his regime as hopelessly corrupt and incapable of defending Afghanistan against the Taliban. Ronald E. Neumann, the U.S. ambassador in Kabul, supported this view and told the *New York Times* that the United States faced "stark choices": a defeat could only be avoided through "multiple billions" over "multiple years."*

Like Neumann, others who still support the war in Afghanistan, which include the media and mainstream political parties throughout North America and Euroland, argue that more state-building on the style of postwar Japan and Western Europe would stabilize the country. Others argue that the model of imperial rule should follow the British style. Neither argument is tenable. Might Afghanistan have been secured with a limited Marshall Plan–style intervention, as is argued by numerous supporters of the war who blame the White House for not spending enough on social projects? It is, of course, possible that the construction of free schools and hospitals, subsidized homes for the poor, and the rebuilding of the social infrastructure that was destroyed after the withdrawal of Soviet troops in 1989 might have stabilized the country. But neither the United States nor their EU allies were seriously interested in such a project. It went against the grain of normal neocolonial policies. The Marshall Plan was a unique response to a severe crisis of confidence in a system that had been wrecked by a ferocious war. It was designed to secure Western Europe in the face of a supposed Communist threat. It was a special operation without precedent before or since: the first time in history that a victorious power (the United States) had helped to revive its economic rivals in order to confront a common enemy whose economic system was at the time perceived as a challenge. Afghanistan was an entirely different situation and was handled as a more traditional colonial operation. Mythmakers, often themselves British, suggested this be done on the British model of "good" imperialism rather than the crude and brutish variety

---

New York Times, November 5, 2006.

of the Americans. This distinction was almost certainly lost on the
benighted Afghans, who had long understood that while the British
could be competent administrators, they were every bit as savage as
their cousins across the Atlantic, a point demonstrated repeatedly
throughout Africa, the Middle East, and India. Their record in assist-
ing the development of the countries they occupied was equally bleak.
In 1947, the year the British left India, 85 percent of India's economy
was rural, and the overwhelming majority of midnight's children were
illiterate. The colonial legacy was summarized crisply by the *Cambridge
Economic History of India,* vol. 2, c. 1757–c. 1970:

> Capital formation (around 6 per cent of NDP) was inadequate to
> bring about rapid improvement in per capita income, which was
> about one-twentieth of the level then attained in developed coun-
> tries. The average availability of food was not only deficient in
> quantity and quality, but, as recurrent famines underscored so
> painfully, also precarious. Illiteracy was a high 84 per cent and the
> majority (60 per cent) of children in the 6 to 11 age group did not
> attend school; mass communicable diseases (malaria, smallpox and
> cholera) were widespread and, in the absence of a good public
> health service and sanitation, mortality rates (27 per 1000) were
> very high. The problems of poverty, ignorance and disease were
> aggravated by the unequal distribution of resources between groups
> and regions.

Rory Stewart, who served as a colonial administrator in British-
occupied southern Iraq, is angered by the stupidity of the occupiers
in both Iraq and Afghanistan and not overimpressed by NGO civil-
society imports to antique lands. He writes, for instance:

> Foreign policy experts will tell you that poor states lack the rule of
> law, a vibrant civil society, free media, a transparent civil service . . .
> employees of major international agencies commonly complain that
> Afghans or Iraqis or Kenyans "can't plan" or "can't implement."
>   At its worst, this attitude is racist, bullying and ignorant. But
> there are less sinister explanations. As a diplomat, I was praised for

"realism" if I sent home critical telegrams. Now, working for a non-profit, I find that donor proposals encourage us to emphasize the negative aspects of local society. . . . Afghans and Iraqis are often genuinely courageous, charming, generous, inventive and honorable. Their social structures have survived centuries of poverty and foreign mischief and decades of war and oppression, and have enabled them to overcome almost unimaginable trauma. But to acknowledge this seems embarrassingly romantic or even patronizing.

Yet the only chance of rebuilding a nation like Iraq or Afghanistan in the face of insurgency or civil war is to identify, develop and use some of these traditional values. . . . This may be uncomfortable for the international community. A leader who can restore security, reconcile warring parties and shape the aspirations of a people may resemble an Ataturk more than a U.S. president. This is not a call for dictatorship. True progress must be sustained by the unconstrained wishes of the people. These should include, in Afghanistan, people with strong liberal values as much as conservative rural communities. These various desires must be protected from both the contorted control of an authoritarian state and the muffling effect of foreign aid.*

Stewart's writings have a touch of imperial romanticism, which might help him outlast many bitter disillusionments. A cool, philosophical frame of mind would immediately grasp that it is not aid alone that muffles but the imperial presence itself. It was always thus.

It is sometimes instructive to study history through the evolution of a city. Take Kabul, for instance, the site of numerous invasions and occupations over three thousand years, a few of them benign. Located in a valley, six thousand feet above sea level, it existed long before Christianity. Historically the city was at the crossroads of adjoining civilizations for countless centuries since it commanded the passes, as numerous conquerors starting with Alexander of Macedonia and followed by Sultan Mahmud, Genghis Khan, Babar, and those with less

---

*Rory Stewart, "The Value of Their Values," *New York Times,* March 7, 2007.

familiar names spent time here on their way to India. Babar loved this city and made it his capital for several years before marching southward. A passionate agriculturist, the founder of the Mogul dynasty, he supervised the irrigation of large tracts of land, planted orchards, and built gardens with artificial streams that made the summer heat and the dust-laden environment of the city more bearable.

The city was a triumph of medieval Mogul architecture. Ali Mardan Khan, a Mogul governor of the seventeenth century and a renowned architect and engineer specializing in public works, built a *char-chala* (four-sided) roofed and arcaded bazaar on the model of the markets that once existed, and occasionally still do, in a number of old Muslim cities, including Cairo, Damascus, Baghdad, Palermo, and Córdoba. It was regarded as unique in the region. Nothing on the same scale was built in Lahore or Delhi. This market was deliberately destroyed in 1842 by the Scottish general George Pollock's "Army of Retribution" (also remembered as among the worst killers, looters, and marauders ever to arrive in Afghanistan, a contest in which competition remains strong). Defeated in a number of cities and forced to evacuate Kabul, the British punished its citizens by removing the market from the map.

A century and a half later, soon after the withdrawal of the Russians, who had built their soulless, multistoried buildings to house their troops and other personnel outside the old city, the Afghan warlords and competing Islamic factions, now fighting each other, came close to destroying the city altogether. Jade Maiwand, a major shopping street that was cut through the center of the city in the 1970s, was reduced to rubble during the warfare of 1992–96. Ajmal Maiwandi, an Afghan-American architect, describes how Kabul has been transformed by history:

> The major destruction of Kabul occurred between 1992 and 1996 after the withdrawal of the Soviet Union in 1989 and the fall of Kabul to various warring factions in 1992. Throughout the war, the urban identity of Kabul was transformed continuously from a modern capital, to the military and political headquarters of an invading army, to the besieged seat of power of a puppet regime, to the frontlines of factional conflict resulting in the destruction of two-thirds of its urban mass, to the testing fields of religious fanaticism which

erased from the city the final layers of urban life, to the target of an international war on terrorism, to a secure gateway into Afghanistan for the internationally backed peace efforts, and presently, to a symbol of a new phase in international unilateralism.*

What Kabul will look like after NATO has left remains to be seen, but the large shantytown settlements that are springing up everywhere provide a clue. The city may well become a tourist attraction on the "planet of slums"† world tour.

Meanwhile architecture is far from the most important of the country's problems at the moment. The U.S. presence today is refracted largely through its military muscle, the air power lovingly referred to as "Big Daddy" by frightened, young U.S. soldiers on unwelcoming terrain, but which is far from paternal when it comes to discriminating between civilians and combatants. The real question is not so much Western arrogance, ugly though it is at the best of times, but what the alternative could be in a society where a Western intervention has unleashed similar opposition as have previous wars and occupations by the British and the Soviet Union. There is no simple solution, but what is clear is that an "international community" that thrives on double standards is seen by the population as part of the problem.‡

Profound difficulties are also to be found among the lucrative blooms in Afghanistan's luscious poppy fields. The NATO mission has made no serious attempt to bring about a significant reduction in the heroin trade. How could it? Karzai's own supporters, few in number though

---

*Dr. Ajmal Maiwandi, www.xs4all.nl/~jo/Maiwandi.html.

†Mike Davies, *Planet of Slums* (London and New York: 2006). This work is a brilliant account of how globalization is transforming our world.

‡A classic example of blindness and double standards was U.S. defense secretary Robert Gates's statement in Australia on February 24, 2008, when he was asked to comment on the entry of Turkish troops into Iraq to combat a Kurdish organization listed as "terrorist" by the "international community": "Our experiences in Iraq and Afghanistan show that military muscle should be complemented by efforts to address grievances held by minority groups. These economic and political measures are really important because after a certain point people become inured to military attacks. And if you don't blend them with these kinds of nonmilitary initiatives, then at a certain point the military efforts become less and less effective. . . . I would strongly urge Turkey to respect Iraq's sovereignty."

they are, would rapidly desert if any attempts were made to stop their trading activities. It would require massive state help to agriculture and cottage industries over many years to reduce the dependence on poppy farming. Ninety percent of the world's opium production is based in Afghanistan. UN estimates suggest that heroin accounts for 52 percent of the impoverished country's gross domestic product, and the opium sector of agriculture continues to grow apace. Indeed, these have been persistent allegations—just as persistently denied by their subject—that President Karzai's younger brother, Ahmad Wali Karzai, has become one of the richest drug barons in the country. At a meeting with Pakistan's president in 2006, when Karzai was bleating on about Pakistan's inability to stop cross-border smuggling, General Musharraf calmly suggested that perhaps Karzai should set an example by bringing his sibling under control. The hatred for each other of these two close allies of Washington is not a secret in this region.

Added to the opium problem are the corruptions of the elite, which grow each month like an untreated tumor. Western funds designed to aid reconstruction were siphoned off to build fancy homes for their native enforcers. As early as 2002, in a gigantic housing scandal, cabinet ministers awarded themselves and favored cronies prime real estate in Kabul. Land prices in the city had reached a high point after the occupation, when the occupiers, NGO employees, and their camp followers built large villas for themselves in full view of the poor.

Then there is, of course, the resistance. The "neo-Taliban" control at least twenty districts in Kandahar, Helmand, and Uruzgan provinces where NATO troops replaced U.S. soldiers. It is hardly a secret that many officials in these zones are closet supporters of the guerrilla fighters. The situation is out of control, as Western intelligence agencies active in the country are fully aware. When the occupation first began, Secretary of State Colin Powell explained that his model was Panama: "The strategy has to be to take charge of the whole country by military force, police, or other means." His knowledge of Afghanistan was clearly limited. Panama, populated by 3.5 million people, could not have been more different from Afghanistan, which has a population approaching 30 million and is geographically quite distinct. To even attempt a military occupation of the entire country would require a minimum of two hundred thousand troops. A total of eight thousand U.S. troops were dispatched to seal the victory; the four thousand "peacekeepers" sent by other countries rarely left Kabul or stationed themselves in more peaceful regions in the north of the country. The Germans concentrated on creating a police force, and the Italians, without any sense of irony, were busy "training an Afghan judiciary." The British, more hated by the Afghans than even the Americans, were in Helmand amid the poppy fields. Incapable of crushing the resistance, they tried to buy off the local resistance until this was vetoed by an enraged President Karzai.

Colin Powell's ignorance also extended to regional and ethnic complexities. During a closed meeting in Islamabad soon after the occupation, he openly failed to grasp the difference between ethnicity and ideology, happily equating Pashtun and Taliban. Khurshid Mahmood Kasuri, the Pakistan foreign minister, corrected the misapprehension by pointing out gently that two senior Foreign Office officials present at the meeting were Pashtuns, definitely not Taliban.

And lastly, while economic conditions failed to improve, NATO military strikes often targeted innocent civilians, leading to violent anti-American protests in the Afghan capital in 2006. What was initially viewed by some locals as a necessary police action against Al Qaeda following the 9/11 attacks is now perceived by a growing majority in the entire region as a full-fledged imperial occupation. The neo-Taliban is growing and creating new alliances not because its sectarian religious practices have become popular, but because it is the only available umbrella for national liberation. As the British and Russians discovered at a high cost in the preceding two centuries, Afghans never like being occupied.

The repression, striking blindly, leaves people with no option but to back those trying to resist, especially in a part of the world where the culture of revenge is strong. When a whole community feels threatened, it reinforces solidarity, regardless of the inadequacies of those who are fighting back. Many Afghans who detest the Taliban are so angered by the failures of NATO and the behavior of its troops that they will support any opposition. A related problem is the undisciplined nature of the mercenaries deployed to assist the NATO armies. They are not responsible to the military commanders, and even sympathetic observers admit that "their behavior, including alcohol consumption and the patronage of a growing number of brothels in Kabul (both very effectively prohibited to U.S. military personnel), is arousing public anger and resentment."* To this could be added numerous incidents of rape, unlawful killings of civilians, indiscriminate search-and-arrest missions, and the rough treatment of women by male soldiers. This has created a thirst for dignity that can be assuaged only by genuine independence.

The middle-cadre Taliban who fled across the border in November 2001 had regrouped and started low-level guerrilla activity by the following year, attracting a trickle of new recruits from madrassas and refugee camps in Pakistan. By 2003 the movement was starting to win active support in the mosques—first from village mullahs, in Zabul, Helmand, Ghazni, Paktika, and Kandahar, and then in the towns. From 2004 onward, increasing numbers of young Waziris were radicalized by the attacks by armed U.S. drones and Pakistani military and police incursions in the impoverished tribal areas. By 2006 there were reports of Kabul mullahs who had previously supported Karzai's allies but were now railing against the foreigners and the government; calls for jihad against the occupation were heard in the northeast border provinces of Takhar and Badakhshan.

But the largest pool of recruits, according to a well-informed recent estimate, has been "communities antagonized by the local authorities and security forces." In Kandahar, Helmand, and Uruzgan, Karzai's cronies—district and provincial governors, security and police chiefs—had enraged local people through harassment and extortion, if not by directing U.S. troops against them. In these circumstances, the Taliban were the only available defense. According to the same report, the Taliban themselves have claimed that families driven into refugee camps by indiscriminate U.S. airpower attacks on the villages have been the major source of recruits. By 2006 the movement was winning the support of traders and businessmen in Kandahar and led a mini "Tet offensive" there that year. One reason suggested for their increasing support

---

*Barnett R. Rubin, "Afghanistan: A U.S. Perspective," in *Crescent of Crisis,* ed. Ivo H. Daalder, Nicole Gnesotto, and Philip H. Gordon (Washington: 2006).

in towns is that the neo-Taliban have relaxed their strictures, for males at least—no longer demanding beards or banning music—and improved their propaganda (producing tapes and CDs of popular singers, and DVDs of U.S. and Israeli atrocities in Iraq, Lebanon, and Palestine).

The reemergence of the Taliban cannot therefore be blamed simply on Islamabad's failure to police the border or cut "command and control" links, as is sometimes claimed by Washington. While the ISI played a commanding role in the retreat of 2001, they no longer have the same degree of control over a more diffuse and widespread movement, for which the occupation itself has been the main recruiting sergeant. NATO's failure cannot therefore be blamed simply on the Pakistani government.

It is a traditional colonial ploy to blame "outsiders" for internal problems: Karzai specializes in this approach. If anything, the destabilization functions in the other direction: the war in Afghanistan has created a critical situation in two Pakistani frontier provinces. The Pashtun majority in Afghanistan has always had close links to its fellow Pashtuns in Pakistan. The present border was an imposition by the British Empire, but it has always remained porous. It is virtually impossible to build a Texan fence or an Israeli wall across the mountainous and largely unmarked twenty-five-hundred-kilometer border that separates the two countries. The solution is political, not military, and should be sought in the region, not in Washington or Brussels.

The cold winds of the Hindu Kush have, through the centuries, frozen both native reformer and foreign occupier. To succeed, a real peace process must be organically linked to the geography and ethnic composition of the country. Those who argue that all that is needed is to throw money at the Afghans to buy off the tribal elders, as the British used to do, have little idea of what is really happening on the ground. The resistance is assuming classical proportions. If one compares Elizabeth Rubin's graphic reports from Afghanistan in the *New York Times* with coverage from South Vietnam in the same newspaper forty years ago, remarkable similarities are apparent. Rubin, like David Halberstam in Vietnam, is alarmed by the high rate of civilian deaths caused by NATO: "The sheer tonnage of metal raining down on

Afghanistan was mind-boggling: a million pounds between January and September of 2007, compared with half-a-million in all of 2006." She later describes the war in Kunar province, where Afghan guerrillas maintain an astonishing level of attacks. American troops come under fire outside their own temporary headquarters:

> The bullets smacked the dirt in front of us. Kearney shoved me into a shack where an Afghan was cooking bread. A few more shots were fired. It was "One-Shot Freddy," as the soldiers refer to him, an insurgent shooter everyone had a theory about regarding the vintage of his gun, his identity, his tactics—but neither Kearney's scouts nor Shadow the drone could ever track him. I accidentally slashed my forearm on a nail in the shack and as I watched the blood pool I thought that if I had to live with Freddy and his ilk for months on end I, too, would see a forked tongue in every villager and start dreaming of revenge.*

Washington's strategic aims in Afghanistan can appear to be primarily focused these days on merely disciplining European allies who betrayed them in Iraq and testing others. In March 2008 the NATO secretary-general, Jaap Scheffer, was full of praise for the Croatians in Afghanistan: "The Croatian participation, and that goes for many other partners, is very important. One of the yardsticks . . . by which nations who are knocking on the door of NATO . . . are measured is are they willing to be a security exporter with us, not only a security consumer but also a security exporter? Croatia is clearly one of those nations who has a good track record of being a security exporter, and I'm happy to hear from my Montenegrin friend that Montenegro, I know that, is also in the process."

The Germans, still training the Afghan police force, would do well to consider whether the skills they are imparting to young Afghans in the "procedural elements of a transatlantic nation-building strategy" today will not be used against NATO tomorrow, as happens in Iraq

---

*Elizabeth Rubin, "Battle Company Is Out There," *New York Times,* February 24, 2008.

when newly minted soldiers, ordered to kill their own people, often desert to the other side.

Clearly the capture of the Al Qaeda leaders cannot be the main goal of the NATO occupiers. Even if the ISI located and handed the leaders over to Washington, NATO would not likely leave the country. To portray the invasion as a "war of self-defense" for NATO makes a mockery of international law, which was perverted to twist a flukishly successful attack by a tiny, terrorist Arab groupuscule into an excuse for an open-ended American military thrust into the Middle East and Central Asia.

Herein lie the reasons for the near unanimity among Western opinion makers that the occupation must not only continue but expand— "many billions over many years." The reasons are to be sought not in the mountain fastnesses of Afghanistan but in Washington and Brussels. As the *Economist* summarizes, "Defeat would be a body blow not only to the Afghans, but"—and more important, of course—"to the NATO alliance." As ever, geopolitics prevail over Afghan interests in the calculus of the big powers. The bases agreement signed by the United States with its appointee in Kabul in May 2005 gives the Pentagon the right to maintain a massive military presence in Afghanistan in perpetuity. That Washington is not seeking permanent bases in this fraught and inhospitable terrain simply for the sake of "democratization and good governance" was made clear by NATO's secretary-general Jaap Scheffer at the Brookings Institution in March 2008: the opportunity to site military facilities, and potentially nuclear missiles, in a country that borders China, Iran, and Central Asia was too good to miss.

More strategically, Afghanistan has become a central theater for uniting, and extending, the West's power, its political grip on the world order. On the one hand, it is argued, it provides an opportunity for the United States to shrug off its failures in imposing its will in Iraq and persuading its allies to play a broader role there. In contrast, as Obama and Clinton have stressed, America and its allies "have greater unity of purpose in Afghanistan. The ultimate outcome of NATO's effort to stabilize Afghanistan and U.S. leadership of that effort may well affect the cohesiveness of the alliance and Washington's ability to shape

NATO's future."* Beyond this, NATO strategists looking to the rise of China propose a vastly expanded role for the Western military alliance. Once focused on the Euro-Atlantic area, "in the 21st century NATO must become an alliance founded on the Euro-Atlantic area, designed to project systemic stability beyond its borders":

> The center of gravity of power on this planet is moving inexorably eastward. The Asia-Pacific region brings much that is dynamic and positive to this world, but as yet the rapid change therein is neither stable nor embedded in stable institutions. Until this is achieved, it is the strategic responsibility of Europeans and North Americans, and the institutions they have built, to lead the way . . . security effectiveness in such a world is impossible without both legitimacy and capability.†

The only way to protect the international system the West has built, the author continues, is to "reenergize" the transatlantic relationship: "There can be no systemic security without Asian security and there will be no Asian security without a strong role for the West therein."

At present these ambitions are still fantasies. In Afghanistan, angry street demonstrations occurred all over the country in protest of Karzai's signing the U.S. bases agreement—a clear indication, if one was still needed, that NATO will have to take Karzai with it if it withdraws.

Uzbekistan responded by asking the United States to withdraw its base and personnel from their country. The Russians and Chinese are reported to have protested strongly in private, and subsequently conducted joint military operations on each other's territory for the first time. "Concern over apparent U.S. plans for permanent bases in Afghanistan and Central Asia" was an important cause of their rapprochement. More limply, Iran responded by increasing export duties, bringing construction in Herat to a halt. In response to Karzai's pleas, Tehran proposed a treaty that would prohibit foreign intelligence oper-

---

*Paul Gallis, "NATO in Afghanistan," CRS Report for Congress, October 23, 2007.

†Julian Lindley-French, "Big World, Big Future, Big NATO," *NATO Review,* Winter 2005.

ations in each country against the other; hard to see how Karzai could have signed this with a straight face.

Washington's options are limited. The most favored solution, balkanization and the creation of ethnic protectorates, might not work in Afghanistan. The Kosovars and others in the former Yugoslavia were willing client-nationalists, but the Hazaras are perfectly happy with indirect Iranian protection, and Tehran does not favor partitioning Afghanistan. Nor do the Russians and their Central Asian allies, who sustain the Tajiks. Some U.S. intelligence officers have informally been discussing the creation of a Pashtun state that unites the tribes and dissolves the Durand Line, but this would destabilize Pakistan and Afghanistan to such a degree that the consequences would be unpredictable. In any event there appear to be no serious takers in either country at the moment.

If this is understood, then a second alternative, both preferable and more workable, becomes apparent. This would involve a withdrawal of all NATO forces either preceded or followed by a regional pact to ensure Afghan stability for the next ten years. Pakistan, Iran, India, Russia, and possibly China could guarantee and support a functioning national government pledged to preserving the ethnic and religious diversity of Afghanistan. A serious social and economic plan to rebuild the country and provide the basic necessities for its people would become a necessary prerequisite for stability.

This would not only be in the interests of Afghanistan, it would be seen as such by its people, exhausted by decades of endless war and two major foreign occupations. The NATO occupation has made such an arrangement much more difficult. Its predictable failure has revived the Taliban, uniting increasing numbers of poor Pashtuns under its umbrella. But a NATO withdrawal could facilitate a serious peace process. It might also benefit Pakistan, provided its military leaders abandoned foolish notions of "strategic depth" and viewed India not as an enemy but as a possible partner in creating a regional cohesion within whose framework many contentious issues could be resolved. Are Pakistan's military leaders and politicians capable of grasping the nettle and moving their country forward? Can they move out of the flight path of U.S. power?

In the meantime the instability in Afghanistan is seeping over the border into Pakistan. Even the secretary-general of NATO is beginning to understand the dangers inherent in this should it continue much longer. In a recent speech in Washington, Jaap Scheffer responded to a questioner by saying, "If instability in Pakistan and instability in the frontier means instability in Afghanistan, the opposite is also true. . . . We need to depart from the notion that Pakistan is not part of the solution, and we should not only brand Pakistan as part of the problem. . . . We have to do everything we can to assist and help the Pakistanis. . . . It's my intention that as soon as there is a new government in Pakistan, I intend to travel again to Islamabad to talk to the president, to talk to the government, to see how we can lift the level of our political dialogue in the interest of minimizing this cross-instability around the borderline there."

The new government in Pakistan inaugurated on March 26, 2008, has already made it clear that it intends to negotiate with the militants in Waziristan. John Negroponte and Richard A. Boucher, representing the U.S. State Department, were not warmly greeted when they arrived in Islamabad to meet Asif Zardari and Nawaz Sharif. The country's largest daily, the *News,* published an editorial, "Hands Off Please, Uncle Sam," that was extremely critical of U.S. interference in the country. Sharif too was surprisingly sharp, refusing to give Negroponte any guarantees or commitments on "fighting terrorism." Sharif told the press, "If America wants to see itself clean of terrorists, we also want that our villages and towns should not be bombed. We do not like the fact that our country is now a killing field. We will negotiate with the militants to try and stop all this." The problem for Pakistan's elected government is that without a settlement in Afghanistan, it will find it difficult to stabilize the tribal areas on its western frontier.

The insurgents in Afghanistan are growing more audacious every month. In June 2008, a guerrilla contingent on motorbikes attacked the prison in Kandahar and freed one thousand prisoners. An embarrassed Karzai immediately *blamed* Pakistan and threatened to cross the border and teach Islamabad a lesson.

In reality, the strategic needs of the United States are now destabilizing the region. What if the people of the region reject these imperial fantasies? Will they, like their states, also be dissolved and created anew?

10

CAN PAKISTAN BE RECYCLED?

IN FEBRUARY 2008, ONE OF AMERICA'S MOST VENERABLE THINK tanks, the Brookings Institution of Washington, D.C., organized an exercise in moral abstraction under the rubric "The U.S.-Pakistan Strategic Relationship." The panel at this event reflected the new pluralism, consisting largely of old friends. In this case, two military philosophers, General Anthony Zinni, onetime boss of U.S. CENT-COM, and General Jehangir Karamat, former chief of staff of the Pakistan army and onetime ambassador to Washington, flanked Richard Armitage, formerly of the State Department, who, as discussed earlier, gained enormous prestige in some quarters after 9/11 for threatening to reduce General Musharraf and Pakistan to the Stone Age. General Karamat, a decent and honorable empire-loyalist, who resisted temptation and never seized power in Pakistan, understood immediately what was expected of him on the Brookings platform. The strategic relationship was not about the inevitable strains in a sixty-year-old marriage, whose course and consequences I've attempted to outline in this book, but about the immediate needs of the United States, which have shaped Pakistani policy for decades.

"Ladies and gentlemen," began poor General Karamat, "the sort of questions that are being asked in terms of the U.S.-Pakistan relationship right now are what is really happening in Pakistan's western border areas, why is it happening, and what is Pakistan doing about it." He tried to explain as best he could that the situation was complex, Pak-

istan was not to blame for the expanding militancy and that the traditional tribal leaders had been virtually eliminated and replaced by militants. He warned gently against any attempt to erode Pakistan's
sovereignty because it would be counterproductive and concluded by
stressing the importance of the "strategic relationship that has a great
future."

General Zinni was at his patronizing worst. He knew the Pakistan
army well, he said. His first direct contact had been with a battalion
that fought in Somalia in the early nineties and had performed
extremely well in a difficult situation. He might have been General
Charles Gordon commending the courage of his Indian sepoys in helping to crush the Taiping rebellion in nineteenth-century China. Zinni
knew Karamat well and was pleased to inform the audience, "General
Karamat is a graduate of Leavenworth, the Leavenworth Hall of Fame
as a matter of fact. He takes pride in that, and I know that for a fact.
That kind of connection, that kind of communication, made our ability to communicate and operate with each other despite the political
climate much more effective." Zinni was effusive in describing how
helpful everyone had been on his 1999 trip to Pakistan when he had
arrived to help out on the Kargil war with India. In reality, the U.S.
general had come armed with an ultimatum from Bill Clinton: withdraw from Indian territory or else. Dennis Kux, another former State
Department official on the South Asia desk, describes what actually
happened:

> Taken aback and dismayed by the Kargil adventure, the U.S. gov-
> ernment responded vigorously—far more so than the Johnson
> administration had reacted during the early stages of the 1965
> Kashmir war. President Clinton telephoned Nawaz Sharif to urge
> him to have his forces withdrawn and sent Gen. Anthony Zinni to
> Islamabad to second this message directly with the prime minister
> and with Gen. Pervez Musharraf, who had replaced Karamat as
> chief of army staff. Brushing aside Pakistan's claim that it was not
> directly involved with the Kargil operation and lacked control over
> the mujahideen, the U.S. general urged Islamabad to see to it that
> the intruders pulled back across the Kashmir line of control. When

not even the Chinese, let alone the Americans, were willing to support the Pakistani position, Islamabad found itself internationally isolated . . . and decided to cut Pakistan's losses.*

It was thoughtful of Zinni not to rub this in on what was, after all, intended as a friendly occasion with a fixed purpose. Zinni backed Karamat's view that Pakistan should not be overpressured on its western border. It had lost a lot of soldiers already. In fact, though Zinni did not say so, more Pakistani than U.S. soldiers or mercenaries have died in the cross-border Afghan war. The Pakistani military deliberately underestimates its casualties. The army claims that one thousand troops were killed during the Waziristan campaigns in 2004 through 2006. When in Peshawar in 2007, I was repeatedly told by local journalists that the real figure was over three thousand killed and many thousands wounded.

The show came to life when Richard Armitage took the microphone. Cutting through diplomatic niceties, Armitage pointed out that Pakistan was in a mess, had been so since 1947, and was no longer a country but four countries (a reference to the country's four provinces) or a bit more if one saw Waziristan as Qaedistan. He accepted only partial U.S. responsibility for this state of affairs and isolated it to the U.S. mode of intervention during the Soviet-Afghan war: "We knew exactly what we were doing in Pakistan at the time, and we knew exactly what was going to happen in Afghanistan when we walked away. This was not a secret." In other words they knew perfectly well that they had handed the country to religious groups and the ISI. What they were doing was using Pakistan as a "Kleenex" (as a senior official informed Dennis Kux) or, more accurately, a "condom" as a retired and embittered general once described the "strategic relationship" to me. As I have repeatedly stressed in this book, U.S. priorities determined Pakistan's domestic and foreign policies from 1951 onward. The long period of foreplay culminated in the Afghan climax. So enthralled were the Pak-

---

*Dennis Kux, *The United States and Pakistan: 1947–2000: Disenchanted Allies* (Washington and Baltimore: 2001). This is an extremely useful and sober, if not fully comprehensive, account of the "strategic relationship."

istani military by the experience that they became desperate to repeat it in Kashmir and Kargil, forgetting that a condom can't do it on its own.

Crucially, Armitage, like Zinni and Karamat before him, opposed as counterproductive the pressuring of the Pakistan government to permit U.S. troops to operate on Pakistani soil, a discussion that had been taking place behind closed doors in Washington for well over a year. U.S. presidential hopeful Senator Barack Obama had made an ill-judged intervention, publicly demonstrating his virility in military matters by supporting the hawks and calling for U.S. attacks inside Pakistan. Armitage said that he saw the future of Afghanistan related closely to a stable, democratic polity in Pakistan, but not a Venezuelan-style democracy, an odd remark given that there is no immediate possibility of this, but certainly revealing of his other preoccupation. None of this appeared to have had an impact on the White House. On April 12, 2008, the American president informed ABC News that the most dangerous area in the world now was neither Iraq nor Afghanistan, but Pakistan, because of the presence of Al Qaeda, who were preparing attacks on the United States. The logic was obvious though not spelled out: preparing public opinion for possible search-and-destroy missions inside Pakistan. The drones, on their own, were not sufficient. The problem, which neither Armitage nor the retired generals addressed at all, was the war in Afghanistan and the problems of governance in Kabul, where a regime fully supported and supervised by the United States is supposedly in charge.

The future of the two countries is certainly interrelated, but as the 2008 elections in Pakistan demonstrated and as some of us have been arguing for some time, the religious groups and parties have little mass support, let alone the armed-struggle jihadi currents. The crisis resulting from Operation Enduring Freedom is now creating havoc inside Pakistan and affecting morale in its army. The solution to this lies in Kabul and Washington. Islamabad and the EU are simply loyal auxiliaries with little real leverage to resolve the crisis.

Britain's most self-important viceroy to India, Lord Curzon, famously remarked that "no patchwork scheme will settle the Waziristan problem. . . . Not until the military steam-roller has passed over the country from end to end, will there be peace. But I do not want to be the person to start that machine." To expect the Pakistan army to do so, and as a result kill thousands of its own people from regions where it recruits soldiers, is to push it in a suicidal direction. Even the toughest command structure might find it difficult to maintain unity in these conditions.

Were this attempted directly by the United States, the Pakistan army would split, and hordes of junior officers would likely decamp to the mountains and resist. The military high command, regularly receiving reports of substantial numbers of soldiers surrendering to much smaller contingents of guerrillas, is well aware that the war in the Frontier Province is extremely unpopular among its troops. The soldiers surrender because they don't want to fight "America's war" or kill coreligionists. Junior officers have been taking early retirement to avoid a second tour of duty on the Afghan border. This being the case today, it is not difficult to imagine the result of a direct U.S. intervention inside Pakistan.

At the time of this writing, the Iraq war has cost $3 trillion. An all-out war inside Pakistan would require a great deal more. Were the Pakistan army to accept money and weaponry to become the steamroller referred to by Lord Curzon, the "jihadi finger on the nuclear trigger" so frequently cited by the West might well become a self-fulfilling prophecy. The regional solution, as I argued in the preceding chapter, is the only serious way out of this crisis.

Armitage accepted that religious extremism had little support in Pakistan, but stressed the crisis of leadership and governance, pointing out the lack of an obvious replacement for President Musharraf:

Unfortunately, the late Benazir Bhutto had a chance as a democratically elected leader, and I think it not for nothing that she found herself in Dubai for a number of years, and Mr. Nawaz Sharif also has had his difficulties. I am not being particularly nasty, I am just pointing out the fact that one of the things that we have to deal with now is that we do not have a ready candidate for soldier of the month.

This view is not much different from my own, with the following proviso. The search for a military pinup to salvage a crisis should come to a permanent halt. The latest incumbent, like his predecessors, has been an abject failure, as the imposition of an emergency revealed. On this, Stephen Cohen, another Brookings expert who specializes in Pakistan, was much sharper in a preelection exchange with me on the *Financial Times* website:

> I'd say that more Americans now see [Musharraf] as a liability, and this begins with the US military who have encountered Pakistan-based Taliban. . . . At best I see Musharraf being eased out by a combination of the Pakistan army, which must find him now to be an embarrassment, and foreign supporters, including the US but certainly China and the Europeans who realise that Pakistan must have coherent and effective leadership to tackle its many problems, not least of which is the growing violence in the society.

While there is truth to this, Cohen, like most U.S. analysts, underestimates the way that continuous Washington-backed military interventions have wrecked the organic evolution of politics in Pakistan, leaving it in the hands of mediocre and mottled politicians who have, till now, shown few signs of learning from past mistakes and whose only skill is in the relentless pursuit of personal wealth. Musharraf signed his political death warrant when he joined up with one such political faction—the Chaudhrys of Gujrat—to help him retain power. It was a signal that, under his watch, nothing was going to change.

And yet, if the present cycle of Pakistani power struggles could be broken, it is not impossible that a new movement or party might emerge to fundamentally change the political system. A precedent of sorts has been established. Who would have predicted the eruption of a large lawyers' movement or Supreme Court judges breaking with tradition and refusing a carte blanche to a cornered military government? It happened when the regime had become discredited and the opposition parties ineffective. The judiciary, despite its limitations, filled the vacuum. The timing was right for the chief justice to accept legal challenges to an unpopular and corrupt regime. His actions reignited popular involvement in the political process, creating the basis for an opposition victory in the general elections of 2008.

It is indisputable that the joint victors of the February 2008 general elections—Bhutto's husband, Asif Zardari, and the Sharif brothers—are tried-and-tested failures. An atmosphere of stifling pusillanimity and conformity prevails inside their political parties where compromises and deals are the prerogative of the leader alone. They were elected primarily because, as is increasingly the case in the West as well, when policy differences in a globalized world are minute, electors tend to vote against the incumbent. Musharraf had outlasted his welcome. His cronies were unpopular. Large-scale manipulation having been vetoed by the new army chief of staff, the elections were cautiously rigged to deny any single party an overall majority in accordance with the U.S.-brokered deal with Benazir.

Benazir had agreed to become Musharraf's junior partner and work with him and also, if necessary, his favored Chaudhrys of Gujrat. This is why Anne Patterson, the latest U.S. ambassador to Pakistan, summoned the widower Zardari after his election victory and reminded him, no doubt in more diplomatic language, that he had inherited not only the Peoples Party from his wife but also her legacy. Musharraf's spin doctors piled the pressure on Zardari by informing the media that corruption cases against him in Europe and Pakistan had not been withdrawn. Only his wife had been given legal immunity. This was somewhat mean-spirited since they worked as a team and immunity for one should have applied to the other, but nothing is ever as straightforward as it seems. Finally, the charges in Pakistan were dropped.

A recycling of the country and its modernization is perfectly possible, but it requires large-scale structural reforms. To isolate Pakistan's problems to religious extremism and dual power in Waziristan or the possession of nuclear weapons is to miss the point, to become marooned in a landscape behind enemy lines. These issues, as I have made clear in preceding chapters, are not unimportant, but the problems relating to them are a direct result of doing Washington's bidding in previous decades. The imbalance is glaring. In 2001, when U.S. interest in the country resumed, debt and defense amounted to two-thirds of public spending—257 billion rupees ($4.2 billion) and 149.6 billion rupees ($2.5 billion) respectively, compared to total tax revenues of 414.2 billion rupees ($6.9 billion). In a country with one of the worst public education systems in Asia—70 percent of women and 41 percent of men are officially classified as illiterate—and with health care virtually nonexistent for over half the population, a mere 105.1 billion rupees ($1.75 billion) was left for overall development.

Throughout the nineties, the International Monetary Fund (IMF) had scolded civilian governments for failing to keep their restructuring promises. Musharraf's regime, by contrast, won admiring praise from 1999 onward for sticking to IMF guidelines "despite the hardships imposed on the public by austerity measures." Impoverishment and desperation in the burgeoning city slums and the countryside—still home to 67.5 percent of the population—were exacerbated further. Some 56 million Pakistanis, nearly 30 percent of the population, now live below the poverty line; the number has increased by 15 million since Musharraf seized power. Of Pakistan's four provinces, the Punjab, with around 60 percent of the population, has continued to dominate economically and politically, with Punjabis filling the upper echelons of the army and bureaucracy and channeling what development there is to local projects. Sind, with 23 percent of the population, and Baluchistan, with 5 percent, remain starved of funds, water, and power supplies, while the North-West Frontier's fortunes have increasingly been tied to the Afghan war and heroin economy.

A cash-flow crisis in May 2008 was temporarily resolved by a Saudi commitment to provide oil on long-term credit.

To PERMANENTLY continue as a satrapy is certainly not going to help Pakistan. Instead, a number of changes, if implemented, could set the country on the road to rapid economic development experienced elsewhere in Asia, while at the same time building and sustaining democratic structures at the level of the state.

First, serious land reform is required to disperse economic and political power to the countryside, reduce rural poverty, and provide aid and subsidies to farmers and peasant cooperatives. Farmers in the United States and Europe have been heavily subsidized, often to the detriment of agriculture in the third world. A subsidy program to small farmers in Pakistan could be of great benefit, but elite attachment to the current market-priorities global system militates against any such plan. Ownership of land is highly concentrated. Only 20 percent of all landholders own more than thirty-five acres, and less than 10 percent own more than one hundred acres. Eighty-six percent of households in Sind, 78 percent in Baluchistan, 74 percent in the Punjab, and 65 percent in the North-West Frontier Province own no land at all. Fifty-five percent of the country's total population of 170 million is landless. This inequity lies at the heart of rural poverty.

The problem is structural. The economy rests on a narrow production base, heavily dependent on the unreliable cotton crop and the low-value-added textile industry; irrigation supplies are deficient, and soil erosion and salinity are widespread. More damaging still are the crippling social relations in the countryside. Low productivity in agriculture can only be reversed through the implementation of serious land reforms, but the alliance between *khaki* state and local landlords makes this virtually impossible. As an Economist Intelligence Unit report on Pakistan noted:

> Change is hindered not least because the status quo suits the wealthy landowners who dominate the sector, as well as federal and provincial parliaments. Large landowners own 40 per cent of the arable land and control most of the irrigation system. Yet assessments by independent agencies, including the World Bank, show them to be less productive than smallholders. They are also poor taxpayers, heavy borrowers and bad debtors.*

The weak economy has been further skewed for decades now by Pakistan's vast military apparatus. For "security reasons," its detailed budget is never itemized in official statements: a single line records the overall sum. In Pakistan, the power of any elected body to probe into military affairs has always been strictly curtailed. The citizenry remains unaware of how the annual $2.5 billion is distributed between the army (550,000 strong, with over two thousand tanks and two armored

---

*Economist Intelligence Unit, *Pakistan, Afghanistan* (London: 2002), 26.

divisions); the air force (ten fighter squadrons of forty combat planes each, as well as French- and U.S.-made missile systems); and the navy (ten submarines, eight frigates)—let alone what is spent on nuclear weapons and delivery systems.

In these circumstances the most recent slogan of the Ministry of Culture, "Grow and Globalize," takes on a satirical, if not surrealist, hue. Unfortunately it is meant seriously. The idea behind it is the sale of large tracts of land to global agribusiness, as has been done in Brazil, while along the way transforming the peasants into employees on short-term contracts. A civil servant from the Finance Ministry in Islamabad was recently reported in the press as saying, "The era of land reform has gone and now the government wants to create new job opportunities through liberalization, privatization, and deregulation of the economy. There is no plan even to discuss land reforms in the upcoming planning document." In the face of this brutal new approach, the old-fashioned feudal landlords have been given a renewed lease on life. In Sind, for instance, they continue to administer justice, dominate politics, rule their fiefdoms with an iron hand, and also, in their own fashion, provide for the common weal by not letting their peasants starve. Some, such as Mumtaz Bhutto (Benazir's uncle), openly contend that those who work their land are better off under a precapitalist system of this sort than under what is offered by globalization. Of course, they will not even consider a third alternative of land redistribution to the poor.

Alongside agricultural reform, a functioning social infrastructure urgently needs to be created for the mass of the population. This requires a transformation on three levels: education, health, and cheap housing. Of these the first two should now be a strategic priority for any government. Figures released by the UN in 2007–8 place Pakistan 136th out of 177 on the Human Development Index, below Sri Lanka, India, the Maldives, and Myanmar. Illiteracy has actually increased and will continue to do so unless measures are taken. The official primary-school enrollment rate of 53 percent is the lowest in South Asia and is almost certainly an overestimate. The Ministry of Education, I was told in Islamabad, pays salaries to nonexistent teachers, charges overhead for deserted school buildings, and has various other scams that inflate the published figures. Even so, the official spending on education is 2.4 percent of GDP, considerably lower than that of Nepal. Despite the parlous state of primary education, more than 50 percent of the allocated nonrecurrent education budget goes unspent each year because of the poor capacity of the system. Many smaller towns have empty, dilapidated school buildings with few teachers. Given this, it is hardly a surprise that desperate, poor families are prepared to entrust their children to madrassas of the Isalamists, where they will be fed, clothed, and educated better than in what passes for a state system. The private educational network is both expensive and class-bound, sometimes rejecting children from poor backgrounds even when they have managed to borrow the money or obtained philanthropic aid. This massive shortcoming in Pakistani society is the responsibility of every government since 1947. The Bhuttos, father and daughter, were no better than Zia and Musharraf in this regard. A high-quality state system with English as a compulsory language (on the Malaysian model) would be an extremely popular measure in every province and would entirely transform the country.

Educational opportunities may be limited in Pakistan, but the poor have almost no health care. Recent figures show that there are just eight physicians and one dentist per ten thousand people and fewer than five hundred psychiatrists for a country with large numbers of traumatized and disturbed people. Malnutrition, acute respiratory illnesses, tuberculosis, preventable diseases of various types, are widespread. One in every eleven citizens suffers from diabetes. Given the lack of facilities, and with nearly three-quarters of Pakistan's specialist doctors working in the United States, government hospitals are a disgrace. Most medical practitioners work in their own clinics or private hospitals for the rich. No official statistics are provided, but Karachi, Lahore, and Islamabad together have up to a hundred or so well equipped of the latter. Conditions in state hospitals in the big cities are grim, and the lack of affordable medicine a permanent curse on the poor. The tragedy is continuous. The coalition government formed after the February 2008 elections announced its twenty top "ministries." These did not include "health and human development."

As for housing, the state provides none except for those currently in government service or the armed forces. The privatization of land in the military cantonments has meant, however, that new military colonies are being created in remote areas outside the cities.

The legal system too is skewed in favor of the wealthy. Recent events with the chief justices notwithstanding, most judges in Pakistan have been vacillating, cowardly, negligent, prejudiced, and above all corrupt. The Zia dictatorship frightened them into submission. His civilian heirs appointed political cronies with the result that, especially during the nineties, justice in Pakistan has never been blind; what was usually weighed in its scales was banknotes, with a few honorable exceptions. It was no secret in the country that in legal cases involving property or corporate claims, senior lawyers, when asked to name a fee, would simply ask the client how many judges he was prepared to buy.

The spate of recent Supreme Court activism that led to Pakistan's only judicial crisis does offer hope on this front, but it is worth remembering that the rot begins at the primary level. Judicial and legal reforms, including a complete separation of powers between the judiciary and the executive, would be a first step toward reviving a dysfunctional state. Proper salaries to reduce the need for "illegal" money would also be helpful. The restoration of the chief justice and his colleagues sacked by Musharraf is an important political issue. But even if the divisions on this question, both within the PPP and between it and Nawaz Sharif's Muslim League, were resolved and the judges reinstated, the structural problems would not go away.

It soon became clear that Zardari was more sympathetic to Musharraf than he was to judicial activists.

The "march" from Karachi to Islamabad was in reality a drive to the capital in cars and buses. It was large, but the government insisted there should neither be a sit-in or a permanent siege of parliament. The leaders capitulated and disbanded the assembly. The result has been to demoralize the movement. Where Musharraf failed, the widower has succeeded.

One of the proud boasts of the Musharraf regime was that it had provided the country with a free media for the first time in its history. This was only a partial exaggeration. Pakistan's first two military dictators had crushed the media in blatant fashion. Zulfiqar Ali Bhutto was not a great friend of press freedom, nor was Nawaz Sharif. While Benazir Bhutto did not interfere with the print media, both she and her husband offered nonstop advice to the programmers of PTV, the state television network, which was impossible to ignore. By way of contrast, Musharraf, during his early days as president, when he was brimming with self-confidence, ended the state monopoly of television. The airwaves were liberated. As a result a range of new stations mushroomed, often providing higher-quality news reportage and analysis than their counterparts in India or Britain. A cocky and arrogant General Musharraf did not imagine that he could ever be threatened by press freedom. He also knew that Pakistanis watched Indian cable channels and news bulletins much more than they did their own state TV. He recognized that reforming the antiquated broadcasting structure would benefit local businesses and create a healthy competition with channels abroad, and indeed this is what happened.

But Musharraf had underestimated the capacity of Pakistani journalists, especially a newer and younger generation untouched by the sleaze of the past, to pursue the truth. Historical crises such as the breakup of the country were, for the first time, openly discussed in the media, and the generals were confronted with hard questions. Inevitably a clampdown followed the early loosening of censorship. The independent media's coverage of the lawyers' revolt was one of the primary targets of the declaration of a state of emergency in 2007. Geo, the largest network, went off the air for many months. The government introduced regulatory procedures that seriously restricted news broadcasting. Musharraf insisted that to remain on air TV news stations had to sign a code of conduct whereby journalists who ridiculed him and other government officials would be subjected to fines and prison sentences. "The media should not agitate," Musharraf said. "It should join us in the war on terror." He was wistfully thinking of CNN and BBC World.

The newly elected government's minister for information announced in April 2008 that legislation was about to be introduced to restore complete media freedom.

The interrelationship between domestic and foreign policy in Pakistan has never been hidden. Instead of a foreign policy dependent on big powers, there should be a regional concentration on South Asia and

the working out of a common approach to international relations. A
rapprochement with India and the creation of a South Asian Union, a
better and more coherent version of the EU, is in the long-term interests of the whole region. At a time when the United States is actively
breaking up states and encouraging client nationalisms in such places
as Kosovo, Croatia, and Kurdistan, regional cohesion offers a noncon-
frontational solution to the Kashmir and Tamil disputes, a reduction in
military expenditures, and an improvement in social standards in all
countries in the area. It would also lead to a political strengthening of
the region as a whole, allowing for healthier relationships with the
United States and China. South Asia should not act as a buffer between
these two great powers, but as a strong and independent region in its
own right. Pakistan's relations with China are an important factor in
this equation. In recent years they have been symbolized by a massive
Chinese investment transforming Gwadar, a small fishing port on the
Makran coast in Baluchistan, into a major port. China's vice premier,
Wu Bangguo, was flown in to lay the foundation stone of the new
development on March 22, 2002, four months after the U.S. occupation of Kabul. When completed later this year, Gwadar will be the
largest deep-sea port in the region, providing the Chinese with an oil
terminal close to the Persian Gulf, which supplies two-thirds of its
energy. Some U.S. intelligence analysts are worried that Gwadar could
become a Chinese naval base providing rapid access to the Indian
Ocean. Such anxieties are reciprocal. With U.S. bases and armies now
on China's borders in Afghanistan, Beijing is beginning to feel the tension. This was one of the reasons that the Chinese prime minister visited Pakistan in April 2005 to sign a set of twenty-two accords that
were designed to boost bilateral relations. A year later Musharraf visited
Beijing. The official agenda centered on trade and counterterrorism,
but Afghanistan and Pakistan's desire for civil nuclear cooperation will
have been discussed in great detail. China is regarded by many in the
Pakistani military leadership as an "all-weather friend," a more reliable
strategic and noninterfering partner than Washington, which has peri-
odically embargoed the supply of military hardware; the final restrictions were only removed after 9/11.

The West's current obsession with Islam is related only partially to

9/11; the larger cause is oil, the bulk of which lies underneath lands inhabited by Muslims. In considering the meanings of Islam, Western analysts would do well to recognize it for what it is: a world religion that is in no sense monolithic. Both as a religion and a culture it encompasses numerous local traditions as different from each other as those in Senegal and Indonesia, South Asia and the Arabian Peninsula, the Maghreb and China. It contains all the colors of the rainbow and its culture has remained vibrant to this day. Saudi Arabia, Egypt, and Indonesia produced three of the finest novelists of the twentieth century, Abdelrahman Munif, Naguib Mahfouz, and Pramoedya Ananta Toer. South Asia has produced poets of matchless quality, including Ghalib, Iqbal, and Faiz. Senegal and Iran have given us an auteur cinema that compares to the best once produced in Europe and often superior to Hollywood. That this has to be spelled out in the twenty-first century points to the provincialism of the West, incapable of looking beyond its own interests and unaware of the world it traduces.

The political realm is murkier, but here also there are causes and consequences. Indonesia, the largest Muslim state in the world, once had the world's largest Communist Party, with a million members and sympathizers. They were wiped out by General Suharto with the blessings of today's Islamophobes.* Who crushed the Iraqi Communists with a leadership that included Sunni, Shia, Jew, and Christian? A U.S.-backed Saddam Hussein. Repression, the implosion of the Communist system, and the new economic orthodoxy produced a vacuum in many parts of the Islamic world. As a result, many turned to religion. A series of articles on Egypt in the *New York Times* in February 2008 highlighted middle-class unemployment as a major factor driving young people to the mosques. The same is true to a lesser extent in Pakistan. For some, religiosity eases the pain.

As for political Islam, it too comes in different shapes and colors. NATO's Islamists in Turkey, neoliberal to the core, are popular in the West. The Muslim Brotherhood in Egypt would be equally happy to work with the United States, but might disagree on Palestine, since

---

*Benedict Anderson, "Exit Suharto," *New Left Review,* March–April 2008.

Gaza is a neighbor. Elsewhere new forces and faces are emerging that have something in common. Muqtada, Haniya, Nasrallah, Ahmadinejad: each has risen by organizing the urban poor in their localities—Baghdad and Basra, Gaza and Jenin, Beirut and Sidon, Tehran and Shiraz. It is in the slums that Hamas, Hezbollah, the Sadr brigades, and the Basij have their roots. The contrast with the Hariris, Chalabis, Karzais, Allawis, on whom the West relies—overseas millionaires, crooked bankers, CIA bagmen—could not be starker. A radical wind is blowing from the alleys and shacks of the latter-day wretched of the earth, surrounded by the fabulous wealth of petroleum. The limits of this radicalism, so long as it remains captured by the Koran, are clear enough. The impulses of charity and solidarity are infinitely better than those of imperial greed and comprador submission, but so long as what they offer is social alleviation rather than reconstruction, they are sooner or later liable to recuperation by the existing order. Leaders with a vision capable of transcending national or communal divisions, with a sense of unity and the self-confidence to broadcast it, have yet to emerge.

There is, of course, Al Qaeda, but its importance in the general scheme of things is greatly overstated by the West. It unleashes sporadic terror attacks and kills innocents, but it does not pose any serious threat to U.S. power. It is not even remotely comparable to the anticolonial national liberation movements that tormented Britain, France, and the United States in Africa or Indochina during the last century. The current turmoil is still confined to those areas of the Middle East where for twenty years or more American power never significantly penetrated: the West Bank, Baathist Iraq, Khomeinist Iran. The real U.S. anchorage in the region lies elsewhere—in Egypt, Saudi Arabia, the Gulf States, and Jordan. There, despite being Muslims, America's traditional clients have held the line and are usually on hand to help out with regional problems. That Pakistan has been part of this group has been at its own cost.

It is foolish to speak, as many Western commentators do, of "global Islam" being "Waziristan writ large," when what is really meant is that the U.S./NATO war in Afghanistan is posing serious problems and that neo-Taliban groups are crossing the border and winning support in Pakistan. Referring to this phenomenon as an aspect of "global Islam" is about as accurate as referring to the judeocide of the Second World War as an aspect of "global Christianity."

An argument often used by Bernard Lewis is that the United States has become a scapegoat for the Muslim world to explain its own decline and problems. To put forward this argument at a time when the Western military or economic occupation of the Arab world, barring Syria and partially Lebanon, is virtually complete is somewhat disingenuous. The founders of Al Qaeda were incubated in Saudi Arabia and Egypt before being dispatched to wage jihad in Afghanistan by Zbigniew Brzezinski, now an adviser to Barack Obama in the 2008 presidential campaign. Pakistan's relations with Saudi Arabia have always been close, with the cash nexus, rather than religion, playing the bigger part. But the Saudi kingdom is also close to Washington. Surely Bernard Lewis is aware that King Faisal sincerely believed that the only way to defeat Nasser and the godless Communists was by making religion the central pillar of the Saudi social order and using it ruthlessly against the enemy. Islam was under threat and had to be defended on all fronts. This pleased his allies in Washington, who were tolerant even of his decision to impose an oil embargo against the West after the 1973 war, something that has never been attempted since.

Even after Saudi oil was fully nationalized in 1980, Washington's politico-military elite maintained their pledge to defend the existing Saudi regime and its state whatever the cost. Why, some people asked, could the Saudi state not defend itself? The answer was because the Saud clan, living in permanent fear, was haunted by the specter of the radical nationalists who had seized power in Egypt in 1952 and in Iraq six years later. The Sauds kept the size of the national army and air force to the barest minimum to minimize the risk of a coup d'état. Many of the armaments they have purchased to please the West lie rusting peacefully in desert warehouses.

For a decade and a half in the late 1970s and '80s, the Pakistan army, paid for by the Saudi treasury, sent in large contingents to protect the Saudi royal family in case of internal upheavals. Then, after the first Gulf War, the American military arrived. It is still there. U.S. air bases in Saudi Arabia and Qatar were used to launch the war against

Iraq. All pretense of independence had gone. The only thing the Saudi princes could do was to plead with the United States not to make public what was hardly a state secret. There was practically no TV coverage of planes taking off from Saudi Arabia bound for Iraq.

Linked to the "scapegoating" argument is a "new" idea that is also promoted by Muslims anxious to please, mainly in the U.S. academy. The struggle, they argue, is not between Islam and the United States but within Islam itself. All this means is that with the United States strongly backing and protecting its friends in the Muslim world, those who oppose client status are fighting back. As the nationalists and the left both have been virtually eliminated, this task has now fallen to Islamist groups of differing stripes. Al Qaeda is one such group, but is a tiny minority within the House of Islam. Nor is this new. Islam has never been united.* That is one reason why it lost Sicily and Spain in the medieval period. The only time it managed to unite its armies was under the Kurdish sultan Salah ad-Din to take back Jerusalem from the Crusaders in the twelfth century and return it to its former status as a city for all three peoples of the Book.

It is simply foolish to expect "Islam" to speak with one voice any more than Christianity or Judaism, Hinduism or Buddhism. The rise of recent Islamist movements with their extremist factions is a modern phenomenon, a product of the last fifty years of world history. It's a phase that will wither away, including in South Waziristan, if the military occupations of Muslim lands are ended. There are bigger problems in the world. To make Islam the scapegoat for U.S. foreign policy disasters is as destructive as the utilization of religion during the Cold War, when the United States itself for the first time stressed its own loyalty to religion. The reason was obvious. Religion was being used to mobilize support in the third world against the godless Communist enemy. President Truman used religion as a weapon against the Soviet Union. In 1952, the U.S. Supreme Court accepted a higher authority than itself when it ruled, "We are a religious people whose institutions presuppose a Supreme Being." The word *religious* rather than *Christ-*

---

*I have explained this in some detail in *Clash of Fundamentalisms: Crusades, Jihads and Modernity* (New York and London: 2002).

ian was used precisely to make a common block with Muslims. President Eisenhower repeated all this in 1954: "Our government makes no sense unless it is founded on a deeply felt religious faith—and I don't care what it is."* In Pakistan and other Muslim states such as Egypt and Indonesia, the USIS openly supported the Muslim Brotherhood and the Jamaat-e-Islami and their student wings. As we have seen, this process reached its climax during the first Afghan war as General Zia, backed by Washington, created, armed, and trained specialist jihadi groups to wage the war against the godless in Afghanistan. Waziristan, in those years, was global anticommunism writ large. The United States could, or so it imagined, wash its hands and retire. The Pakistani state was lumbered with this unsavory legacy. Then came the 9/11 blowback, which, contrary to the views expressed by George W. Bush at the time, was not an attack on pure innocence by irrational evil, but the outcome of what had transpired in another epoch.

In 2003, after a lengthy trip to Pakistan, I wrote:

> The Army is now the only ruling institution; its domination of the country is complete. How long can this be sustained? . . . The officer corps is no longer the exclusive domain of the landed gentry— a majority of officers come from urban backgrounds and are subject to the same influences and pressures as their civilian peers. Privileges have kept them loyal, but the processes that destroy politicians are already at work. Whereas in the recent past it was Nawaz Sharif and his brother, or Benazir Bhutto and her husband, who demanded kickbacks before making deals, it is now General Musharraf's office that sanctions key projects.

> Of course, high—even stratospheric—levels of corruption are no bar to longevity, if a military regime has sufficiently intimidated its population and enjoys solid enough support in Washington, as the Suharto regime in Indonesia testifies. Can Musharraf look forward to this sort of reign? The fate of his dictatorship is likely to depend on the interaction of three main forces. First will be the

---

* *Christian Century* 71 (1954).

degree of internal cohesion of the Army itself. Historically, it has never split—vertically or horizontally—and its discipline in following a 180-degree turn in policy towards Afghanistan, whatever the sweeteners that have accompanied it, has so far been impressive. It is not impossible that one day some patriotic officer might deliver the country of its latest tyrant, as Zia was once mysteriously sent on his way to Gehenna; but for the minute, such an ending appears improbable. Having weathered the humiliation of its abandonment of the Taliban, the high command looks capable of brazening out any further acts of obeisance to orders from the Pentagon.

What of parliamentary opposition to military rule? Vexing though the upshot of the October 2002 election, for all its fraud, proved to be for Musharraf, the parties that dominate the political landscape in Pakistan offer little hope of rebellion against him. The cringing opportunism of the Bhutto and Sharif clans knows few limits. The Islamist front ensconced in Peshawar and Quetta is noisier, but not more principled—cash and perquisites quickly stilling most of its protests. Popular discontent remains massive, but lacks any effective channels of national expression. It would be good to think that their performances in office had discredited the PPP and Sharif's clique forever, but experience suggests that should the regime at any point start to crack, there is little to prevent these phoenixes of sleaze from arising once more, in the absence of any more progressive alternatives.

Finally, there is the American overlord itself. The Musharraf regime cannot aspire to play the same role as regional satrap that Zia once enjoyed. Pakistan has been ousted as imperial instrument in Afghanistan, and checked from compensating with renewed incursions in Kashmir. But if Islamabad has been forced into a more passive posture along its northern borders, its strategic importance for the US has, if anything, increased. For Washington has now made a huge political investment in the creation of a puppet regime in Kabul, to be guarded by US troops "for years to come," in the words of General Tommy Franks—not to speak of its continuing hunt for Osama bin Laden and his lieutenants. Pakistan is a vital flank in the pursuit of both objectives, and its top brass can look forward to the kind of lavish emoluments, public and private, that the Thai military received for their decades of collusion with the American war in Indochina. Still, Washington is pragmatic and knows that Benazir Bhutto and Nawaz Sharif were just as serviceable agents of its designs in Kabul as Zia himself. Should he falter domestically, Musharraf will be ditched without sentiment by the suzerain. The Pax Americana can wage war with any number of proxies. It will take an uprising on the scale of 1969 to shake Pakistan free of them.*

Events have not contradicted this analysis, with one exception. It was impossible to predict the pleasant if unexpected surprise that the country witnessed in the judicial upsurge. Its impact was a renewal of hope, and the effective media coverage of the movement left Musharraf exposed. He now needed a mixture of repression together with a civilian cover and had little option but to accept a U.S.-brokered deal with the late Benazir Bhutto. He was by now largely discredited in the country, and the imposition of the emergency was the last straw for many of his supporters. The assassination of Bhutto increased his unpopularity. Defeat soon followed.

However flawed the February 2008 general elections in Pakistan may have been, they were a blow to Musharraf as well as the Islamist alliance, which lost its stronghold to the secular Awami National Party, the heirs twice removed of old Ghaffar Khan, who had taught the Pashtuns to value nonviolence and to combat imperialism. The Peoples Party emerged as the largest party with 120 out of a total of 342 seats in the National Assembly, closely followed by the Sharif Muslim League with 90 seats and the ANP with 13. The pro-Musharraf Muslim League won 51 seats and the MQM 25. The defeat was decisive. Had there been no ballot rigging, it would have been a complete rout, especially for the MQM in Karachi, where violence and chicanery were on open display. The religious coalition obtained 6 members of parliament, and even if the Jamaat-e-Islami had not boycotted the election, their representation would not have been much higher.

---

* "The Colour Khaki," *New Left Review* 19 (January–February 2003).

Till the Bhutto assassination, the election campaign had been largely lackluster. The mainstream parties had few differences on ideological or policy grounds, either on the domestic or the international level. The Peoples Party had long abandoned its populism. The key interlinked issues were Musharraf's presidency and the reinstatement of the chief justice and others sacked during the emergency. The PPP was divided on this issue. One of its Punjabi veterans, Aitzaz Ahsan, was a central figure in the campaign to bring the judges back. Bhutto's widower, on the other hand, had been sentenced to years in prison by the same judiciary and loathed them. At a meeting of party leaders in April 2008, he made his views clear to Ahsan.

Leaving aside that the ANP, like the PPP, is not unfriendly to Washington, its electoral triumph in the Frontier Province confirms what some of us have consistently argued. The world's sixth most populous country and a nuclear state is not on the verge of a jihadi takeover. If neocons in the Bush administration or their successor want their prophecies of gloom and doom fulfilled, all they need to do is to occupy parts of Pakistan, destroy its nuclear facility, and impose a puppet regime. The hell that is Iraq would rapidly shift eastward. Definitely not recommended.

The delighted politicians of the PPP and the triumphant Muslim League rapidly agreed to form a coalition and divide the ministerial spoils. True to form, Nawaz Sharif, himself out of parliament, selected tried-and-trusted supporters or relatives for the work that lay ahead. Zardari, empowered by his widow, was able to choose the new prime minister. During her exile, Bhutto had selected an amiable and unquestioning Sindhi landlord as her proxy. He was widely expected to be the PPP choice. Makhdoom Amin Fahim, a pir-cum-landlord, politician and religious divine rolled into one, is hardly a social liberal. Uniquely, even for Pakistan, all his four brothers-in-law are the Koran. Fahim's family claims descent from the first Muslims to enter the subcontinent, the cohort of Muhammad bin Kasim who took Sind in 711. Women in early Islam owned and inherited property equally with men, a tradition that took root in parts of Sind. Landowners there devised an ingenious solution to prevent women from marrying outside the family, which could lead to the parcelization of the estates. The young heiresses were literally married off to the Koran—similar to nuns becoming brides of Christ. This preserved the girls' virginity, which in turn provided them with magic healing powers; but above all it ensured that the property remained under the control of their fathers and brothers. The problem posed by the four wealthy sisters of the PPP leader was thus piously solved.

Zardari decided against Fahim for geopolitical reasons. He felt a Punjabi landlord would be better placed to run the country and selected another divine-plus-politician from the saint-ridden city of Multan. The choice was Yousaf Raza Gillani, a politician well attuned to the spirit of the age and cut from the same cloth as many of his contemporaries. Gillani's qualities had been recognized by General Zia-ul-Haq, and like Nawaz Sharif, he became an early favorite of the dictator's, serving loyally on various committees designed to buttress the regime. After Zia's death, Gillani was a loyal supporter of the Muslim League, but fell out with Nawaz Sharif and joined the Peoples Party. He stayed with them and turned down offers from the Chaudhrys of Gujrat to jump ship and join their Muslim League. His instinct served him well in this case. His loyalty to the PPP when it was out of power has been handsomely rewarded by the party's godfather.

The immediate impact of the electoral defeat suffered by Musharraf's political factotums was to dispel the disillusionment and cynicism of the citizenry. The moral climate seemed to improve. But not for long. The fervor and naïveté soon turned to anger. The worm-eaten tongues of some politicians were soon back on display. Two major issues confronted the victors. The first concerned the judiciary. Nawaz Sharif had pledged that, if elected, his party would reverse the midnight actions carried out during the emergency and restore the chief justice of the Supreme Court and the other sacked judges to their former positions. Soon after their election triumph, the widower Bhutto and Nawaz Sharif met in Bhurban and publicly agreed that this would be a major priority and the judges would be brought back within thirty days of the new government taking office. There was general rejoicing in the country. Since November 3, 2007, until just after the election, the chief justice, Iftikhar Muhammad Chaudhry, had been a prisoner of the regime, detained in his house that was sealed off with barbwire barricades and a complement of riot police permanently on guard. His landlines were cut and his cell phones incapacitated by jamming devices. Colleagues and lawyers defending him were subjected to similar treatment. One of them, Aitzaz Ahsan, railed against the Bush regime in an op-ed in the *New York Times* on December 23, 2007:

> People in the United States wonder why extremist militants in Pakistan are winning. What they should ask is why does President Musharraf have so little respect for civil society—and why does he essentially have the backing of American officials?
>
> The White House and State Department briefings on Pakistan ignore the removal of the justices and all these detentions. Meanwhile, lawyers, bar associations and institutes of law around the world have taken note of this brave movement for due process and constitutionalism. They have displayed their solidarity for the lawyers of Pakistan. These include, in the United States alone, the American Bar Association, state and local bars stretching from New York and New Jersey to Louisiana, Ohio and California, and citadels of legal education like Harvard and Yale Law Schools.
>
> The detained chief justice continues to receive enormous recognition and acknowledgment. Harvard Law School has conferred on him its highest award, placing him on the same pedestal as Nelson Mandela and the legal team that argued Brown v. Board of Education. The National Law Journal has anointed him its lawyer of the year. The New York City Bar Association has admitted him as a rare honorary member. Despite all this, the Musharraf regime shows no sign of relenting.

The new government ordered the immediate release of the dismissed judges and the removal of all restrictions. This was widely seen as a prelude to their reinstatement. Musharraf and his backers in Washington panicked. If the chief justice and his colleagues resumed office, John Negroponte informed the new government (via Assistant Secretary of State Richard Boucher), Musharraf might be legally removed and that was unacceptable. He had to stay on, at least as long as Bush remained in the White House. His departure would be regarded as a setback in the war on terror.

This accelerated the political process and brought out into the open the differences on this issue between the PPP leadership and the Sharif brothers. At a subsequent meeting with U.S. officials in Dubai, in the presence of Musharraf and Benazir Bhutto's fixers, the latter were asked to confirm the exact nature of the deal agreed by the late Benazir with the Americans prior to her return to Pakistan. Her husband had been sidelined during that period and appeared to be unaware of all the details.

Asif Zardari had his own worries. The National Reconciliation Ordinance that pardoned corrupt politicians had been part of the deal between Bhutto and Musharraf. It was a much-hated ordinance and the Supreme Court was due to hear an appeal questioning its legality. Zardari, only too aware that this and the possibility that cases against him in European courts might be resurrected, capitulated. Simultaneously, U.S. officials in Pakistan offered inducements to the chief justice in the form of a senior position on the International Court of Justice with all the perks of the post or even an academic post in the United States. The chief justice told them that he was not interested.

Asif Zardari and Nawaz Sharif met in London in April 2008 to iron out their differences. Each was accompanied by trusted aides. Two elected Muslim League parliamentarians flanked Nawaz Sharif. Two unelected political fixers, Rehman Malik and Husain Haqqani (the first a submissive courtier, the second a crucial link to Washington), sat with Zardari. No consensus could be reached on the restoration of the judiciary and this inevitably produced cracks in the alliance. After consulting senior colleagues, Nawaz Sharif withdrew Muslim League ministers from the central government, citing disagreement on this issue. It is extremely rare in Pakistan for any politician to relinquish office on an issue of principle. Nawaz Sharif's popularity in the country soared. Zardari's action provoked the deepest indignation among the supporters of the judiciary and a number of senior figures in the PPP were clearly unhappy at the public embrace of Musharraf. But having accepted Zardari as their temporary leader they had rendered themselves powerless. As the party's guardian, the Bhutto family had deprived their ward of any intrinsic political identity and no group inside it was capable of formulating an independent political program. PPP politicians had grown so accustomed to the Bhutto harness that they could take no step without it. This is a pity. As I have argued earlier, the Bhutto family has long exhausted its historical function. Were the PPP to rid itself of this incubus, democracy could only be enhanced, even if it took a few years for its leaders and members to overcome their political numbness and become articulate again. In the meantime, the initiative lies entirely with Zardari and his close advisers. They make the key decisions, utilizing Prime Minister Gillani and the PPP cohort in parliament as a rubber stamp. For the moment this suits both Musharraf and Bush. What happens after their departure remains an open question.

The campaign to defend the judiciary was the first serious nationwide mass movement against the arbitrariness of military rule since 1969. The Supreme Court decisions that challenged the Musharraf regime had restored the country's self-respect. Its secular character had disproved the myth that jihadi terrorists were on the verge of taking over the country. But the judges were much less popular in the ruling circles of the United States and Europe, where elite opinion was neoimperialist in outlook and obsessed with occupation and war. Pakistan's judges were not regarded as helpful by these groups. Musharraf's use of emergency powers to dismiss the "turbulent" chief justice had accelerated the decomposition of the regime. For defending the civil rights of the poor, the chief justice was referred to by some Western liberal newspapers as a "judicial activist" or a "firebrand."

Washington and its allies regarded the war in Afghanistan and Pakistan's role in relation to it as the central priority. Everything else was seen as a diversion. What would be the attitude of the newly elected Pakistani politicians to the tempest in Afghanistan? Would they refrain from moves that might embarrass the United States and give Washington a free hand? In March 2008, Admiral Eric T. Olson, the head of the United States Special Operations Command, arrived in Islamabad for consultations with the Pakistan military and surprised locals by demanding a roundtable meeting with the country's elected leaders, another first in the country's history. Olson asked the politicians how they viewed the urgent U.S. need for cross-border incursions. None of the Pakistanis who responded regarded this as a good idea and they made their opposition very clear. The seniormost civil servant in the Frontier, Khalid Aziz, told Olson that "it would be extremely dangerous. It would increase the number of militants, it would become a war of liberation for the Pashtuns. They would say: 'We are being slaughtered. Our enemy is the United States.'"

For Nawaz Sharif the possibility of the killing of Pakistani citizens in the Frontier Province by U.S. troops ruled out this arrangement as a serious option. He believed that negotiations with the militants in Waziristan and a gradual military withdrawal from the area were essential to deter terrorist attacks in the large cities. The PPP was more equivocal on, but it too was firmly against, NATO raids inside Pakistan. The ANP leaders in the Frontier, who had hitherto been supportive of the U.S. presence in neighboring Afghanistan, were not prepared to give Washington a blank check and supported negotiations with Baitullah Masood, a pro-Taliban militia leader in South Waziristan, accused by the CIA of masterminding Benazir Bhutto's assassination, a claim denied by some of Bhutto's closest colleagues. Two senior ANP leaders, Asfandyar Wali Khan (the grandson of the late Ghaffar Khan) and Afrasiab Khattak, were summoned to Washington for meetings with National Security Adviser Stephen Hadley and John Negroponte. There was only one point on the agenda: cross-border raids. Washington was determined to find Pakistani politicians who would defend them. Both ANP leaders refused. Later, Khattak informed the *New York Times,* "We told them physical intervention into the tribal areas by the United States would be a blunder. It would create an atmosphere in which the terrorists would rally popular support." That this needed saying is worrying.

Owais Ghani the governor of the Frontier Province and, interestingly, a Musharraf appointee, also reiterated this view, "Pakistan will take care of its own problems, you take care of Afghanistan on your side. Pakistan is a sovereign state. NATO is in Afghanistan. It's time they did some soldiering."

On May 18, as if to underscore that the United States was not overly worried about the views of elected politicians, a Predator drone bombed Damadola in the Bajaur Agency in Pakistan and killed over a dozen people. The United States claimed that they had targeted and killed a "significant leader." Akhundzada Chattan, the member of parliament from the Bajaur Agency and a PPP veteran, called a press conference and denounced the United States in strong language for "killing innocents." Local PPP leaders backed him up strongly, especially when he repeatedly insisted that "the protest lodged by the Pakistan government against the missile raid is not enough. The government should also sever diplomatic ties with the U.S. and expel its ambassador immediately."

Chattan said that a clear pattern had now been established. As soon as the Pakistan government and the local insurgents began to talk to one another and discuss a durable peace, NATO targeted the tribal areas inside Pakistan and killed innocent people. He warned Washington to cease these activities and issued an appeal to the tribal elders, the insurgents, the Pakistan army, and the new government to cast aside all other differences and unite against "foreign aggression." This dissent in the PPP suggests that Zardari's ascendancy is perhaps not as secure as he might imagine. It is also another reminder that the decision of successive Pakistan governments to keep the tribal areas formally separate from the rest of the country is counterproductive. Such an anomaly prevents political parties and other organizations from functioning in the region, leaving political control in the hands of tribal leaders, usually with dire results.

As if these developments on the Afghanistan border were not big enough problems by themselves, the country as a whole is in the grip of a food and power crisis that is creating severe difficulties in every city. Inflation is out of control and was approaching 15 percent in May 2008. Gas, which is used for cooking in many homes, has risen by 30 percent in the past year. Wheat, the staple diet of most people, has seen a 20 percent price hike since November 2007 and, while the UN's Food and Agriculture Organization admits that the world's food stocks are at record lows, there is an additional problem in Pakistan. Large quantities of wheat are being smuggled into Afghanistan to serve the needs of the NATO armies. It is no secret in Pakistan that some of the smugglers include the newly elected parliamentarians. Their triumphant, smiling faces conceal odious calculations. Politics is a way to make money. The few hopes aroused by the election have faded. The poor are the worst hit, but middle-class families are also beginning to be affected.

• • •

POLITICS IN A land of perpetual dictatorships and corrupt politicians is undoubtedly depressing, but with some positive aspects. For one, politics has revived an interest in stories from the popular literature of an earlier period of Muslim rule in the region. The following tale, first told by a sixteenth-century storyteller, repeated to me in Lahore in 2007, sums up, with a few modifications, life in Pakistan today: A man is seriously dissatisfied with a junior magistrate's decision. The latter, irritated, taunts him to appeal to the *qadi* (a senior judge). The man replies, "But he's your brother, he won't listen to me." The magistrate says, "Go to the mufti [expert in Muslim law]." The man replies, "But he's your uncle." The magistrate says, "Go to the minister." The man replies, "He's your grandfather." The magistrate says, "Go to the king." The man replies, "Your niece is engaged to him." The magistrate, livid with anger, says, "Go to hell then." The man replies, "That's where your esteemed father reigns. He'll see to it I get no satisfaction there."

Official history is mainly composed of half-truths and outright lies, in which everything is attributed to well-meaning rulers and noble, pious sentiments. Those who write this are worshippers of accomplished facts, rallying to the side of victors. Sometimes a general, sometimes a politician. Success justifies everything. There is another history that refuses to be repressed.

Pakistan's satirists, writers, and poets generally refuse to silence their voices. They serve as the collective conscience of the country, and life without them would indeed be bleak. They often sight victory in times of defeat. The Punjabi poet and novelist Fakhar Zaman, who as a PPP activist served his time in prison during the Zia dictatorship, is one who refuses to relinquish hope:

How can he who lost his eyesight paint?
How can he who lost his hands sculpt?
How can he who lost his hearing compose music?
How can he whose tongue was cut out sing?
How can he whose hands are tied write poetry?
And how can he whose feet are fettered dance?

With muffled nose and mouth how can one inhale the scent of
    flowers?
But all this has really happened:
Without eyes, we painted
Without hands, we sculpted statues
Without hearing, we composed music
Deprived of a tongue, we sang
Handcuffed, we wrote poetry
With fettered legs, we danced
And the fragrance of flowers pierced our muffled mouths and
    nostrils.

INDEX

About the Author

Writer and filmmaker Tariq Ali was born in Lahore and studied politics and philosophy at Oxford University. He was a prominent leader of opposition to the war in Vietnam and more recently the war in Iraq. Today he writes regularly for a range of publications including the *Guardian,* the *Nation,* and the *London Review of Books* and is on the editorial board of *New Left Review.* He has written more than a dozen books including nonfiction such as *Can Pakistan Survive?, The Clash of Fundamentalisms, Bush in Babylon,* and *Pirates of the Caribbean,* and fiction including *Shadows of the Pomegranate Tree, The Book of Saladin, The Stone Woman,* and *A Sultan in Palermo,* as well as scripts for both stage and screen. He lives in London.